From Mau Mau to Harambee

Memoirs and Memoranda of colonial Kenya

TOM ASKWITH

Edited by
 Joanna Lewis
 African Studies Centre
 University of Cambridge

CAMBRIDGE AFRICAN MONOGRAPHS   No 17

FROM MAU MAU TO HARAMBEE was first published by the African Studies Centre, University of Cambridge, Free School Lane, Cambridge, CB2 3RQ, England, in 1995.

Copyright © Tom Askwith, 1995
Editorial copyright © Joanna Lewis, 1995

Design & Production by Salah Bander

All Rights Reserved
   Crown copyright is reproduced with the permission of the Controller of HMSO

British Library Cataloguing in Publication Data
1. Africa   2. Kenya   3. Colonial History   4. Askwith, T.
I. Lewis, J   II. African Studies Centre

ISBN   0-902993-30-5

Cover illustration: *Water colour depicting a community development project by Tom Askwith*

Printed in Great Britain by
RANK XEROX
42 Sidney St, Cambridge,
CB2 3HX, England.

Contents

Dedication	*i*
Thanks	*ii*
Map of Kenya	*iv*
Glossary	*v*
Preface - John Lonsdale	*vii*
Introduction - Joanna Lewis	1

PART 1 Memoirs of Colonial Kenya

Chapter 1 The Country and its People: a Personal View 27
  The Tradition of Community

Chapter 2 Colonisation 33
  1. The Railway Line
  2. Missionaries
  3. British Administration
  4. The White Settlers
  5. How the Tribal Areas Became Exhausted

Chapter 3 The Second World War and the drift towards Mau Mau 45
  1. Racial Discrimination
  2. Life in Post-War Nairobi
  3. The United Kenya Club & Inter-racial Co-operation
  4. A Meeting with Jomo Kenyatta
  5. Race Relations

Part II Mau Mau and Memoranda 57

Chapter 4 Warnings and Remedies
  1. The Plight of the Landless African
  2. Correspondence with the Government
    i. African Vagrancy Memorandum
    ii. Some Observations on the Growth of Unrest in Kenya
    iii. Remedies
  3. Extract from *East African Royal Commission 1953-55 Report*

Chapter 5 Declaration of the State of Emergency 90
Address to European Electors' Union

Chapter 6 The Rehabilitation Programme 111

PART III The Story of Community Development
Chapter 7 Promoting Local Leadership 125
1. Introduction
2. Progressive Farmers
3. CD Assistants (men)
4. CD Assistants (women)
5. Chiefs and Leaders
6. CD Officers
7. Group Leaders
8. Orientation
9. Techniques
10. Community Education
11. Women's Emancipation
12. Youth Centres
13. Sport and Recreation

Chapter 8 Restoring Fertility to the Countryside Through Self-Help 159
1. Introduction
2. Early Experiments
3. Machakos
4. Kitui
5. Central Nyanza
6. Elgon Nyanza
7. The Kalenjin
8. Taita
9. The Kikuyu
10. Scope and Value of Community Development

Chapter 9 Conclusion 209

Appendices 213
Retrospect 218
Bibliography 222
Index 224

Dedication

This book is dedicated to my colleagues who worked in social development in Nairobi immediately after the Second World War: the community development officers and their staff who laid the foundations of community development in the early 1950s: the rehabilitation officers and their staffs who worked in the Mau Mau Works Camps: the community development officers and their staffs who expanded the work of community development throughout Kenya during the ten years immediately prior to the declaration of Independence, and the staff at the two Jeanes Schools who trained the subordinate staff to guide and develop these programmes: the dozen homecrafts training centres, and the administrative staff who were responsible for supporting this unprecedented expansion.

Their work went largely unsung and this little book is intended to make amends. The gratitude of the village people must be their reward.

T.G. Askwith

Thanks

My thanks are due to the numerous individuals who have been kind enough to read either the whole of parts of the script and give me the benefit of their advice and comments. They will not all necessarily approve of the final conclusions I have reached, but they have helped me, with hindsight, to see the problems confronted in clearer perspective.

In particular, I would like to mention the following: Dr John Lonsdale of Trinity College, Cambridge, for the continuing support and encouragement he has given to the publication in the first place.

My protegé, Dr Joanna Lewis, if I may be privileged to refer to her as such in view of the great difference in our ages. Her 'Colonial Politics of African Welfare in Kenya 1939-1952: a crisis of paternalism' has proved the perfect lead-in to the arguments contained in part 2 and 3 of the book and a valuable accompaniment to part 1. The narrative, therefore, flows naturally from the middle thirties to the time of Independence. She has done much to restore my confidence that the campaign we conducted forty years ago was indeed worth while. She has also done even more to present the material in a readable form.

Elspeth Huxley for her advice, and more particularly, for the background material provided by her classic 'Red Strangers' which gives such a wonderful picture of Kikuyu life as a back-drop to my narrative.

Anthony Kirk-Greene, MBE, of St Antony's College, Oxford, who served in Nigeria, whence the original concept of community development emerged.

My former colleague, Don Diment, OBE and Veronica Owen, former head of Limuru and Malvern Girl Schools.

But more especially I want to express my deepest appreciation to my wife Patricia, who has not only tackled the monumental task of typing the many preliminary drafts of the script, but also many articles and memoranda prior to that. One must appreciate that this involved the even more difficult task of deciphering my handwriting and correcting my spelling and punctuation.

But her greatest contribution has been to stand by me when things were tough, as they so often were, and give me encouragement over the last 55 years. What has been even more important is that she has taught me how to laugh about it and not to take myself too seriously.

She, and often the children, have accompanied me on safaris to see community development schemes in action all over Kenya. She has opened countless women's training centres and youth clubs and given hospitality to numerous colleagues. For all this I shall be for ever grateful.

T. G. Askwith

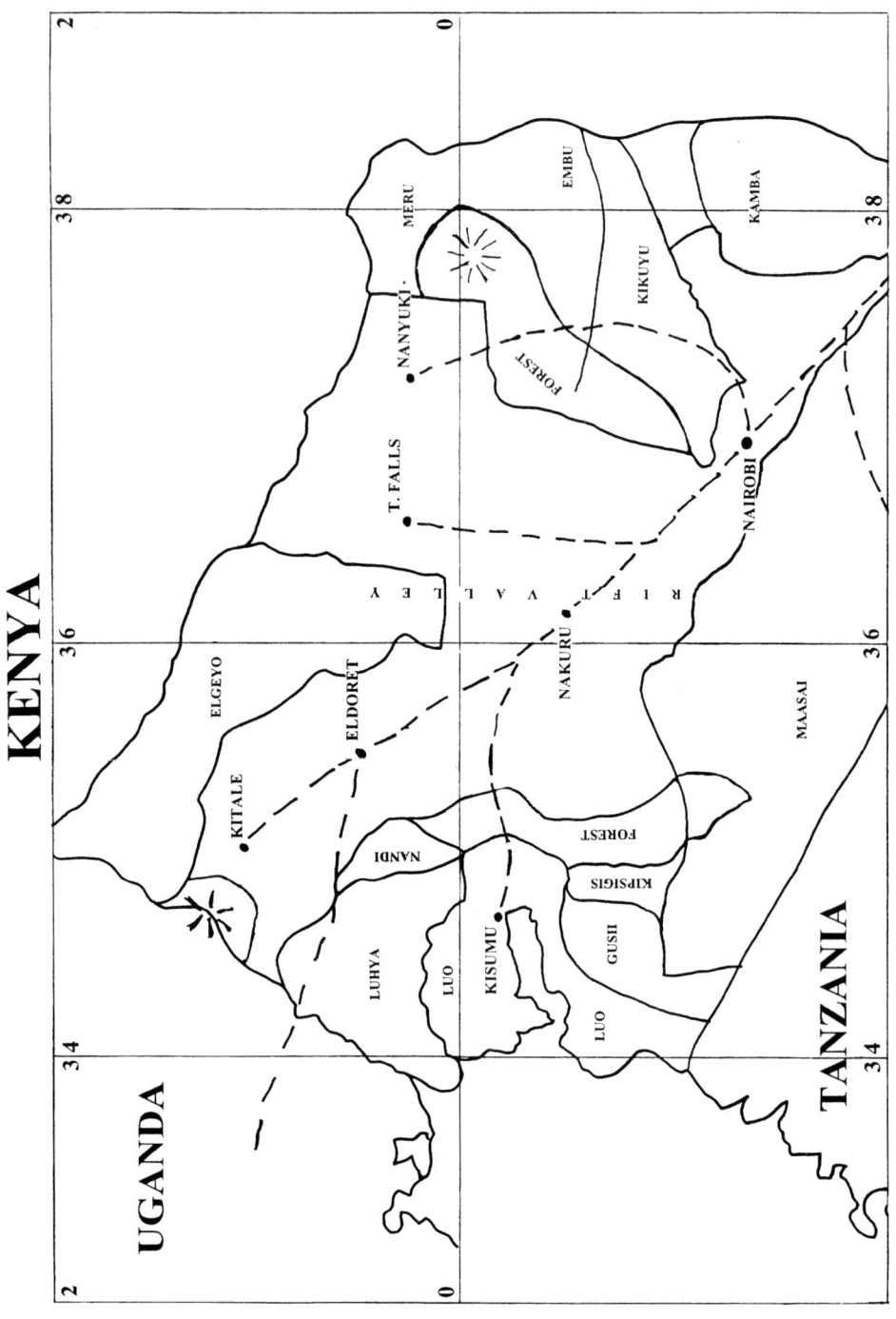

MAP OF KENYA

Glossary

askari	soldier
Dini Ya Mswamba	Church of Msambwa
harambee	progress
Maendeleo Ya Wanawake	working together for progress
manyatta	Maasai homestead
miazini	market/trading point
mikora	name for underclass in Nairobi
moran	Maasai warrior
mweytha	communal activity

Abbreviations

CID	Criminal Investigation Department
Cmd	Command Paper (British Government)
CMS	Church Missionary Society
edn	edition
KAU	Kenya African Union
MRA	Moral Rearmament Movement
OBE	Order of the British Empire
SAS	Special Air Service
Shs	Shillings
VE	Victory Europe
UNICEF	United Nations Children's Fund

Preface

All students of history are baffled by the question how far an age makes men and women, how far individuals create their age. We are all men or women of our time, but times change and real people whose personalities we can recognise have had their part to play in changing them. Not only is the relationship between individual human agency and the broader social structure necessarily difficult — and therefore intriguing to — puzzle out, but personal memoirs are often the most frustrating — and therefore fascinating — sources from which to attempt to draw evidence one way or the other. They reveal but in revealing also conceal, quite to what extent it is the historian's job to discover. That is why those of us who are interested in the past, amateur detectives all, feel drawn to autobiography, memoir and biography: they present in what we hope will be their most intimately personal form all the most baffling issues of historical explanation.

Tom Askwith's memoir of his life and work in colonial Kenya will not disappoint those who read him with these issues in mind. For Kenya between the wars, when he first went out as a cadet, had an apparently firm colonial structure, ruled by British officials like himself, and without more than an occasionally queasy question in their minds on whether their duty to Africans was compromised by their service to the small but powerful minority of white settlers. By the end of his career, it was clear to all that Kenya would soon be an independent state, ruled by its African majority, a country in which whites could expect no privileges other than those of individual citizenship.

So Askwith's times had certainly changed. And he had played no small part both in changing them, and, perhaps at least as importantly, in changing the way that people, his fellow whites especially, tried to explain their times to themselves, in order to inform their personal sense of purpose.

But this is precisely where the fascination of historical detection begins in the case before us. For in these pages we will find statements of Askwith's faith in colonial tutelage which seem too morally confident for him to look kindly on the end of empire; we will later find memoranda on rising African discontent in the post-war period that will impress us with their informed sympathy, their liberal convictions, their historical breadth — surely arguments that ought to change policy but of which the colonial government took not the slightest notice; and an account of Askwith's vigorous stewardship of his office as

Commissioner of Community Development, with this then revolutionary acknowledgment of the essential part to be played by African women in sustaining their society through change, but which* leaves us asking how precisely it was that this state-sponsored intervention from below, so essential if the community development project was to achieve its aims. In these three successive sections of the memoir we are, then, faced with the problem of how to relate personal belief, to professional action, political argument to policy influence and bureaucratic intention to social outcome.

And there is, if that were not enough, what for many people will in itself be enough, Tom Askwith's own story, ordinary enough perhaps in the days of Empire, impossibly exotic now. The African Studies Centre of the University of Cambridge is glad to publish it, together with the scene-setting introduction by Joanna Lewis, whose doctoral research on the colonial politics of African welfare in Kenya 'rediscovered' Askwith for a modern audience.

John Lonsdale
Trinity College
Cambridge
1995

* *should read:*
from above was translated into the politics of African self-interest from below,

Introduction [1]

The highs and lows of human achievement, whether we focus on the individual or the collective enterprise, appear to be found in the way outsiders have involved themselves in the affairs of Africa and Africans. Selfish plunder shadows selfless sacrifice. The most brutish brutality accompanies the noblest of humanitarian principle. Systematic discrimination partners indiscriminate benevolence. A formal Empire which the British barely constructed in Africa from the 1880s to the 1960s, with not a little help from African agency contained all these contradictory yet interacting features.[2] What dominates the legend of Empire as it is remembered today is the shamefulness of this episode, producing on occasions an awkward relationship not only with an imperial past, but also between Africans and Britons whose lives remain so inextricably interlinked.[3]

One institutional by-stander in the rise and fall of Empire in Africa is the University of Cambridge, a repository of the spoils of Empire. However, researchers at the African Studies Centre are beginning to flesh out the academy's capacity to spawn individuals committed to the struggle for racial justice across the continent of Africa. Clarkson's anti-slavery movement owed much to the enlightened thinking of Peter Peckard, Master of Magdalene College, later University Vice-Chancellor and his connection with Olaudah Equiano the freed-slave, and William Pitt the younger.[4] Activism to help some of Africa's poorest reveals itself as a strong branch in this tradition. Students at Queens' College (in the 1840's home to Cambridge's first African student Alexander Crummell) currently help support the education of girls living in some of rural Zimbabwe's most vulnerable communities. A student branch of Action Aid helps fund a school for boys in Uganda; while a university-wide organisation, Link Africa, endeavours to bridge the gap between the privileged in Cambridge and teaching needs in Africa.

One man, whom it could be said to have been part of this institutional connection with Africa, is Tom Askwith. After matriculating from Peterhouse in 1929, Askwith spent most of his working life in Kenya, a British colony in Eastern Africa. Countless men have passed through Cambridge and then stepped into the colonial service, many returning to attend the Colonial Office summer schools held in Cambridge after the Second World War. Tom Askwith was part of this flow but what makes his career as a colonial administrator interesting to the historian is the way his own particular blend of paternalism, progressive outlook and a politics of inclusion, interacted, not always smoothly, with the specific institutional, social and political cross-winds of his time.[5] For Askwith was instrumental in promoting a concept of community development based on the devolution of resources to Africans but was instrumental in the context of first, the use of coercion by the state in response to Mau Mau and then secondly, decolonisation.

A Career in the British Colonial Service

Askwith spent twenty five years in Kenya, a period which culminated in what was to be the beginning of the 'end of Empire'. Kenya was a settler colony. Europeans, mainly British, endeavoured to farm parts of the territory and had taken over an area known as the White Highlands where African families were excluded from farming on racial grounds but were allowed to live as 'squatter' families providing cheap labour. The administration of the colony consisted of a 'thin white line', short of resources and often subject to the will of the local settler population.[6] Askwith spent his first years in the colony cutting his teeth as a district officer. Rotating between peripheral up-country stations, he was part of the old Empire of settlement where an 'end of Empire' could scarcely have been contemplated at the time. His postings included Kisumu, Taveta (on the border with Tanganyika), Kisii, Kakamega, Isiolo (Northern Frontier Province famed for its dust storms, spitting cobras and weekly delivery of water by ox-cart), then on to Machakos and finally Kitui.[7]

At the end of the Second World War, Askwith was promoted to the tricky post of Municipal Native Affairs Officer for Nairobi, for he was considered a reliable administrator by his superiors. He insisted that his adjutant be an African and he worked very closely with Dedan Githege in Nairobi. Askwiwth held this demanding job until 1949 when he made the decision to takeover from Pat Williams as Commissioner for Community Development. This new department had grown out of the Welfare Organisation which had been patched together as a compromise structure in 1946 and possessed only a handful of field-staff.[8]

What distinguishes Askwith as an administrator from this period onwards is the way he was able to discern the signs of dramatic African social change. Askwith applied his knowledge of the periphery to the problems of the centre. In Nairobi his working philosophy gradually came to be dominated by a commitment to alleviating African poverty and a growing opposition to racial discrimination. Subsequently, Askwith pioneered a strategy for improving basic living standards among rural African communities, using traditional methods and structures, as well as targeting policies towards African women. And he did so with the help of community development assistants (African and European, male and female), supportive technical officers and converts among the district administration. Throughout his working life he never veered in his total belief in the merits of this strategy. Meanwhile his collaborative network included local organisations, pressure groups in Britain as well as international non-governmental organisations.

As Commissioner, Askwith succeeded in expanding the Department of Community Development against entrenched local opposition. Until 1951, he simultaneously held the post of Principal at the Jeanes School, Kabete, an adult training centre originally founded by American missionaries in 1926 to train teachers in community 'uplift'. Then, after the outbreak of what became known as the Mau Mau Rebellion, Askwith found himself in charge of the government's rehabilitation campaign. Part of a wider counter-insurgency operation, Askwith's mandate was to put together a package of rehabilitation measures designed to win back the 'hearts and minds' of those men and women who were implicated in the rebellion.[9]

Immediately Askwith was dispatched to Malaya to examine counter-insurgency tactics there. His subsequent plan was accepted. Suspects were detained in a series of works camps and guarded villages where specially trained Rehabilitation Officers would put into operation a home grown strategy involving education and manual labour, designed to turn them into enlightened peasant farmer and farmer-wife. By 1956, 60,000 had passed through this procedure known as the 'pipeline'. Under pressure to speed up the process, the Kenyan Government approved a departure in official policy towards those imprisoned for Mau Mau crimes who refused to confess - the use of force to make the recalcitrant 'hard core' prisoners work. Askwith expressed disapproval and was subsequently relieved of rehabilitation but not community development: this virtually meant 'the sack'. When eleven detainees were beaten to death at Hola Camp, an official enquiry recommended that the original system be restored. Soon afterwards all detainees were released. Tom Askwith retired and left Kenya in 1961 having also served as Permanent Secretary to Benaiah (Apolo as he was widely known) Ohanga, the first African Minister who was in charge of the Ministry of African Affairs. Askwith received no decoration for public service; his rank would otherwise have entitled him to the CMG.

Opposition to the use of force may have been detrimental to his career but after the Hola Massacre it was an Askwith version of paternal rule that the Colonial Secretary of the time, Ian Macleod, preferred to follow.[10] Although a Tory, Macleod was committed to the post-war settlement in Britain including the welfare state and he became a stern opponent of racism and later, of racially-based immigration laws. He was particularly appalled by the murders. Morality, economics and national reputation now came together on the question of Empire. Open to the arguments of the trade unions and international labour organisations, he became convinced that racial rule was no longer justifiable or viable and he set in motion a timetable of independence for African countries at a speed that perhaps even surprised Tom Askwith.[11]

Tom Askwith certainly surprised me in May 1989. I was in the first year of my Ph.D struggling to work out what direction my research would take when I learnt that Kenya's former Commissioner for Community Development was in Cambridge, astonishingly to coach the Peterhouse First VIII rowing crew. Here was a chance for my first taped interview with what I viewed as a living relic of an imperial past. Being Welsh, female and of unconventional dress, I assumed my subject would be disproving and there would be inevitable barriers to meaningful dialogue. As I climbed the ancient wooden staircase that led to his guest room, I distinctly remember wishing I were somewhere else, wondering why I ever got into this, daring myself to turn back even at the point of knocking on the door. I need not have worried for he answered all my naive questioning with patience, clarity and a fervour that had remained unquenched. Soon my research settled on a period of administration in Kenya which spanned much of Askwith's career, a career which he has now recorded in this book.

Biographical Sketch

Tom Askwith was born in Surrey on May 24th, 1911 of English upper-middle class stock. His paternal grandfather was Deputy Chief Cashier of the Bank of England, whilst his father opted for a career with London Life Insurance. The First World War interrupted with tragic results. After joining the Royal Horse Artillery, his father was killed on the fields of Ypres in 1917, leaving his mother to bring up two small boys alone. They were fortunate in that Haileybury College paid for the boys' public school education from its War Memorial Scheme. The War shaped their development in other ways, too. According to Askwith, the effect of war shortages produced an underweight, lanky adolescent, lacking in powers of concentration and missing a father's guiding presence.[12]

Askwith, however, was not about to resign himself to a life of mediocrity. Showing self-determination and initiative, he persuaded two of his school masters to help him prepare privately for his school certificate examination despite the fact he had not been placed in the examination class. He surprised everyone by passing with high grades. Thus, in 1929, he matriculated to Peterhouse, where a prominent Fellow of the College, Carey Francis, had just abandoned his privileged existence in academe in favour of the Church Missionary Society. Coincidentally, Francis also found a new life in Kenya. He worked as headmaster, first in a small country school near Kisumu, then at the prestigious Alliance High School outside Nairobi. When he retired, he chose to work among the children of the poor in the slums of Nairobi.

At Cambridge Askwith read engineering, the profession of his mother's family. In retropsect he sees himself as 'a late developer ' but extremely fortunate to have had the benefit of much guidance and encouragement from his tutor at Peterhouse, Paul Vellacote, later to become Headmaster at Harrow and Master of Peterhouse. Askwith gained new confidence when his skill as an oarsman became apparent. He rowed to victory over Oxford with the University First VIII two years running; won the Grand Challenge Cup at Henley in 1932; represented Britain at the Olympic Games twice (reaching the final on both occasions); and won all the main sculling events at Cambridge, plus the Diamond Sculls at Henley in 1933.

Trainee salesman at Whitbreads Brewery was a post that could not hold him. For after graduating, Askwith quickly found a 'nine-to-five' working life monotonous: a 'troglodyte' existence in which the 'predictable game of rugger and Saturday night drinks party could not satisfy'.[13] Thus in 1936, along with a number of contemporaries from Peterhouse, he joined the British overseas administration and was sent to Kenya. At Cambridge they had ritually been exposed, like many before them, to the ethos of serving one's country and naturally saw themselves as keepers of this tradition. A career in the overseas civil service satisfied the keenness to serve with the thirst for adventure.

The Empire had always functioned as an outlet for the aspirations of the young and idealistic (yesterday's district official, today's VSO worker or Himalayan backpacker) as well as being the destiny of the entrepreneur, the mercenary, the disgraced aristocrat or the sexually frustrated.[14] Askwith, however, quickly found romance of the long-lasting variety. It was at a dance held at Government House that he first met Pat Noad, at that time secretary to Sydney 'Sad Sod' Fazan, the Provincial Commissioner for Nyanza. They were engaged to be married on September 3rd, the first day of the Second World War.

Askwith's decision to join the colonial service and that of his contemporaries was not simply inspired by a search for adventure and the fulfillment of one's perceived class duty, but also a social conscience which was shaped by the time. For he had been encouraged by his tutors and masters, men who had escaped the fields of Ypres but felt the loss and horror, to look at the world around him and to be aware of his own generational 'good fortune'. Living through the trauma of the Second World War added to this feeling.

It was at the end of the Second World War when transferred to Nairobi that Askwith saw poverty and racial inequality in unacceptable doses. He became concerned with finding ways to remove the hardship and discrimination which his African assistants let him see among the slums of Nairobi. As a mark of his administrative capabilities, he was able to make connections: connections between the rural areas and the problems of the town; connections between British social history and the landscape around him; between European discrimination and African disaffection. He became more convinced that Africans themselves, through traditional mechanisms and structures of command, could organise improvements in standards of living, whilst the government ought now to make serious efforts to impart the technical wisdoms of the day through African women.

If the ultimate goal of his remedy was the standard requirement of colonial paternal rule for the time - administrative control that could engender respect for its authority - his sequencing of this colonial concept of progress contained an unorthodoxy. For control and respect for authority, according to his view, would only stem from material improvements and not the other way round. In other words, empire loyalism was better nourished through the sweet taste of material progress rather than induced by coercion and fear. This rested on his belief that progress (as understood at the time) was a concept that Africans could comprehend, a belief of course not shared by all colonial servants. He and others tried to discredit the old assumption that Africans were generically lazy; instead they could be energised by community self-help rather than coerced by compulsory edicts and forced labour. What Askwith ultimately came to see was that community development taken to its logical conclusion meant free Kenyan citizens and not obedient colonial subjects.

Private and Public Spheres
Dangerous as it is to plot a direct relationship between private experience and public action, for those who risk to speculate, part of the explanation for Askwith's maverick stance as colonial administrator may lie in at least three interacting private spheres. First, his adolescent years endeared him to a philosophy of self-help. He had experience of taking the initiative, of going it alone. He had benefited from being given a chance and he knew that individual potential could often remain hidden. He had felt physically disadvantaged but worked to overcome this. Thus, as his experience of Kenya deepened, he embraced the concept of community development although this put him at odds with some in the administration. He was at times ridiculed and perhaps was eventually no longer considered 'one of us'. However, drawing on his past, he maintained the view that Africans had to be allowed to carry out improvements for themselves, even if that meant watching mistakes being made. Askwith was not afraid to take this risk.

Secondly, Askwith's above average awareness of the central role of women in maintaining communities as well as stabilising family life, stemmed perhaps partly from being brought up by his mother and from sharing his life with a strong and capable woman. Pat Askwith worked voluntary and unpaid, like so many 'colonial wives', in various capacities in connection with her husband's work. Pat knew Kenya well and she shared her husband's philosophy. Theirs was a team effort, just like the team effort Askwith preached for African development workers. Pat had first arrived in Kenya aged nine months when her father, Jock Noad, took up a post as Public Works Department Engineer in Nyeri and it was sitting in a soap-box carried by porters that she went on her first safari around Mount Kenya. At eighteen years of age, although considered a potential candidate for Oxford University, in the post-Munich climate of 1938 she was anxious to get back to her father in Kenya, her mother Hope having died in 1936. She first met Tom in Nairobi at a dance and next heard of him when, playing a game of tennis, a small plane flew overhead and someone said "That's Tom Askwith having a flying lesson".[15] Finally, she met up with him again when he was transferred to Kisumu where her father now worked; Askwith shared a house and passion for sculling with Martin Byers, a family friend.

As Commissioner for Community Development Askwith supported programmes which acknowledged the central role of African women in food production, education and small-scale income generating enterprises. In 1949, he quickly pointed out that the post-war community halls run by African Social Welfare Workers, usually ex-soldiers, had failed as an educative mechanism and they ought now to be run by trained African women. He did not show any reluctance to deal with European women as professional colleagues and was responsible for developing a new category of colonial female servant, the Homecrafts Officer. Quite remarkably for the time, considering the institutionalised chauvinism which abounded in 1955, he even lobbied to have these women upgraded to district officer status. Not suprisingly, the idea of District Officers in skirts failed to gain approval.[16]

Thirdly, Askwith mixed with a range of individuals and groups inside the colony which perhaps extended beyond the orthodoxy of his time. His social circle did not conform to convention. He had few close acquaintances among the settler community and only when in Nairobi was he a regular churchgoer. Although he had great respect for the Missions and their social welfare work, he did not care for their 'doctrinaire approach' and their 'antipathy towards certain African traditions'. Having friends as well as work colleagues among the African educated elite by the early 1940s, Askwith was more aware than most Europeans of the offence and damage caused by racial discrimination. This predisposed him to entertain the idea of more political inclusiveness in the colony and taught him much about the path to racial reconciliation. His own prejudice was soon replaced with a commitment to dismantling the barriers between black and white which he did so in his own quiet way. He was involved in setting up the first meeting-place for all races in Nairobi which became known as the United Kenya Club. By the late 1950s, Askwith came to understand that racial rule was a serious barrier to the development of the country's potential resources, both material and human. Passionate about athletics, he worked hard to organise track-events on an inter-racial basis and was at one time Chairman of the Kenya Sports Association. Throughout his time in Kenya, Askwith pursued interests such as sculling and water colour painting, becoming Chairman of the Kenya Arts Association.

The Book

The following memoir *From Mau Mau to Harambee* offers the reader a blend of autobiographical reminiscence, official documentation and descriptive data drawn from Tom Askwith's twenty-five years spent as an administrator in colonial Kenya. For the student of Empire, it offers some fascinating primary source material in the form of official letters, a speech to a key European political group inside the colony and an extract from an official report into land and population. Also, there is much secondary source material to be gleaned from the testimony of a British colonial official in charge of community development for over ten years. The memoir is therefore to be read as representation and as data.

1. General Recollections

The book divides into three parts. In Part I Askwith offers the reader a brief introduction to Kenya, its ethnography and physical characteristics. He follows this with an account of some of the main features of British colonial rule up to the outbreak of major unrest in the colony in 1952. What we have is an insight into the worldview of a colonial official; one strand in the ruling ethos of an elite living isolated and physically challenging lives scattered on 'islands of white'.[17]

To the critics of empire, more familiar with its failures, its excesses and its violent imposition of an alien system of rule, this account of the balance sheet of the colonial period will undoubtedly appear self-satisfied and partial. It does however bear witness to the motivation and self-image which kept colonial officials committed to their life of exile. Imperial servants were energised by a sense of being the harbingers of progress as Askwith reminds us in his retrospective stock-taking. His discourse of achievement will embarrass a younger British generation more familiar with institutional failure at home and the spectre of ethnic conflict in Africa, often blamed on the inheritance of a ludicrous national boundary system. But it is not quite the same 'gung-ho' discourse of the Colonel Blimp genre, celebrated in the anecdotal orgy of Trench's *Men Who Ruled Kenya*.[18] Colonial ideologies of rule were not always unitary and unchanging, as Askwith's career reminds us; they could be customised according to individual encounters and were increasingly contested privately by some officials, as the myth which the rhetoric served began to tarnish in the face of a racial system increasingly unable to cope with African social change.

Askwith's personal account of colonial rule in Kenya is built upon a belief in the high-intensity nature of the impact of the British in Kenya. Askwith stresses the disruption to traditional concepts of community in indigenous societies which found themselves operating under an alien system of taxation, an alien pattern of chieftainship in collaboration with the government and an alien form of local government based on municipal England. Men took up paid employment on white settler farms or in Nairobi, not only to pay poll tax but also to find money to pay for their children's schooling (mainly for their sons), an overwhelming priority for many families.

Askwith identifies a dramatic population expansion with the benefits brought by British rule: the control of famine, disease, tribal warfare and slavery combined with the growth of cash-cropping to produce a rapid growth in the population.[19] However, this generated intense pressure on the available land for cultivation. Barred from holding land in the White Highlands, many Africans, especially Kikuyu, felt the effects of land shortage. After the Second World War, returning African soldiers added to the numbers looking for land and for paid employment in Nairobi. Askwith is keen to stress the offence to Africans caused by racial discrimination. Askwith also reminds us of the great gulf of ignorance and suspicion created by a system that enforced racial segregation and of the effect this had on men such as Jomo Kenyatta, destined to be Kenya's first post-independence national leader. Askwith briefly documents his own efforts to bridge the racial gap as the government official in charge of African welfare in Nairobi and as co-founder of the United Kenya Club in Nairobi.

2. Memoranda and Mau Mau

Part II of the book covers the build-up to the Mau Mau uprising in 1952 and the declaration of a State of Emergency. In Chapter 4, Askwith looks at the Administration's response to Mau Mau. First, we have his own contribution in the form of three fascinating memoranda which he submitted to the Government in Nairobi for consideration between 1950 and 1952. In these documents we find warnings of the deep social malaise in the colony and the need for constructive policies to address social issues.

The first of these, 'African Vagrancy', was sent to the African Affairs Committee, a new think-tank established at the Secretariat. Although lacking powers of legislature it nevertheless brought together for the first time members of the African elite with government officials to discuss issues of African administration. It was the nearest the colonial state came to comprehending the problems that found expression in Mau Mau. Askwith had submitted a sensitive profile of those whom most Europeans in the colony casually dismissed as 'spivs' or the typical lazy native,. Thus he began to bridge the gap in official minds between 'them' and 'us'. Unemployment, no social security in old age, wages paid at levels which did not allow a man to support a family in Nairobi, nor to send the next generation to school, were all producing demoralised men without hope, Askwith explained, who were vulnerable to options which took them outside the law.

In addition to embellishing these men with a social and domestic context, Askwith continued in this vein by making a comparison between events in English history at the time of the early Industrial Revolution. He suggested an in-depth social survey be carried out to gather data on what was happening. Clearly, few Europeans knew much about how people lived in down-town Nairobi. Askwith realised that his knowledge would have to be converted into bureaucratic jargon to be taken seriously. A survey was eventually set in motion but it came far too late. Ultimately, of course, as the document 'Remedies' reminds us, Askwith's reform package for the 'economic hardships facing the working man'- more land, higher wages, old age pensions for landless elders and special schools for their children - all required fundamental adjustments in the racial restrictions and political economy of the colony.

Similarly, 'Some Observations on the Growth of Unrest in Kenya', written two years later, illustrates how Askwith was desperately trying to communicate African experiences, fears and vulnerabilities to white officialdom in Nairobi and also in Whitehall. Worthy of mention is the language he uses. He does not use the derogatory term 'native', for this implied a self-sufficiency that urban Africans did not have, plus a view of racial inferiority that Askwith did not subscribe to. And he further erodes the barrier of African otherness for Africans are humanised in the text. They are introduced as servicemen, young men, fathers of children, craftsmen. He endowed them with multiple roles, social responsibilities and universally recognised concerns.

Askwith's skill as an administrator enabled him to relay key matters of African concern, matters that Africans and Europeans, when in dialogue together, could rarely articulate due to the wall of prejudice that existed between black and white. For example, restrictions on the purchase of freehold for building town houses irked Nairobi's better salaried African citizens. The imminent restrictions planned for the independent schools were a blow to the less well-off who depended on the flexibility and low cost fees of these establishments to buy their sons and daughters a European education. Askwith explained why the issues of racial discrimination ought to be seriously considered. Restrictions on cultivation and landholding were not only unproductive, he insisted, but were creating public resentment and private defeatism. And he explained simply how economic and social pressures were producing a generational split among the Kikuyu - an observation that touched upon the crucial breakdown of the moral economy of the Kikuyu at this point - unearthed in John Lonsdale's revolutionary essay on wealth, poverty and virtue in Kikuyu political thought published in *Unhappy Valley, Book Two*.[20]

As we know from the impressive literature on Mau Mau, Askwith's warnings went unheeded. However, a social and economic survey of the Kikuyu was set in motion, although it came too late. The significance of the existence of these warnings lies in what this tells us about the climate and capacity of the administration on the eve of imminent social breakdown. As some of the recommendations subsequently made by the African Affairs Committee illustrate, such as an appeal to teachers to instil more discipline in the schoolrooms, white officials had become increasingly tentative in their views of what was best for African society and equally unimaginative in their prescriptions. This lack of confidence and a lack of flexible discourse with which Africans and Europeans could discuss the breakdown of Kikuyu society was part of a crisis of colonial paternal rule. The problem of African social change had already gone beyond the collective capacity of the British to debate it, let alone control it. A collision of some sort was virtually inevitable.

Askwith has chosen to include a transcript of an address delivered in 1953 to the African Affairs Committee of the Electors Union, a key European political organisation in the colony. This transcript illustrates how even moderate minds upheld the view and certainly expressed this view in public, that Mau Mau was, at its core, a subversive organisation. It was demonised as communist, modelled on European terrorist organisations and committed to inciting mass disobedience. Mau Mau did produce a state of emergency and the colonial government embarked upon a counter-insurgency programme of the 'carrot and stick' variety. Initially more of the 'stick' was applied with mass-detention, expulsions and interrogation, heightening the degree of social terror experienced by tens of thousands of Kikuyu. However, Askwith was quickly put in charge of organising the 'carrot' side in the form of an extensive so-called Rehabilitation Programme involving confessional cleansing, re-education and settlement in guarded villages. Here the crisis may have found a partial solution in the community development ethos supplied by Askwith, at last given a budget and target population to work upon. Land and economic security restored a degree of calm which was remarkable in the circumstances.

3. The East Africa Royal Commission 1953-55 Report

Askwith has given us an opportunity to revisit 'Agrarian Administration', chapter 24 of the *East Africa Royal Commission 1953-55 Report* (Part V 'Conditions for the Development of the Land').[21] Askwith feels that a vindication of his work is necessary and that this report illustrates how his brand of community development - the Africanisation of agrarian administration and the recognition of the central role of African women - were, at least on paper, taken up by the colonial authorities.

If we take the Report as a whole, we can see an attempt to consider a wide range of issues which have a resonance with Askwith's earlier memoranda: some of the investigative headings for example were 'The Changing African'; 'Existing Fears'; 'Age Structure'; 'Birth Control'; 'The Basic Poverty of East Africa'; 'Education of Girls' and 'Race Relations'. The rebellion in Kenya had clearly sharpened colonial minds and made available manpower and resources for a sweeping study of African administration. Also, the Report was a product of advances in technology which enhanced the information-gathering potential of bureaucracies at this time. Faster travel and better communication all played a part in the quick turn-around of data such as we find in the collection of tables on African population densities by district, province and territory. Above all, the text illustrates the confidence and assertive mood of this period. What the report testifies to is the belief in the capacity of state intervention to direct social and economic change.

Moving to the particular chapter which Askwith has included, we can see that colonial minds were able to cooly assess the situation and give detailed attention to the issue of agrarian change. We read of a desire to move away from administration by edict and 'compulsion' in favour of 'patient propaganda' and 'persuasion' through example. We hear how 'peasants' were more likely to be converted by 'men of their own race', well-trained and enjoying the confidence of the local population. And we find tacit approval of Askwith's community development. African standards of living, according to the Report, could be improved by a two-way process: 'the encouragement and stimulation of local initiative rising from the individual, the family or the clan unit' coupled with 'advanced techniques, guidance and direction by teams of specialist officers'. The stress was upon African agency - the support of local councils, young farmers' clubs, traditional chiefs and elders - for 'it is to the Africans that the government will have to look to'. And apparently it was also to African women, for we have one page on the need to enlist the co-operation and confidence of the women with an acknowledgement of their major role in cultivation.[22]

However, we ought to pause at this point and consider how influential and representative was this particular official rhetoric. This section of the Report takes up 12 pages, with one page on women coming at the very end. The one paragraph on community development contains a cautionary note warning that vague notions of 'social uplift' could produce a dispersal of 'well-meaning effort'. When analysing the language in this section as a representation of a colonial discourse of rule, what is excluded becomes as important as what is included. For the term 'peasant' conveniently papers over a set of complex relationships forged in the context of racial inequality and the concept of the 'native' living in self-sufficient tribes. These wisdoms and prescriptions were 'white' intentions and required much from the African population in the sense that they demanded that Africans see the state, as embodied in the African crop adviser for example, as somehow separate from its racial and arbitrary personification of the District Officer ordering them to move off their holdings because they were hopeless farmers. The notion of self-help was attractive to some perhaps not because it gave Africans the chance to learn by trial and error how to improve their standards of living, but because it fitted the political economy of the colony rather well: resources for development were often commandeered by the settler community, leaving little for the African Reserve areas.

Nevertheless, the Report alerts us to the importance of the 1950s in understanding the periodisation of the state in modern Africa. Further research on agricultural administration in Kenya for example, may illustrate to what extent the colonial state succeeded in building a transitional bureaucratic framework which managed social and political change for a time, as well as providing economic stability. If, in some areas, the colonial state became more focused, assertive and able to give space to Africans and civil society, albeit in loyalist forms, then decolonisation becomes more a product of its moment of renaissance on the ground, rather than of decay; whilst the apparent high degree of legitimation immediately enjoyed by the post-colonial state becomes easier to comprehend.

4. Community Development
In Part III of *From Mau Mau to Harambee* we have Askwith's detailed account of community development in colonial Kenya. Chapter 6 contains an overview of the main components and ethos of community development. Askwith's drive came from his conviction that standards of living could be raised most effectively by blending traditional communal practices with modern technical wisdoms. He believed that if people generated their own small-scale initiatives after technical officers ran campaigns of awareness-raising, then the big

administrative challenges of the day - soil erosion, disease and transport constraints - would gradually be solved. So too would the perceived lack of experience in British-style local government be remedied, for managing and choosing these community initiatives would, according to this view, form a collective lesson in self-government and citizenship. Through a process of trial and error, courses at Jeanes School were tailored for African Community Development Assistants - men at first, but later women also - who would work under the guidance of specially trained community development officers. In the policy designed for youth for example, we see the influence of the British public school regime. Here were rudimentary attempts to include women and the youth in order to nurture what would now loosely be termed, a civil society through which the state could work.

Finally, in Chapter 7, we are given a detailed account of the progress of community development in the colony, moving from region to region. Its core feature was the revival of mutual assistance in order to mobilise labour for the construction of a school, a terrace, a cowshed, a social centre and so on; projects believed to improve the potential economic prosperity and quality of life of a community. Crucial to Askwith's programme was the success of a pilot scheme in Manyasi Valley, Central Nyanza. This provided him with the much needed proof that the presence of Community Development officers working with technical staff, using film and radio, could set in motion a regional wave of development projects such as cattle enclosures to collect manure, wash-stops to prevent soil erosion, kitchens with raised stoves as a safety precaution. Askwith could boast that the only materials brought in had been nails.

In the early 1950s, this work suffered a setback when Askwith's field-staff budget was deleted by the Legislative Council, the colony's parliament, as a cost-saving measure. However, in the slide towards Mau Mau, his budget was restored by the Secreteriat under pressure from the Colonial Office in London, where Askwith's memos and reports had been read with more enthusiasm than in Nairobi. Successes multiplied and Askwith gives us many examples of these. The story of Machakos district is a good illustrative case. Here the pressure on land was a serious problem. With technical assistance on offer, the community development workers managed to create a revival of *mwethya* - communal labour to help a neighbour. The result was hundreds of miles of ridges dug which improved the absorptive capacity of the soil. As Askwith reminds us, this remained an enduring legacy. At Independence such strategies for development became a national movement called *harambee*. Similarly, the *Maendeleo ya Wanawake* women's groups went from strength to strength, becoming a potent branch of civil society and more recently taken over by the ruling party in Kenya. As a study by environmental geographers in Machakos concludes, '...the colonial approach to resource management did ultimately result in widespread acceptance of terracing, dam-building and the use of mwethya type self-help groups'.[23]

The late colonial state and society

Tom Askwith's memoir and memoranda help us understand the way an individual interacted with the bureaucratic structure which employed him, the relationship of private and professional action to political conviction, and how a strand of personal ideology belonging to an individual administrator who gradually moved away from mainstream thought and became less than representative, could in a particular context, make a difference to the pattern of colonial history and beyond. Tom Askwith's story will perhaps encourage historians of empire to look more closely, not only at the form and significance of the late colonial state and society, but also the relationship between the late colonial state and society with the post-colonial period.

1. Colonial paternalisms in crisis
Taking the colonial state first, Askwith's administrative career illustrates the potential of individual action within a bureaucracy: he was much more than a unitary structural category of colonial servant. He fought off the dragging inertia of bureaucratic constraints and made a potent challenge to the established ethos, as the memoranda illustrate. He was primed to execute this challenge for a number of reasons. First, as already discussed, his social encounters were wide-ranging and proved ultimately transformative. He had connections with liberals in the colony, with voluntary organisations and the church. After moving to Nairobi he enjoyed the company of educated Africans. And so his racial thinking began to show elastic properties. Experiencing the awkwardness of racial restrictions in Nairobi, a feeling sharpened by liberal criticisms coming from Britain, Askwith became committed to improving race relations, beginning with the inauguration of the first meeting place for all races. In Nairobi his observations led him to appreciate the central role of women in development. Workers in Nairobi usually lived without their wives; their wages being insufficient to support a family in the urban setting. Askwith soon understood that colonial policy ought to be about enabling Africans to live in families, for women not only provided material care but, as Luise White notes, they could also discipline husbands.[24]

Askwith's African assistants made sure he saw extreme levels of poverty and urban squalor that offended his humanist sensibilities: 'Men sleeping ten to a hundred square foot room, men wearing shirts and shorts that were fifty percent patches, the nauseating smell of choked-up sewers, beer halls over-flowing with men drowning their sorrows at weekends'. He collaborated with the East African Women's League and similar groups in the colony. He worked closely with the Press Liaison Officer and Jeanes School.

Taking advantage of improvements in communications, he corresponded directly with the Colonial Office on a number of matters and always made sure he kept them informed of his work. He also capitalised on the support community development now had from international non-governmental organisations such as UNESCO, for example. And he looked to other colonies to learn about their approaches to African welfare, all of which increased his potency as an administrator, since he was able to capitalise on the advances in bureaucratic management which technical developments made possible.

Secondly, it was because of Askwith's skill as an administrator that he was in the right place at the right time when in 1953, he was given the responsibility for organising the rehabilitation programme. This gave him a dramatically increased budget and administrative apparatus. He was always adept at communication. To get his old colleagues to take community development seriously, he would blitz them with circulars, memos, articles and points of information. When he achieved a community development success story he immediately publicised it, taking advantage of the improved printing technology available. For example, he informed everyone in the administration of how in the Manyasi Valley project, farmers had begun to make significant alterations in their farming and domestic practices because of the presence of a community development team.

Thirdly, Askwith was not afraid to be different. In an unprecedented move which infuriated provincial commissioners, he held a conference for community development field officers in Nairobi to discuss their work. Provincial Commissioners regarded these officers as being under their jurisdiction and so did not appreciate local matters being discussed out of their domain. Nevertheless, this sort of initiative which struck a blow against district feudalism, served Askwith well. After this conference, Askwith was able to make an appraisal of what exactly was happening at the social centres set up after the Second World War where retrained demobilised soldiers worked as social welfare officers. They had not been a success. The attendance of African women however had been quite remarkable. So Askwith inaugurated a change in policy. The centres would be run by trained African women who also would work as part of agricultural and health teams designed to inject the ethos and wisdoms of community betterment into rural homes. This was a policy that the Colonial Office had first discussed in 1925 and again in 1939. It was Askwith who was able to cut through a generation of administrative incoherence and put this policy into action.

Thus Askwith's career highlights a crisis in paternal rule, for his memoranda and promotion were a response to African social breakdown. The colonial state at the time was a liminal structure. Neither totally a modern system of government responsible for providing the welfare of its citizens, nor a force merely maintaining the status-quo in order that the tribe could sustain and police its own welfare, established colonial paternalisms of rule seemed to some, no longer to work. The African tribe in Kikuyuland was showing sig s of breaking down. A new generation of wealthy landowners no longer app ared willing to patronise the landless poor in the traditional manner. Meanwhile, settlers were evicting more squatters who were forced to return to the congested reserves. Wages in Nairobi remained largely insufficient to look after a family so the cost of domestic reproduction was pushed back onto the tribe. Racial paternalism could no longer deliver. Askwith and others believed they had found an answer. He shared the same view on local government as Arthur Creech Jones, Secretary of State for the Colonies in the 1940s: through adult education in 'citizenship and civics', Africans would learn how to improve the organisation of their society and do it willingly; they would instinctively organise their own welfare and social needs, as Askwith believed they had always done.

Askwith and those like him were facing up to the reality that whites could no longer govern by edict. Africans had to be trained in good government and in technical skills to organise their own community development. Meanwhile, specialist officers could induce communities to organise their own welfare schemes provided that people were given more say in how things were done. This was different from the authoritarian paternalism of the district. Instead it demanded a relaxation in racial prejudice and recognition of responsibility and maturity, albeit perhaps in the inevitable context of a recognition of mutual patriarchal self-interest. Askwith's challenge was to show that, if given a chance and helping hand, African men and women would experience the liberation of community self-help rather than the oppression of compulsory labour. Ultimately of course, this could not happen within a racially divided society and Askwith came to the same conclusion.

2. Local remaking and external agency
If Askwith's career illustrates this crisis in colonial paternalisms of rule, it may also illustrate how the crisis was partially solved in the late colonial period. His community development and rehabilitation programme may have produced in some areas, a local compromise between state and society by providing a transitional framework in which social breakdown gave way to social order. Decolonisation may point to a degree of success in administration rather than total failure. For agrarian administration in late colonial Kenya may provide an interesting example of how one branch of the state tried to devolve resources from above to the people below. When more is known about the self-remaking of the Kikuyu in the 1950's and 1960's, scholars may be well placed to explore

further the relationship between external agency and local reconstruction, an ongoing issue throughout the post World War II period, linked to the role of the state. Askwith clearly believed that communities had to develop themselves, by trial and error and through self-expression. But integral to this approach was the belief that an administrative framework gave the scope and support necessary for this process to take place. We do not yet know to what extent in the re-ordered village communities were mobilised in new ways and took new forms, or else were energised simply because state power was shared out between established monopolies of control.

The level of calm which reigned in Central Province by the late1950s in relation to the high degree of violence and social terror experienced by the Kikuyu was a remarkable achievement in local remaking, and as yet no one knows the proportionate role of community to state, of indivdual to society. Rehabilitation and community development involved the colonial state giving African communities greater capacity to provide their own solutions to the breakdown of tribe, albeit within a framework of external threat of discipline and Western concepts of development. What many came to accept was that through this enabling process, good colonial subjects were increasingly behaving like free Kenyan citizens. Central Province may be representative of a decaying colonial state or a manifestation of a renewed state structure providing a transitional framework. While the ideology of the colonial state waned and withered, its integrative capacity as a modern bureaucratic power may have increased. If so, the speed of decolonisation is a mark of the regeneration of the late colonial state, and the relative high degree of legitimation experienced by its predecessor, a direct legacy.

Community development and rehabilitation in Central Province may not only highlight peculiarities in the periodisation of the state apparatus in Africa post 1945 but this episode may also be of use those currently fathoming out the realms of possible relationships between the state and the restructuring of society. What we know already about the origins of Mau Mau highlights the destructive power of poverty and insecurity in relation to local communities and their complex moral economies which has no more horrific reincarnation than recent events in the crowded villages of Rwanda. The colonial state's belated response to social breakdown among the Kikuyu contained contradictory elements: the use of force, coercion and intimidation along with Askwith's rehabilitation package. What it did therefore was to tackle the heart of the problem - access to land - and it invested resources in 'rehabilitation' of combatants, men women and children, following the lines of its policy towards ex-askari after the Second World War.[25] Violence and coercion are usually at the heart of state formation and consolidation as well as the promise of greater economic security; a dualism which runs through all systems built out of patriarchal domination.

We may also understand more about the role of local violence and how to confront it. Recently, commentators have observed a marked increase in violence throughout the world, particularly in Africa, and have explained this as a proliferation of warlordism, a macho-military factor gone high-tech, and as a return to a form of non-ideological violence.[26] Askwith had his finest hour in the midst of an intense period of violence, the Mau Mau Rebellion. This was condemned at the time for being an atavistic return to an ancient barbarity that lay dormant in the mind of 'the native'. We know now it was a strategy adopted reluctantly to recast tribal civic virtue so that the poor could learn self-mastery and temper sources of power and wealth that were no longer identifiable and local. As John Lonsdale was first to observe 'power which is unknowable is always feared to be antisocial'.[27]

The struggle to fix civic virtue, to reclaim a right to act for the good of the community and to purge the errant in the face of an apparently arbitrary source of external power may not be just specific to the violence of Mau Mau in the 1950s.[28] By including cleansing ceremonies in the rehabilitation process, the authorities were perhaps not just cleansing combatants in the eyes of others, but unwittingly also the power of the state in the eyes of the detainees. Breaking the culture of violence today in parts of Mozambique and Angola will require new moral economies built upon the restoration of local forms of power and of economic security. But as a recent report on Mozambique has warned, the shortcomings of current rehabilitation efforts are not just related to funding; what is more at fault is the focus. Not enough is known about the level of community that exists in societies disrupted by war; reintegration strategies have to include components that strengthen the wider fabric of the community.[29]

However, what is the state's current capacity to intervene from above, and provide outside resources in order to rebuild and raise the standard of living within the local community? A number of global trends may be undermining its capacity for such intervention. Mozambique, now that war and multi-party elections have come and gone, is an extreme illustration of this phenomenon. First, the state's economic resource base has remained limited. With few signs of foreign investment, the formal sector has stayed minimalist and the manufacturing capacity remains low.[30] International capital no longer moves in to exploit local resources. Secondly, and partly as a consequence of this economic crisis, the state appears increasingly fragmented, and, with a history of corruption on a grand scale, more vulnerable to competition from other sources. Crime consortiums and banditry, World Bank and IMF strictures, NGOs and UN agencies providing some level of social welfare, all combine to erode the capacity of a state structure to devise and implement national programmes of reconstruction and reconciliation.[31]

Askwith's tale of bureaucracy and administration, however, alerts us to a number of dynamic processes currently at work in the continent which may well add a local twist to the future relationship between local remaking and external agency where violence and poverty have destabilised communities. For such processes may, in some situations, revive the integrative power of the state; in other contexts, these processes may ensure that such integrative power is located elsewhere. Thus in Africa today, we have a situation where a range of scenarios now exist in relation to the structure and capacity of the state. Askwith reminds us of how technological advances in mass communication currently offer a tremendous force for change.[32] From the outbreak of the Second World War, the application of a communications revolution changed the pattern of administration and the relationship between local remaking and external agency in the Empire. Askwith used the developments in modern technology well, which allowed for the proliferation of cheap print and more film and radio, and he put them to the service of his projects. The present communications revolution in electronic media may have a similar potency in respect of control of news and restriction on information flows which could encourage more open and inclusive state structures, less able to conceal, abuse or marginalise; instead sustaining a more plural form of political organization.[33] Alternatively, such technological developments could enhance the capacity of the state to control information and resort to crude forms of ideological indoctrination.

A second source of dynamism may be found in the few examples of reconciliation and political inclusion in the continent. Although Askwith's discourse of imperial achievement recorded in this memoir may support the view that one current feature of Western decline is the retreat of self-confident elites, less able to sustain power-generating projects through the state, it is also testimony to the unique contribution of a colonial servant inspired by his belief in the politics of inclusion and community development, spread through the influence of modest example.[34] The politics of inclusion has no more potent incarnation today than the example of Nelson Mandela and Bishop Tutu. In South Africa the balance between personal freedom and group rights; between the state and new political forces, is being carved out of difference, and the state has a crucial role as mediator between forces which bitterly contest the past. But this is not just a cult of heroism. It is a bottom-up phenomenon as Donsi Khumalo, a member of the Pretoria Metropolitan Council, testified to when he told his audience 'we have an individual responsibility for healing the wounds of apartheid'.[35] And it may provide a stimulus to the Southern African region as a whole in its encouragement of the multiplicty of political players and reconciliation. Recently, an Ecumenical

Delegation of Angolan Women held their first meeting in South Africa. Their country has been at war for twenty-eight of the last thirty years. In an unprecedented move, they called on the warring parties in Angola to stop fighting, to stop importing arms and to bring women into the process of national reconciliation.[36]

****

Tom Askwith confronted the bully. At one single moment he saw the contradictions at work in the institution which employed him. He opposed the use of force against Mau Mau prisoners who refused to work, even though he could quite easily have turned his back. In that small action he perhaps illustrated a spirit of the time which became 'the winds of change'. More recently it is the winds of retirement that Tom and Pat Askwith have enjoyed in Cheltenham, England. One of their two sons works on development projects similar to those his father began in Kenya. Tom continues to answer the numerous letters from persistent inquirers about colonial times. The money he raises from his water-colour exhibitions is routinely donated to a hospital in Kenya. Generously, he gave all his personal papers to Preston Chitere, a Kenyan academic, in the hope that African students would have easy access to this material. He returns regularly to Cambridge to keep an eye on the college First VIII. Both he and Pat have laboured together to present his memoirs to the African Studies Centre at Cambridge. In the same town back in the late eighteenth century, Peter Peckard, Master of Magdalene College, delivered a powerful sermon damning racial injustice and dismantling difference, by simply asking 'Am I not a man and a brother?' Tom Askwith must surely be seen as heir to this tradition, a tradition we ought not to forget.

Joanna Lewis
Churchill College
July 1995

Endnotes

1. I am grateful to John Lonsdale and Keith Hart for commenting on earlier drafts of this essay and to Peggy Owens for her proof-reading skills. The primary source evidence which forms the basis for much of the subsequent remarks, unless otherwise stated, is referenced in detail in ch.6 of Joanna Lewis, *'The colonial politics of African welfare, 1939-52: a crisis of paternalism'* (unpublished Ph.D, Department of History, Cambridge University, 1993).

2. John Lonsdale, `The conquest state, 1895-1904`, in William R Ochieng, (ed) *A Modern History of Kenya 1895-1980 in honour of B A Ogot* (London 1989); Terence Ranger, `Revisiting The Invention of Tradition`, ch.2 pp.62-111, in Terence Ranger and Olufemi Vaughan (eds) *Legitimacy and the State in Twentieth-Century Africa* (London, 1993).

3. For an illustration of this interlinkage in relation to the crisis in Angola see K. Hart & J. Lewis `Introduction` to Keith Hart & Joanna Lewis (eds) *Why Angola Matters* (London, 1995).

4. For a preliminary account of research in this area see S.Bander and K.Hart, `The Cambridge Anti-Slavery Caucus`, proposal for research funding, African Studies Centre, 1995.

5. Recent work on the lives of two colonial officials Frank Brayne and Sir Malcolm Darling, both ex-Cambridge, also illustrates the contribution made to colonial government by two colonial officials who moved beyond the mainstream thinkers of their time; Brayne in promoting `appropriate technology` and `community uplift` in the Punjab in the 1920s: Clive Dewey, *Anglo-Indian Attitudes: The mind of the Indian Civil Servant* (Hambledon, 1993).

6. Tabitha Kanogo, *Squatters and the Roots of Mau Mau* (London, 1989); A. H. M. Kirk-Greene, `The Thine White Line: the Size of the British Colonial Service in Africa`, *African Affairs*, 79, 314 (1980) 25-44.

7. Correspondence from Pat Askwith, 16th December 1994.

8. See Joanna Lewis, `The origins of community development in colonial Kenya`, *Journal of African History*, (forthcoming).

9. For a recent account of this period linked to the issue of the nationalist movement see Wunyabari Maloba, *Mau Mau and Kenya: an analysis of a peasant revolt* (Indiana, 1993).

10. John Kent, *The Internationalisation of Colonialism: Britain, France and Black Africa, 1939-56* (Oxford, 1992).

11. Robert Shepherd, *Iain Macleod; a biography* (London, 1994).

12. Correspondence with Tom Askwith, 8th May 1994.

13. Mss. Afr. s.1770, T G Askwith, *Memoirs*, Rhodes House Library, Oxford.

14. For example see David Cannadine, *The Decline and Fall of the British Aristocracy* (London 1990); Ronald Hyam, `Empire and Sexual Opportunity, *Journal of Imperial and Commonwealth History*, 14, 2 (1986) 42-90.

15. Correspondence from Pat Askwith, 16th December 1994.

16. Minutes of Rehabilitation Advisory Committee meetings in1955, quoted in Joanna Lewis, `On

rehabilitating Mau Mau' (East African Seminar Series, Cambridge University, unpublished paper, 8th March 1994).

17. Dane Kennedy, *Islands of white; settler society and culture in Kenya and Southern Rhodesia, 1890-1939* (Durham, 1987).

18. Chenevix Charles Trench, *The Men Who Ruled Kenya: The Kenya Administration, 1892-1963* (London 1993); for a gender sensitive analysis of colonialism's culture,see Helen Callaway, 'Purity and Exotica in Legitimating the Empire. Cultural Constructions of Gender, Sexuality and Race', ch.1. pp.31-61, in Ranger & Vaughan (eds) *Legitimacy and the State in Twentieth Century Africa*; for a portrait of the local complexities and peculiarities of colonial encounters and culture as a process which has continued into the post colonial period, see Nicolas Thomas, *Colonialisms Culture: Anthropology, Travel and Government* (Oxford, 1994).

19. See John Iliffe, *Africans: the history of a continent* (1995) for a compelling account of how Africans struggle to people a harsh and hostile environment has produced a dramatic growth in the population in recent history, a feature of the twentieth century which influenced decolonisation and more recently the collapse of apartheid.

20. John Lonsdale, 'The Moral Economy of Mau Mau: Wealth, Poverty and Civic Virtue in Kikuyu Political Thought', ch.12 in *Unhappy Valley: Conflict in Kenya and Africa. Book Two: Violence and Ethnicity* (London, 1993) pp.315-467.

21. The other chapters in Part V are : Agricultural Potential, Present Land Use, Alternatives to Customary Land Use, Tenure and Disposition of Land; *East Africa Royal Commission 1953-1955, Report* (Cmd.9475, 1955).

22. Ibid, pp.371-378.

23. Marilyn Silberfein, *Rural Change in Machakos* (Lanham, 1989); for evidence as to how this movement was carried on see Jerry Crowley, *Go To The People; An African Experience in Education for Development* (Gaba Publications, Eldoret, 1985) which describes a more recent attempt in this genre with a specific Christian agenda.

24. Luise White, 'Separating the Men from the Boys: Constructions of Gender, Sexuality and Terrorism in Central Kenya, 1939-1959', *International Journal of African Historical Studies*, 23, 1 (1990)

25. This type of external intervention is often under-resourced in more contemporary situations. Mozambique for example, had 100,000 demobilised soldiers, many of whom were illiterate. Its Ministry of Labour was given a copy of a four volumed World Bank sponsored report on training trainers, re-training and rehabilitation. But it received no money for such projects from an institution which reputedly has liquid reserves of $18.5 billion earning $1.3 billion per annum. Instead the problem was left to non-governmental organisations, like an Italian agency in Maputo training 680 ex-soldiers over nine-months to be plumbers, electricians, metal workers and mechanics; Victoria Brittain, 'Troops given tools to fight battle for survival', *The Guardian*, 19th July 1994; John Vidal, 'The Bank that likes to say sorry: Bretton Woods at 50', *The Guardian*, 22nd July 1994, pp.16-17.

26. John Keegan, 'Better at Fighting', *Times Literary Supplement*, 24th February 1995, pp.3-4. Countries like Ethiopia and Somalia may illustrate a new type of warfare conducted by military minorities who care little of what people think he argues reviewing a history of the Indian Army by S. L. Menzes, *Fidelity and Honour* (New Dehli, 1994); Robert D. Kaplan, 'The coming anarchy', *Atlantic Monthly* (February, 1994) 44-74.

27. John Lonsdale, *Unhappy Valley*, p.301 ; also `Mau Mau's of the Mind revisited`, (unpublished paper, Cambridge University, 1994).

28. For example see K.B. Wilson, `Cults of Violence and Counter-Violence in Mozambique`, *Journal of Southern African Studies*, 18, 3 (1992) 527-582; and Stephen Ellis, `Liberia 1989-1994; a study of ethnic and spiritual violence`, *African Affairs*, 94, 375 (1995) 165-197.

29. see `Conclusions` in Joao Paulo Bourges Coelho & Alex Vines, *Demobilisation and Re-integration of ex-combatants in Mozambique*, (Refugee Studies Programme, Oxford University, February 1994) p59.

30. Stephen Chan, `The Regional Context: Chances for a Stable Mozambique`, one day seminar `Mozambique: Post-Election challenges, SOAS, 2nd June 1995); for an economist's account of the failure of the post-colonial state to develop peasant production in Ghana, see J.H. Frimpong-Ansah, *The Vampire State in Africa: the political economy of decline in Ghana* (London 1991).

31.. William Finnegan, The Harrowing of Mozambique (London, 1992); see Joanna Lewis, `ON-U-MOZ, get set, go! Confessions of a UN Election Observer` (forthcoming Prickly Pear Press, 1995).

32. see Antony Giddens, `Modernity and Utopia`, *New Statesman and Society*, 3, 129 (1990) pp.20-22 on the importance of administrative capacity in the history of modernity.

33. Wole Soyinka described the state apparatus in his country Nigeria thus: `more than three decades after Independence, nothing works because nothing is intended to work`, Adewale Maja-Pearce, *Times Literary Supplement*, 24th February 1994, p.27; Robin Theobold, `Lancing the Swollen African State: Will it Alleviate the Problem of Corruption?`, *Journal of Modern African Studies*, 32, 4 (1994) 701-706.

34. see Ken Jowitt, `Our Republic of Fear`, *Times Literary Supplement*, 10th February 1995, pp.3-4.

35. Donsi Khumalo addressing the Action for Southern Africa Forum, University of London, 4th March 1995.

36. Kathryn O'Neill, (Christian Aid) `The role of the church organisations in Angola` , paper given at African Studies Centre One-day International Seminar, `Angola 1995: the road to peace`, Pembroke College, Cambridge, 1995.

PART I
Memoirs of Colonial Kenya

Chapter One

The country and its people
a personal view

Kenya, as seen on the map, is a rhomboid about the size of France, bounded by the Indian Ocean in the south-east, Tanzania on the south-west, Lake Victoria in the west and Ethiopia in the north. Down the centre runs the great cleft of the Rift Valley which starts in the Jordan valley and runs down the Red Sea, crosses Ethiopia, Kenya and Tanzania and peters out in Malawi. So put simply, the country consists of a series of zones running from north to south with the Rift Valley dividing it down the middle.

What about its inhabitants? They are, of course, very varied but may be divided into three main groups; the Bantu, who are mostly cultivators, the Luo who practise mixed farming, and the nomads. Each inhabit the area which best suits its own culture. Moving from east to west, one first encounters the coastal tribes, who are Bantu, then one crosses the huge Taru desert which is uninhabited, until one reaches the highlands, dominated by Mount Kenya in the north and the Aberdare mountains in the south. The eastern slopes are watered by the monsoon rains twice a year and so are blessed by the deep loam of former forests and are inhabited by another Bantu group consisting of the Kikuyu, Kamba and allied tribes.

Beyond the Aberdares lies the Rift Valley which lies at an average of 5000 feet. The soil consists of volcanic dust and is of low agricultural value. It was all originally inhabited by the nomadic Maasai. To the west of the Rift Valley the land rises to over ten thousand feet and is mostly forested. It is well watered by winds off Lake Victoria in the west. Beyond the forests lies a belt of land inhabited by two semi-pastoral tribes allied to the Maasai, the Kipsigis and the Nandi. To the west of them again the land descends to 5000 feet and becomes richer agriculturally. It is inhabited by Bantu people, the Abaluhya in the north and the Gusii in the south. In the belt of land bordering the Lake live the Luo who enjoy a mixed economy derived from agriculture, animal husbandry and fishing. Finally, in the vast northern deserts live the nomadic Turkana, Boran and Somali with other kindred tribes.

The most fertile areas are those on the Eastern slopes of Mount Kenya and the Aberdares and the hills fed by rains from Lake Victoria in the west. The least fertile ones are obviously the deserts in the north and east. The Rift Valley is essentially infertile except for livestock as otherwise it would have been inhabited by agricultural people in the first place. Arthur Hazlewood in *The Economy of Kenya, the Kenyatta Era* classifies the fertility of the various zones as follows:-

> 100% of the land in Nyanza and Western Province falls within the "High and Medium potential range", 90% of Central (Kikuyu) Province falls within the same category while only 20% of the Rift Valley Province is so included.

As in other parts of the world the inhabitants have in the past been constantly on the move. Sometimes small family groups infiltrated into other areas as a result of pressure of population. More regularly families moved to virgin land as their fields became exhausted by over-cultivation.

Similarly, they were constantly in danger of attack from other tribes or from clans of their own tribe. These attacks were mainly for the purpose of stealing cattle, but sometimes, as in the case of the Maasai, to acquire women. In this way they adjusted their economies when they had become decimated by drought and consequent famines or by diseases of their livestock, which were regular occurrences. Even in the 1930's it was possible to see the remains of protective stone walls around homesteads, although the stockades which had originally been constructed from timber had disintegrated. Stock theft was still a common occurrence although it was becoming less a matter of necessity and more a form of sport.

The people could be divided into linguistic groups which probably shared a common ancestry. First there were the Bantu speaking peoples who had moved from the south into the coastal strip next to the Indian Ocean, to the slopes of Mount Kenya and to the highland belt between the Kalenjin and the Luo, the former originating from Ethiopia. Next there were the Luo themselves who had moved, over the centuries, from the upper reaches of the Nile in Uganda and the southern Sudan along the lake shore and into Tanzania. Finally, there were the Maasai who had moved south from the northern Sudan, and some claim from Egypt itself, into the Rift Valley and the plains extending into Tanzania.

Each group of people settled in areas suited to its culture; the agriculturalists in the fertile forest areas, the pastoralists in the plains and the nomads in the deserts. There were, naturally, no fixed boundaries between them, instead, by common consent, they left belts of no-mans-land. These were usually those areas of country where one climatic zone gave way to another. In the area near Nairobi, for instance, where the forests began to give way to the savannah of the Rift Valley, the Kikuyu left a belt of forest land uncultivated. This enabled the young warriors to climb the trees and keep watch for marauding Maasai. As soon as an invasion party was seen trotting towards Kikuyu country armed with long spears and painted shields, their lion mane headdresses giving them added height, probably shouting in unison as they forged their way through the long grass, the outposts would leap down from their lookouts in the trees and sprint back to sound the alarm in the villages. As many as could would then make their escape into the surrounding undergrowth. The Moran would round up the cattle and slaughter the old and helpless, but take the younger women with them after setting light to the huts. The Kikuyu, not surprisingly, lived in terror of the Maasai as people in other parts of Kenya feared the Arab slave raiders. The Arabs themselves were reluctant to pass through Maasailand, instead they skirted the plains to the south.

The Tradition of Community

There is a salient point about the structure of East African society; the people were all dominated by a sense of community. This is not to suggest that they were communist inclined or held all their property together but that they were controlled in all matters concerning society as a whole by their councils of elders to whom they gave great respect. What is more, by custom there was a clear division of labour, particularly as between men and women. In general the women were responsible for everything relating to the home, which, apart from the preparation of food, extended to the collection of firewood and water and the lighter agricultural tasks. Strangers have sometimes concluded that the men were an idle lot and left all the work to the women but they have overlooked the fact that men had to keep themselves fit and in readiness to attack their enemies as required. At the same time they did undertake the heavy duties relating to building the perimeter defences of villages, cutting the timber for houses, and hunting. We still see vestiges of this tendency in our own society where it is usually the men who go fishing, shooting or even coursing! The women were, in fact, proud of their strength, and were well aware of the fact that this was a bonus when men were looking for a wife. Visitors from abroad, particularly politicians eager to find fault, often made fools of themselves in this respect. On one occasion a British MP was actually unwise enough to criticise the men of a certain tribe for expecting their wives to carry enormous loads of firewood. It was the women, however, who objected most to such remarks, considering them a reflection on their physical ability.

The division of labour was a sensible system so long as the country was constantly in a state of war. When that danger was removed the young men were indeed left with little purpose in their lives and society began to suffer from the same kind of unrest which more sophisticated ones experience in times of mass unemployment.

Another overriding principle of traditional society was that of self-sufficiency or what is referred to as a subsistence economy. This simply means that each village depended on the country side in its immediate vicinity to meet its physical requirements. All the essentials for the maintenance of life were available there, water, firewood, honey for beer, thatching grass, game, fish and herbal medicines. Any family could call on the assistance of its neighbours for any job beyond its own capacity. Failure to respond could incur the ultimate penalty - banishment. Anyone who was exiled in this way would almost inevitably perish.

Such were the sanctions which held society together and although life was often extremely hard it had possibly more stability than that under colonial rule however benevolent it happened to be, as we shall see in due course. But a common characteristic of all these people was that although from time to time circumstances forced them to move in a body, their horizons were limited. So the way of each community was dictated by its environment and most have remained in the same neighbourhood from generation to generation; the pattern of existence had to be adapted to its characteristics. Experience dictated which timber was termite-resistant and thus suitable for building, which types of grass or reed made the best thatching material, which gourds were most suitable for containers to carry water, and so on.

A particularly significant aspect of these tribal groups was that they were communities in the absolute sense of the term, a sense which has long disappeared in our society. This is to say they relied on a common loyalty and sense of co-operation. They had developed a highly integrated social and economic organisation.

These were some of the principles that western immigrants to Kenya, reared in an individualistic society, found most difficult to grasp. It was only when they learned to base their development schemes on the traditional structure of society that they succeeded in solving some of the problems resulting from the introduction of colonialism.

The main differences between the people inhabiting the various areas, apart from their languages, always a symptom of isolation, were in their ways of life. The Maasai, Turkana and Somali were all nomadic, largely dependent upon the milk, blood and meat of their livestock whether cattle, sheep, goats or camels. The Bantu group, as forest clearers, were mainly vegetarian. The

Luo would naturally supplement their diet with fish. All to a greater or lesser extent, apart from the Kikuyu and Maasai, would hunt the abundant wild game.

Strangely, the diet adopted by the different tribes seemed to affect their temperaments: the Maasai and Somali being more aggressive and conservative; the semi-pastoral people like the Kalenjin were warlike but not so aggressive; the Luo robust and extrovert; the Kikuyu tending towards secrecy, but adaptable and keen to learn all they could from immigrants. The original inhabitants of the forest land had been hunters but had been absorbed by the Bantu people when they settled there.

At the time just before the arrival of the colonists, the population of Kenya amounted to only a small fraction of what it has become today and the reasons for this will be analysed in the next chapter. Lord Lugard in his *Dual Mandate in British Tropical Africa* estimated the population of Kenya in 1919 to be 2.6 million and the Report of the *Kenya Land Commission* published in 1934 calculated that it was increasing at a rate of 3% per annum. The 1962 census gave a population of 7 million. By 1969 this had risen to 11 million increasing at 2.8% per annum.

There were other factors that we have to appreciate. Two of the most important were superstition and fatalism, both of which helped the people to rise above the calamities which so often overwhelmed them. women did not help in the enforcement of discipline and obedience to tribal authority as it did in medieval Britain, but it was generally believed that no accident, sickness or misfortune ever occurred unless the individual had offended someone in some way. What is more, this "someone" might include an ancestor who was regarded as as much alive as one's neighbour. People lived in dread of offending, sometimes unconsciously, in some way or another and in consequence were perpetually in need of being cleansed of their guilt.

These points are important to bear in mind when we consider the problems of Mau Mau and community development in due course.

Chapter Two

Colonisation

It was largely the search for ivory and the trading of slaves that stimulated the interest of foreigners in East Africa. This was in a way connected with inter-tribal war since victorious tribes found they could dispose of their captives to the Arabs at a profit. In turn, the Arabs used the slaves as a means of transport for the ivory they acquired on their forays. Currency was often cowrie shells which they brought up from the coast, or beads. Joseph Thomson, one of the most remarkable young Scottish explorers, when he reached Nyanza on the shores of Lake Victoria described how the local populace was rather less friendly than the people he had met a few days earlier and it was quite possible that the column was again mistaken for a slavery party. A number of slavers had been known to operate with impunity in the district, including one particularly unsavoury character called Sudi the Slaver. The activities of tribal war as chief fought against chief enabled them to get captives to sell for firearms and trade goods.

Indians acquired ivory for their carvings from the Arabs. The Portuguese started trading somewhat later, but were mainly concerned with provisioning their merchant ships en route to Goa. But it was the threat of German control of the headwaters of the Nile which tipped the scales. Dr David Livingstone had been urging Britain to put a stop to the slave trade for some time without much success. Now she finally agreed to build a railway from Mombasa to Uganda via Kisumu on Lake Victoria, to provision the garrison established by Captain, later Lord Lugard. The main purpose of this force was to bring influence to bear on the Khedive in Cairo and so maintain Britain's control of the Suez Canal, her commercial lifeline with India.

A point to remember is that administrative control over this vast area was achieved by very few men with very little bloodshed. When one considers the slaughter of the indigenous inhabitants which has occurred in most areas of the world, including our own islands, at the hands of invaders, the cost in human lives in Kenya was small. A more important consideration is what was achieved to improve the quality of their life. Professor P T Bauer in his *Equality, The Third World and Economic Delusion* has this to say: 'Colonial conquest was usually attended by bloodshed. The extent of the bloodshed and the forms of coercion differ greatly in the various areas. In the British colonies it was generally slight, especially in East Africa' [emphasis mine - TGA].

Joseph Thomson had this to say of his experiences when he reached the country surrounding present-day Nairobi in 1883:-

> When Kimameta and the traders had last visited Ngong they had taken advantage of the villagers who came to sell their produce at the forest edge and captured some. Some were redeemed by their relatives, the remainder were taken to the coast and sold into slavery. The traders followed the incident by attacking several villages, killing a number of people and kidnapping others.

Since the Maasai look on agriculture as a menial occupation and to this day seldom till the soil, fresh vegetables had to be bought from the Kikuyu, who were understandably distrustful of leaving their forest enclaves because of the enmity of the traders and the large number of Maasai ever present around the camp. The only way markets could be established was to penetrate the forest and approach them direct. Thomson undertook this somewhat dangerous enterprise and set foot in one of the most lovely woodland scenes he had ever seen. A two-hour march brought his well armed party face to face with the Kikuyu for the first time.

The Railway Line

The British Government faced the problem of reimbursing itself for the cost of building the railway line, which at one point reached an altitude of 10,000 feet above sea level, and cost about 5.5 million. The rolling stock had to be remarkable too, since the only fuel was wood, and a special type of locomotive, the Garratt, with twin sets of driving wheels, was evolved to tackle the gradients. Construction of the line down the face of the Rift Valley involved a funicular lift at one point. So what with the problems of overcoming attacks by man-eating lion and the repeated theft of copper telephone wires to adorn the local women, the engineers had many difficulties to overcome and at considerable cost.

The fact that the railway, for a large part of its length, ran up the rift Valley through some of the finest scenery and in glorious climatic conditions suggested to the authorities, however, that it might contribute to large scale agricultural development as was the case in Canada and the United States, and this spelled colonisation.

A great point in its favour was that the surrounding countryside was apparently virtually uninhabited, except for a few roving Maasai. Joseph Thomson reported that after a long period of inter-necine battles in the 1880's the Laikipiak were decimated to such an extent that they ceased to maintain their separate identity. Cattle were dying in their hundreds [probably from rinderpest: TGA.] The dreadful stench emanating from heaps of putrefying carcases made life in the manyattas almost unbearable. According to Thomson, the Laikipiak were torn between the belief that the strange white man was the perpetrator of the disease systematically destroying their herds, and the possessor of the medicines which would cure them.

The British government agreed to the settlement scheme as long as the Maasai, who lived along the railway line, could be peaceably persuaded to move and join their kindred to the south of Nairobi. After somewhat protracted negotiations this was successfully achieved, although certain sections suffered considerable losses in both human and animal terms in the course of their moves, first to Laikipia and then to the south. The way was now clear for the opening up of the area to what became known as 'white settlement'. In addition to the Maasai grazing areas it was decided to include in the areas available for white settlement the buffer zones between tribes referred to earlier, for two reasons; firstly because both nature and man abhor a vacuum, and secondly since a human barrier between tribes could be as, if not more, effective in doing away with tribal skirmishes and cattle rustling as the forest belts. This was a decision fraught with political difficulties at a later date.

Farmers were encouraged to come out to develop these plains where the agrarian, economic and social problems were almost completely unknown. One of the greatest challenges was how to persuade people to leave their homes in the fertile areas and work for foreigners, for they had no understanding or indeed need of money. They had all they required to sustain life within their home areas.

Someone hit on the idea of introducing a poll or head tax, which is not usually a popular idea in any country. To obtain the money with which to pay it the individual concerned would have to work; the old people, were, of course, exempted. It was argued that with the removal of inter-tribal war the young men had little to occupy their time and should contribute to the cost of government and help pay for the security they now enjoyed.

In fact, no great objection was raised to the tax which was probably regarded as a legitimate charge made by the new rulers in return for security, although many obviously believed it went straight into the pockets of the District Commissioners! They found it would involve working for the settlers for a few months of the year and in addition to their wages they were provided with food and even the right to graze a number of cattle and livestock on the settlers' land as squatters and to cultivate a few acres as well, if they wished, so it seemed worthwhile. It must be remembered that the term 'squatter' comprises those Africans with a legally recognised right to live and cultivate on a white settler's farm and does not mean 'trespasser'.

The pattern of their lives, in fact, would probably be similar to that of farm labourers in England at that time, although sociologists might suggest that this was hardly a standard of living to aspire to. Nevertheless, it was higher than they often enjoyed in their traditional homelands.

A point which was probably not entirely lost on them, however, was that they would be living on and cultivating land originally occupied by their traditional enemies the Maasai, or else on land left unoccupied as a first line of defence against them.

But the advantage of being free from hunger would have been a major consideration. In the case of most Africans the period immediately prior to the onset of the rains was almost invariably one where everyone had to tighten his belt if he wore one in case he had to make his food reserves last till the following harvest. Existence was often measured by the period which separated one famine or pestilence and the next.

At that time, of course, it was the basic needs of life which were the most important, but there was another factor which counted a great deal among the young men - the opportunity for the first time in living experience to travel, and, what is more, in safety. This was a most exciting prospect. Most people had never in their lives been further than a dozen miles from their homes on hunting expeditions, unless they had had the misfortune to fall in with an Arab caravan. Few had any idea what a train was, for instance, except by report, and had certainly no idea that there was such a thing as the sea in which vast boats floated. Now there were opportunities to work hundreds of miles from home and to return as heroes to tell their stay-at-home companions and girl friends all about the world outside.

Of course eventually, the experience of travel and adventure began to pall, especially when instead of being able to go out simply to earn enough to pay one's poll tax, one became saddled with the need to earn quite large sums for, say, a bicycle or fancy clothes and, of course, later to pay the children's school fees. It was this problem which became the ruling passion of their lives. African parents would often half-starve themselves to ensure that their children got the opportunity of education. This phenomenon, therefore, deserves to be looked at more thoroughly.

The Missionaries

It is not always appreciated that the first white pioneers to brave the hardships and dangers of the deserts which separated Kenya proper from its gateway at Mombasa were missionaries. The first white man to catch a glimpse of the craggy peak of Mount Kenya piercing the clouds on the far horizon was a Swiss missionary named Dr Krapf. He described his first experience of landing on the coast of Africa as follows:-

> They lifted me out of the boat and bore me on their shoulders to the land with singing, dancing, brandishing of arrows and every possible mode of rejoicing. Ascending from the shore across a grassy soil we arrived at a wood of lofty trees. The narrow footpath in the wood led to three entrances in a triple palisade which encircled the village. The Wanyika had made a favourable impression on me for they were both quick and well behaved but wore extremely little in the way of clothes, even the women not being sufficiently clad.
>
> When I declared to the chiefs that I was not a soldier, nor a merchant who had come to trade but a Christian teacher who wished to instruct the Wanyika... in the true knowledge of God, they looked at me with something of a stupefied expression.

Later he illustrated the attitude of some Wakamba he was staying with as follows:-

> If I wished to read they would ask if I was trying to spy into their hearts or whether I was looking for rain and enquiring after diseases. When I wrote they wanted to know what I had written and whether it contained sorcery.

These brave men and their loyal families came patently as messengers of peace. They taught the secrets of eternal life - not in fact an idea very far removed from African concepts of the hereafter, for they had a firm belief in the survival of their ancestors and were convinced that God lived on the unattainable summit of Mount Kenya. Missionaries also built hospitals and schools financed by contributions made by the congregations of the little parishes in Britain. So these missionaries had something more than their Christian message, they had a particular and unique form of magic. They could, by making marks on a piece of paper, or even in the sand, convey messages to others without even uttering a syllable. They could also send messages to people far away by means of a runner with a cleft stick. Writing must, they argued, also hold the secret of how the white man was able to cure sicknesses more effectively than their own doctors. If only they too could acquire this skill they might be able to compete with the white man by learning the secret of his powers.

Hard on the heels of the missionaries came the adventurers, the explorers and hunters, some of whom came in search of ivory like the Arabs before them, although they did not necessarily come for money. Some simply looked for excitement in order to escape the dullness of industrialized Europe. We as a nation have never been lacking in such enterprising individuals and it is probably true to suggest that the great majority of those, both men and women, who came out to Kenya were motivated simply by the spirit of adventure. Whether they came to work for the government or, having some capital, to settle, or, like the missionaries to respond to the evangelistic urge which lurks under the surface of many who wish to serve their fellow creatures, or even those who simply hoped to make their fortunes, none were deterred by the risks involved, believing or hoping that they would be the lucky ones and not perish from blackwater fever or a Maasai's spear.

British Administration
With the completion of the main railway line to Uganda branch lines were built to other parts of the country which showed promise of being able to provide exports. From these a web of roads linked the more remote areas. The government divided the country into administrative districts according to the tribal pattern prevailing and appointed chiefs and headmen to take charge of the particular clans which inhabited them. In due course, councils were elected by the people to advise on the development of the districts and indigenous courts of law to deal with disputes.

Technical staff were appointed to promote the cultivation of new crops with a saleable value. Hospitals and schools were built to relieve the missions of some of their burdens. Veterinary Officers began to immunise stock from East Coast fever and rinderpest.

Some important observations were made by the Pearson Commission to the World Bank regarding this period. Professor Sir Arthur Lewis has argued that the tropics were transformed during the period 1830 to 1913. In 1913 sub-Saharan exports were only 6.2% of tropical trade. By 1937 they were

13.3% and by 1955 sub-Saharan exports constituted 16.2% of tropical trade.

P T Bauer in his book *Equality, the Third World and Economic Delusion* points out that:-

> Social and economic change was so rapid that the governments and their advisers had little time to examine some of its implications and consequences. This circumstance may partly explain the land policies of the British colonial governments.

Had the colonial governments been less pressed by rapid change their land policies might have been based on a more thorough understanding of social realities.

The extreme material backwardness of pre-colonial Africa exacerbated the difficulties and complexities of sudden change. The huge area depended on muscle power for transport and communications, usually human muscle.

As I have already noted, the basic ingredients of modern social and economic life including public security and health, wheeled transport, modern forms of money and scientific agriculture were brought to sub-Saharan Africa by westerners in the nineteenth and early twentieth centuries. They were introduced by the colonial administration or by foreign private organisations or persons under the comparative security of colonial rule and usually in the face of formidable obstacles.

The work of actually building the railway had largely been undertaken by Asians from India. They came as artisans and skilled labourers, and when the line was completed set up in business, building little general stores in even the remotest parts of the colony, undeterred by loneliness and the dangers of their situation. They even provided an unofficial banking service for the locals, and were an essential element in the development process as builders, mechanics and even in certain areas as farmers.

The White Settlers

Finally, of course, came the white settlers who have been described so often that there is little need for me to deal with them in detail, except to refer to a few aspects, which seem to have been overlooked by historians.

To begin with, they were not allocated all the best land. I have referred to this already indirectly with reference to the comparatively low rainfall and hence poor fertility of the Rift Valley, where most of them became established. The Rift Valley was the least fertile of the highland regions.

The foundation of ordered government in the tribal areas had scarcely been laid and the first settlers had barely completed their mud-plastered and thatched-roofed farmhouses when Kenya was confronted with its first major crisis - war against Germany, in Tanganyika.

All who could enlisted and wives took over responsibility for farms in desperately lonely places and in sole charge of the squatters. Often quite young and with children, the only doctor scores of miles away over rutted tracks, they bravely survived while their husbands were away. How often do we give a thought to how they endured those long four years? It was no holiday in the sunshine as enjoyed by tourists these days. What is more, when we read about exploitation do we appreciate the loyalty of the squatters who helped these young people to survive? Does it sound like the oppression of the slave plantations? I imagine that all of them - black and white - felt they were in it together. After all, thousands of Africans joined up too and as many died from malaria as from bullets.

After the war the farmers returned to their homes to try to go on from where they had left off. They were joined by even younger men often sickened and disgusted by years in the trenches of Flanders, yearning for peace and a clean air to breathe and a worthwhile existence. Such men also joined government service and many felt an urge to help the inhabitants to enjoy a better life too, free from warfare and famine and disease, with hope for the future instead of fear.

But their troubles were not yet over. Over the horizon came locusts in vast ominous clouds which laid waste to the land, to the crops, the young coffee trees and the grassland and to anything which grew. No one knew how to stop them. All they could do was beat their tin cans and hope to frighten them away - but the locusts were even hungrier than the humans.

Every kind of disease of cattle or wheat had to be overcome. The banks had to be persuaded to help them to carry the burden. The Asian shopkeepers in the tribal areas carried out much the same function with the African population.

Then, to cap it all, came the world slump when the bottom fell out of the coffee and flax markets. It was the end for many. Even the government servants had to take a cut in their salaries; recruitment was halted.
But at last things began to improve. No one had illusions any more but with

luck they might survive. Already, but scarcely appreciated, the population in the tribal areas began to expand, a sure sign that there was at least enough food about. The market for printed materials and sewing machines took off. The Raleigh advertisement of an African with a broad grin on his face speeding away from a lion must have sold a lot of bicycles.

How the Tribal Areas Became Exhausted

While the Rift Valley and the neighbouring areas were being opened up through the enterprise of the settlers, similar campaigns were being conducted in the tribal areas. Not only was a structure of government being set up, but cash crops suitable to the climatic conditions of the respective areas were being introduced; cotton and sugar in Nyanza, for instance, and wattle in the Kikuyu area, maize everywhere. But certain crops such as coffee and tea were regarded as only suitable for cultivation in plantations if standards were to be maintained. This proved to be a bone of contention at a later stage but it certainly did contribute to the recognition of Kenya coffee and tea as standards of excellence on the world's markets. Later, as we shall see, they were developed as peasant products, under close supervision, with considerable success.

Naturally, pressure on the land began to increase not simply on account of the expanding population but also because of the volume of cash crops being cultivated. The cause of this population explosion needs to be evaluated.

First of all, I think all would agree that the medical missionaries have done as much as any other agency to reduce the deaths among infants and older people. The chance of survival of newborn babies was in the past very slim and those who reached what we call middle age were classed as elders. Apart from what the missionaries provided there were at first no medical services for the public as a whole. Mortality was due to a multiplicity of diseases aggravated by malnutrition and at times starvation.

The second great killer was famine. We know only too well how horrific famine can actually be when it has occurred in such countries as Sudan, Ethiopia and Somalia. During the colonial period in Kenya, however, starvation was kept at bay simply because grain could be transported along the new network of railways and roads from areas of adequacy to those of scarcity. The alleviation of shortage is, after all, mainly a matter of transportation, relief works and fair distribution.

The third great killer, of course, was inter-tribal war, which was effectively abolished during the colonial period.

It was, then, the removal of these scourges by colonisation that led to the unparalleled growth of population. A process had been started which would inexorably expand year by year and, at the same time, naturally aggravate the demands made upon the soil. The old beneficial practice of shifting cultivation had come to an end when there was no more virgin land available to cultivate. The inevitable consequence was soil erosion and the removal of the top soil by torrential rains. The growing herds of cattle, sheep and goats completed the destruction of the grazing.

In the meanwhile the demands for labour on the farms in the newly settled area of the Rift Valley, on the coffee and tea estates planted, for the main part, in the buffer areas between tribes, and in the semi-desert areas where sisal was planted meant that most of the able-bodied men left their homelands for longer and longer periods. Others went to the towns, to the docks, the railways and the expanding industries. The more educated of them went to work in offices while others enlisted in the army, police and prison services. All were expected to supplement their low wages with the produce of their holdings.

A giant efflux had taken place leaving only the old, the women and the children and the local government staff in the tribal areas. The women were the least able to carry this burden of agricultural development and to grow cash crops in addition to their household obligations. Inevitably, the condition of these tribal areas, once the most fertile parts of the country, began to deteriorate alarmingly and could no longer satisfy the needs of a family.

One can only conclude, therefore, that it was those very humanitarian measures undertaken to remove the evils which had kept the population in check - warfare, disease, famine, slavery and so forth - which had themselves become the cause of destruction. It was not exploitation, as some have suggested, that was to blame but an undermining of the balance of nature which had previously limited the population to the carrying capacity of the land. To those who argued that the settlers should give up their exclusive rights to land to provide for the increasing number of landless people, it was objected that the latter would quickly destroy it in the same way as had happened in the tribal areas.

This apparently insuperable problem was exacerbated by the fact that the inhabitants, conditioned by centuries of calamities, were not prepared to limit the size of either their families or their stock. They regarded the former as the future supporters of the tribe and the latter as their traditional measure of wealth and source of dowry. Each in their own way had represented a form of insurance which they were not prepared to abandon.

Chapter Three

The Second World War and the drift towards Mau Mau

The approaching economic and social calamity was apparent but it was delayed by the outbreak of the Second World War. Thousands were recruited for service. Kenya became the base for troops from all over Africa and the United Kingdom for the assault on Abyssinia and later for the support of the North African and Burma campaigns. Enormous sums were expended by Britain and these tended to mask the deterioration occurring in the tribal areas, although great expansion took place in the settled areas and towns.

Fortunately the war was not the long-drawn-out affair of the first one insofar as Kenya was concerned, but when Abyssinia fell Kenya became the granary for East Africa and, to a lesser extent, for the Middle East. At last the industry of the farmers was beginning to pay dividends.

The war ended with the country in much better economic shape than ever before, but yet one more cloud appeared on the horizon. This time it was much more serious, however, and presaged war in the country itself, war much more vicious than anything in the past - civil war and terrorism.

The thunder of political unrest and crime gave warning of the impending storm, but few took any notice of it. As has been pointed out, the first settlers, as soon as the inhabitants got over the shock of their arrival, were not regarded as a menace. In fact, they were seen to be a positive advantage and life had become much more secure and agreeable than previously. This state of affairs was not to last, however. Those who had enlisted and fought in Burma had seen something of the outside world. They began to see that they could run the country just as capably as these foreign usurpers as they were described in the world's press. Why not overthrow them and take over their farms?

During the war many had enlisted and enjoyed a standard of living higher than anything they had known before. They were able to send remittances home and for a long time the dangerous imbalance in the economy was not apparent. When peace came they were paid their gratuities and often given training for civilian employment and business, but all this could not guarantee them jobs nor meet the demands of the next generation who were leaving school in ever increasing numbers. An explosion was inevitable.

Racial Discrimination

There was also the question of discrimination in the matter of wage and salary rates. They came back into an economy with the same pattern of remuneration as when they enlisted years before. It still took no account of the man's family which the produce of his land was expected to support. What if he had no land, as was the case with the children of some of the squatters?

A further source of resentment was that fostered by the lack of better paid jobs for those leaving the secondary schools in particular. Parents who had scraped and saved to give their sons an adequate education, often at the cost of being separated from their families for most of their working lives, found that at the end they had nothing to show for it. This bred a burning sense of bitterness in the whole system, resulting in an alliance being formed between the better educated landless and those who lacked any qualifications at all, the "mikora". Neither of them had anything to lose by revolution and, perhaps, something to gain.

It may be argued that there was insufficient land for the Settlers' needs. To this one must reply that the acquisition of a few farms was probably all that was needed to meet the needs of the landless which would have been money well spent in the interests of peace and security.

Life in Post-War Nairobi

I was appointed to take charge of the welfare of the African inhabitants of Nairobi just before the end of the war. For the next four years one was to see the growth of the ulcer which shortly afterwards was to burst in the shape of Mau Mau. While in certain ways one became a helpless spectator of events, in another one had an unrivalled view of the spread of the problems which in a few years were to engulf the entire body of African society.

One of the first recommendations I made to the City Council on taking up my new post of Municipal Native Affairs Officer for Nairobi was to recommend the appointment of an African to assist me. I insisted that firstly, he should be a Kikuyu and so representative of the dominant tribe of the area: secondly, that he should be remunerated on such a scale as to render him possibly the best-paid African in Kenya at that time. But one realised that money could not by itself provide the service which was required, and I must record the immense debt I feel towards Dedan Githege. He was entitled Assistant , but in fact he was far more than that and acted as my confidant and advisor. Everything I was able to achieve, such as it was, was due to his wise advice. In the process, of course, I sometimes made myself unpopular with the councillors who were nearly all white and many must have thought my recommendations were sometimes far too radical. But this view was undoubtedly shared by most of my colleagues in the Administration and I was prepared to accept it as a natural feature of the task.

I was fortunate in being freed from most of the bureaucratic duties which beset most civil servants at that time. It was my task to keep a finger on the pulse of African public opinion. As a result I was able to spend the first hour of each working day in simply talking to Dedan and any other member of the African community who might keep us informed of what was going on, whether socially, politically or economically.

The second hour would be spent in reading the vernacular newspapers and in particular the correspondence columns. In this way I gained an insight into the state of public opinion which was at least as reliable as the Special Branch reports, compiled from information gleaned from informers who were, as likely as not, activated more by private interest and the hope of reward than the public good.

A Meeting with Jomo Kenyatta

A case in point was the incident when Jomo Kenyatta was persuaded to oppose the railway strike in Nairobi in 1947. Dedan told me at one of our morning sessions that this was imminent and moreover that Jomo Kenyatta was due to address a mass meeting at the Kaloleni Hall during the preceding weekend. It was quite clear what he was suggesting; that he might be prepared to speak out against it. It seemed worth trying. Dedan said he would ask him to come and see me.

On the Saturday morning a car drew up outside our office and a crowd of passers-by immediately began to collect. Out stepped Jomo resplendent in his beaded cap, fly-whisk and double breasted suit. Amid much cheering and waving of the fly-whisk he walked slowly and with great dignity up to the office. Dedan welcomed him at the door. In order to make the occasion as casual as possible I waited a while before going in to Dedan's office to greet him.

We talked of this and that until I brought the conversation round to the subject of the impending strike. I commented that if it came off it might be difficult for us to maintain peace in the city since the Railway administration would, I supposed, replace the Kikuyu, who were the ones who advocated the strike, by members of other tribes in order to keep the line working. This might well cause inter-tribal riots and that would be the end of the goodwill I understood Jomo was trying to build up between the various ethnic groups. He nodded, but made no comment, and after a while he left, with the greatest goodwill on both sides.

Next day he attended the mass meeting at Kaloleni Hall. As usual he was an hour late, I suppose to increase the state of excitement and anticipation. It was reported that he spoke for two hours, but without a mention of the strike which was all that anyone wished to hear about. At last he brought the subject up. "I hear" he said "that there is talk of a railway strike in Nairobi." He paused and raised his ebony stick with its ivory handle above his head. There was a deathly silence. "If anyone supports such an idea" he continued ominously "I shall knock his block off", or words to that effect.

The silence continued and shortly afterwards he left. There was no strike, which demonstrated the power that he wielded over the Kikuyu. One wondered whether it was also intended as a reminder to the government of the fact and perhaps that he stood on the side of law and order, a sign which all in authority had waited to hear from him. The overture was not accepted, however, and those who hoped that discussions might take place between him and the government to try to avert the impending crisis, which is dealt with later, were disappointed.

The United Kenya Club and Inter-racial Co-operation

Discussions did, however, take place between Jomo and some of the senior members of the United Kenya Club, but although I was Chairman I could not as a civil servant participate. Hugh La Fontaine, a former head of the Administration, who was also a foundation member of the club was their prime mover, but they got nowhere. Jomo obviously wanted talks to take place at a much higher level, but he did by his presence indicate that he wished to negotiate. The Government was presumably equally determined not to do so.

The United Kenya Club had been formed for social not political purposes, although it was difficult to avoid political discussion from intruding during our weekly lunches and social gatherings. Its purpose was to provide a meeting place for those of goodwill and free of racial prejudice on a basis of complete equality. Membership of the three main ethnic groups was kept to equal numbers. Applicants for membership were subject to veto if any member of the committee considered that he or she might not conform to the Club's requirements.

This led to an embarrassing situation at a later stage when Derek Erskine, a very senior Nairobi citizen, knighted for his outstanding contribution in that respect, applied for membership. He was black-balled! The reason for this was that during a recent electioneering campaign he had referred to Africans in the terms of Rudyard Kipling's famous poem as 'the lesser breeds without the law'. This had been published in the local press and understandably caused great offence.

What the African members did not appreciate was that Derek in his flamboyant way referred to those who were not enfranchised, namely the African section of the population, and so suffered discrimination in consequence.

I, as Chairman, had the thankless task of breaking the news to Derek and he, typically, asked if he might meet the committee and apologise for the unintentional offence caused, which he could very well appreciate. The committee agreed and went further, and later invited him to re-apply for membership.

A sequel to this unfortunate incident was that Derek later made it possible for the Club to move from its corrugated iron shed to its present handsome quarters near the University, where it continues to flourish. On a later visit to Nairobi I visited the Club and was invited to talk to the members about the early days. After the lunch I could not help expressing my surprise to the Chairman that the original constitution and object of the Club were still maintained even though one of its original purposes, to overcome racial discrimination, was no longer a problem. He replied that, on the other hand, there was still a need to reinforce the measures initiated by Jomo Kenyatta to ensure that inter-racial and, let us admit it, inter-tribal harmony should be maintained. It is enormously encouraging to see this policy apparently succeeding, and long may it continue to do so.

The success of the Club was due to a series of outstanding members, many of whom became Chairmen in their turn. I cannot speak of the more recent ones, but I remember with great affection those of my own time. Bethuel Gecaga, now a very prominent business man who always avoided the limelight and took no part in politics; Bill Kirkaldy Willis, Bethuel's foster father, the last of a long line of medical missionaries in Kikuyuland; Hassan Nathoo, a great enthusiast who eventually moved his thriving dental practice to London; Shirley Victor Cooke, a Member of Legislative Council, who delighted in urging liberalism on the government in no uncertain terms. He was in the tradition of a number of the earlier District Commissioners who felt it incumbent upon them to champion the cause of their African wards, however unpopular they might become in high places in the process; S.O. Josiah, City Councillor and continuing friend, with whom I had much in common, having lived so long in Luo country and been married by Archdeacon Owen in Kisumu in 1939.

The Archdeacon was, incidentally, a lifelong campaigner against child labour on the tea estates at Kericho. This seemed to be more as a matter of principle than conviction, for he had never visited a tea estate to see conditions for himself and in fact refused to do so. The children were, however, very well treated and were provided with good schooling by their employers.

However, to return to the matter of Nairobi and the United Kenya Club. We Europeans rather expected to be subjects of obloquy among certain sections of the white community when we joined, but I am afraid it never occurred to me that Africans often suffered the same fate. They would be referred to as black Europeans, traitors to the cause of African Independence, whereas in the case of Europeans it was more a suggestion, though equally wounding, of letting one's side down. In the case of the Asians it was, I think, different and they were more concerned that their wives might be confronted with what they regarded as the laxity of Western society. But we all learned from each other. I remember being very impressed by a charming young Asian doctor and his wife. They were obviously devoted to each other. When we first met I asked him conversationally when they had first met, and, obviously embarrassed, he admitted that it was on their wedding day.

Some of the members of the Club also served on the African Advisory Council which was my main link with the African community in Nairobi. After a full day's work in my office I used to spend most evenings and many weekends in the locations attending meetings of one kind or another with representatives of the enormous number of social or tribal groups. This was fascinating, if exhausting, but only in this way could one learn about the social and economic problems of the people at first hand.

The Advisory Council was the sounding board upon which, to change the metaphor, one floated ideas for improving the way of life of the citizens. But one had to be careful not to take this excellent means of consultation for granted. This book is not concerned with such a complex subject, but it may be of interest to recall an incident which occurred in the early days of my appointment.

I had made a suggestion to the City Council, regarding some comparatively trivial matter relating, I think, to hawkers' fees. When a member of the Advisory Council noticed a record of this fact in the minutes he asked why it had not been referred to them in the first place. All that I could say was that I was very sorry but it was a complete oversight. To my surprise this was greeted by complete silence, followed by a burst of applause. I then realised that apparently it was a new experience for a white man to apologise for his actions, a situation not unlike that in our own country where politicians never seem to admit they are in the wrong. In any case it seemed to create an entirely new relationship between the councillors and myself which made our future negotiations infinitely easier.

At the end of my four years of office I was very touched to be presented with an appreciation signed by the Vice Chairman and members of the Council which I value more than any other memento in my possession.

It had not been an easy period, marked as it was by the growth of unrest which we had been powerless to deal with. I summarised this in a series of reports to government which I include later. I received no acknowledgement but unofficially I was informed that they contributed to the setting up of the *Royal Commission on Land and Population* just before the outbreak of Mau Mau. This, however, did not seem to address itself to the main problem, which was the chronic shortage of land among a section of the Kikuyu which, in my view, was the main cause of the crisis.

Race Relations in Nairobi

But before dealing with this I would like to digress a little to consider the attitude of the better-educated Africans I met while in Nairobi in relation to their participation in government. While I do not believe the actual outbreak of violence had much relation to the nationalistic campaign which had been growing ever since the Harry Thuku riots soon after the first World War, this was a matter on which I could never agree with the majority of my colleagues.

Some of my seniors used to emphasise that the only aim of the 'politicians', as the nationalists were rather disdainfully termed, was to obtain power and good jobs for themselves. That this was an important objective is undoubtedly true, but it overlooks the fact that they were by no means unrepresentative of the views of the population as a whole. The assumption seemed to be that if they were removed as they were in the Jock Scott operation at the outbreak of Mau Mau, the population would thereby become law-abiding supporters of the government. This was, of course, by no means the case and it took six years of bloodshed and reforms before a sense of common purpose was achieved.

One principle which never seemed to be appreciated was that the last thing the better educated members of the community wanted was the destruction of the social and economic base built up with the help of the immigrants. Where would they be if this was eliminated as later occurred in countries like Uganda? They, as much as any other Kenya residents, looked forward to a prosperous, secure future, but could not see this materialising except through an independent government.

The landless, as will be suggested later, were a different kettle of fish and saw their future simply in terms of physical survival and so of land. Their idea of Utopia was reversion to tribal life where they could live in simple dignity, even though this might necessitate great hardship. After all, they were no strangers to it, for that was what they had learned to accept.

So it seemed to me to be of the utmost importance to give careful and sympathetic attention to the feelings and aspirations of the comparatively small educated elite. The City Council had, with the financial assistance of the Colonial Development Fund and the guidance of my predecessor Tom Colchester, established a number of admirable housing estates for the better-paid Africans and their families. Over the succeeding years they became integrated more and more into the local government machine. The sympathy and understanding of men like Alderman Vasey did much to facilitate this process but much of his work was undermined by his colleagues.

There were casualties among the African representatives. My old friend Tom Mbotela, the son of a freed slave, given succour by the CMS at their mission at Frere Town just outside Mombasa is a case in point. He was probably too much of an inter-racialist for the stomach of some nationalists and was murdered.

The Churches were persuaded to play a most valuable role in the establishment of multipurpose community centres in the different housing estates and the names of many of them such as Bill Owen and Stanley Booth-Clibborn, late Bishop of Manchester will be remembered with affection and gratitude by the older generation of Nairobi-ites. But finally I must refer with the greatest respect to Carey Francis, possibly the finest headmaster in the history of African education in Kenya. I am particularly proud of the fact that he was a member of my college, Peterhouse, where he was obviously destined to have a most distinguished academic career. He gave it all up, joined the CMS, was appointed headmaster of Maseno near Kisumu in 1928 and then moved to take charge of the Alliance High School, just outside Nairobi, in 1940 which, as its name implies served the brightest students of all the Protestant churches.

Carey maintained an exceptionally high academic and personal standard in both schools - too high for some of his students, perhaps. He even continued to send notes to some of them about their standards of behaviour when eventually they became Ministers. Nevertheless, all the pall bearers at his funeral in 1966 were both his former pupils and Ministers in the government. Typically, his last years after retirement from the Alliance were spent teaching in a little slum school in Pumwani, at the heart of the Nairobi housing estates. He was, of course, a member of the United Kenya Club and an outspoken critic of government policy from time to time.

But speaking of public life, my relations with the first African Minister to whom I was appointed Permanent Secretary were, I think, particularly happy ones. Beniah Ohanga, a teacher from Luo country, did not have any particular desire to take on such an important position. He was a kindly and unambitious man who felt, I think, when asked to serve, that he owed it to his country to take on the job. His responsibilities were taken over by the Minister for African Affairs in 1956.

One began to appreciate, however, the pressures which are inevitably imposed upon political representatives. By tradition he was expected to enjoy financial favours in recognition of his status and to pass on a proportion to his supporters. This is the same the world over. But at the time such men had additional burdens to bear. In the first place, like the foundation members of the United Kenya Club, he had to get used to being referred to as 'a white man's toady'. I remember this arose at our first meeting when my new Minister asked me how he should address me. I said everyone knew me as Tom, but he felt this would be quite unsuitable. After a little thought he said "I know. I will address you as Bwana Tom" which seemed to me a pleasant combination of formality and informality. It must be remembered that in Swahili "Bwana" does not carry the subservient connotation which it later acquired and was more equivalent to the French "Monsieur". So "Bwana Tom" I became and he was Beniah between ourselves. I could never get used to the term "Yes, Minister" except on official occasions.

Our relationship, both official and demi-official, was the cause of some unexpected situations. On one tour of Nyanza we arranged a reception at the Kisumu Hotel for his constituents. Now this was at the time when the larger hotels closed their doors to anyone but white visitors. But Kisumu was different and the manager of the hotel was a friend of mine, as was John Riddoch, the mayor of the town, who was to be invited, with other members of his council. So the occasion seemed likely to become a pioneering one.

There was however one problem which I was unaware of at the time. Barbara Castle, I discovered, was due to arrive at the end of a tour of Uganda that same evening to stay at the hotel. She would obviously think that the political reception was all a put-up job especially to embarrass her, for she was one of the foremost critics of British colonial policy in the Labour Party at that time.

There was nothing one could do about it, but when we met I apologised that the inevitable noise might disturb her at the end of her tiring journey. Naturally she denied this and I could not help noticing that she seemed to be thoroughly enjoying mixing with such a cheerful cross-section of Kenya society on her first evening in the country.

I may have rather over-stressed the matter of discrimination between Africans and the other races in Kenya but it was such a crucial issue at the time. While obviously there were many immigrants, both official and unofficial, whose attitude towards the indigenous inhabitants was abominable, the same could be said of a few of the people of this country today. We argued, however, that it was of fundamental importance to remedy the situation, particularly among those who had received a good education and had a right to expect greater understanding and opportunities.

Mainly it was simply ignorance and lack of interest which divided people of different cultures, as in other parts of the world, but one felt that senior officials and politicians at least should work to overcome such defects; few did so. Moreover those who did were classified by that most degrading term 'do-gooders'. In Kenya at that time such individuals were regarded as the lowest form of life. What a contrast is to be found in present day Kenya.

PART II
Mau Mau

Chapter Four

Warnings and remedies

The Plight of the Landless

To re-cap briefly, the population of the Kikuyu, stimulated by the removal of famine, tribal warfare and disease continued to expand at a tremendous rate. It increased beyond the capacity of either the farms or industry to absorb. Young men, often without land or place in society, began to leave home and flood into Nairobi and other towns. Unable to find employment they battened on their relatives and in so doing depressed the general standard of living still further. The power of nature and the aggression of mankind having been to some extent curbed there was nothing to prevent the uncontrolled expansion of the population, with potentially disastrous consequences. Measures had to be evolved to increase the productivity of the land to meet the needs of this growing number of mouths. But it was not enough simply to increase productivity unless this provided for those most in need. The whole population must benefit and not just those in control of the means of production.

But the effects of these factors only became apparent with the servicemen returning home after the Second World War, their good pay coming to an end and their gratuities spent. They began to feel the same sense of deprivation as their counterparts in the United Kingdom and elsewhere. In the case of the Kikuyu resentment was even stronger since, apart from the shortage of land as a result of the increase in population, there was also the accelerating pace of soil erosion.

Let us look again at the squatters on the farms in the Rift Valley. They, like their kindred in the homelands, had multiplied and so had their stock until the white farmers felt unable to give employment for all the progeny of their original squatters. Where were they to go? "Back to where they came from" said the employers, but that was generations ago, and anyway by this time there was no room for them. So they migrated to the town in search of jobs. Meredyth Hyde-Clarke, Labour Commissioner in 1947 stated that 'the African reserves were already over-populated and over-stocked and were incapable of absorbing large numbers of dispossessed squatters with their stock'. The

Squatter Policy Committee in 1947 agreed that the squatter problem was primarily another aspect of Kenya's agrarian crisis.

It was the first unambiguous assertion by the government that the squatter problem would not go away and could not simply be resolved by moving disgruntled Africans back to overcrowded reserves.

The problem in the tribal areas was aggravated by the sub-division of land on the deaths of landholders. Individuals not only found themselves the owners of dozens of small pockets of land but their total area was quite inadequate to provide them with a livelihood. For some time now, as has been noted, the men had had to spend their whole life in employment in order to earn funds needed for their children's education. Now they found their reduced holdings even failed to give their wives enough to feed their children, let alone cultivate cash crops in addition.

These hardships provided the seeds of revolt and they germinated in the form of Mau Mau. It was nobody's fault unless one accepts the view of those who claim that settlers should never have been encouraged to farm in the Rift Valley in the first place. But then, without them Kenya would never have become the rich agricultural country it is today.

So there grew up a class of men who were landless and jobless and had no means of support except their friends and relations. When those sources failed they took to crime and the collection of funds to support bogus political societies. Their sisters became prostitutes to serve the ever-growing mass of unattached men, or brewed illicit beer to drown the sorrows of the populace.

Of course, the government was warned of the impending catastrophe, as will be described in due course, but it was too late, and the murder of Chief Waruhiu, a leading Christian in 1952, sparked the explosion which was to engulf Kikuyuland in a savage and bestial war, partly atavistic and partly civil, for the ensuing six years, and lead in the end to Independence.

We should now consider whether any action could have been taken to avert the impending catastrophe. The position was depressing to say the least of it. I had received no acknowledgement of my assessment so for all I knew it was simply regarded as alarmist and rejected accordingly.

But one cannot help wondering whether in fact anything could have been done to prevent the worst occurring and the answer was probably 'No'. The disease had already spread too far. This does not imply that social or economic action could not have been taken at an earlier stage. The warning signals had been apparent long before I submitted my own report. Norman Humphrey had emphasised the problem of landlessness in Kikuyuland years before. So far as I know no one disputed his assessment but nor was anyone prepared to face up to the logical solution of providing more land for settlement schemes.

There had certainly been the Mau Scheme at Olenguruoni which had failed through lack of co-operation in its administration by the participants but this was a somewhat different situation. It was set aside to prove alternative land for those earlier Kikuyu residents from the area around Limuru whom the previous Land Commission had come to the conclusion were right-holders.

Actually, Limuru was one of the barrier zones I referred to earlier between the Kikuyu and the Maasai and it is questionable whether the Kikuyu had any more right to land there than anyone else. But that is by the way. The question is whether anything could be done to deal with the plight of those who had no means of support.

I sent a report on the situation to the Government. In my assessment I had been careful to suggest that only those who could prove that they had no alternative means of livelihood should be provided with land in a settlement scheme, and even then under strict control lest the land should be badly cultivated. The Settlers had always been adamant about the sanctity of the White Highlands but the Mau scheme was in a Forest Zone and so, perhaps, exempt.

Nevertheless, no one seemed to recognise the fact that, apart from introducing some form of social assistance, which would have been expensive, there seemed no alternative but the provision of land.

I had suggested a survey to determine the extent of the problem and find out how many families were in fact landless, but no action was taken on this either. The only acceptable remedy seemed to be endless and futile repatriation of unemployed vagrants to the Reserves.

When the second *Royal Commission on Land and Population* was set up, as I have mentioned, the matter of landlessness was never mentioned, nor was I invited to give evidence. This appeared to be the last opportunity for government to face up to the problem before the country was engulfed by civil war. The Secretary of State could have been urged to allow exceptions to the residence of certain categories of people in the Scheduled Areas, such as landless ex-squatters, for instance.

It had been proved through such settlement schemes as Makueni for the

Wakamba that they could be managed perfectly adequately without danger of misuse but the elected white settler Members of Legislative Council seemed adamant in their stance. In such circumstances armed rebellion seemed inevitable.

Measures were later taken by the Labour Department to improve the conditions of employment in the town but these did not affect those eventually involved in Mau Mau for they were unemployed, as I have tried to show.

It almost seemed that the elected Members of the Legislative Council were determined to fight the issue to the death and on the other side the leaders of Mau Mau were equally prepared to do the same. These are the classic conditions for the declaration of war and that is what resulted.

Correspondence with the Government

1. The following text is of a memorandum I sent to The Chief Secretary referred to above:

January 12th, 1950
African Vagrancy Memorandum

The present alarming tendency of a section of the African population, principally composed of Kikuyu, to attempt to create a state of anarchy, makes one wonder what has led to this state of affairs.

One has the history of the post-war years. The discharge of the askaris with little incident; the quiet period while gratuities were spent; the ensuing period of political agitation for more land and an alteration in the squatter laws - matters which concerned Kikuyu principally; the attempt to bring the administration to a standstill by terrorising certain Kikuyu Chiefs; the organisation of the Mombasa strike by Kikuyu; the attempted fermentation of a Nairobi and colony-wide strike by Kikuyu; the period of thuggery and disorder in Nairobi ended by the removal of the workshy from the town; finally the recurrence of similar lawlessness on the outskirts of the town, put down, one fears only temporarily, by widespread Police action.

One cannot help wondering whether these conditions are not similar in cause and character to those ruling in the middle ages in England. The following extract from Professor Trevelyan's *English Social History* is significant :-

> The bands of 'sturdy beggars' who alarmed society in the early Tudor reigns were recruited from many sources - the ordinary unemployed, the unemployable, soldiers discharged after the French wars and the Wars of the Roses, retainers disbanded at Henry VIII's command, serving men set adrift by impecunious lords and gentry, Robin Hood bands driven from their woodland lairs by deforestation and by the bitter enforcement of the King's peace, ploughmen put out of work by enclosures for pastures, and tramps who prudently pretended to belong to that commiserated class.
>
> The cause of the growth of this class in the middle ages was clearly simple poverty among people who were landless and without means of support, after the dissolution of the Monasteries.

With regard to remedies, Professor Trevelyan has this to say :-

> It was soon found that the whipping of sturdy beggars was by itself no solution. The double duty of providing work for the unemployed and charity for the impotent was gradually

> recognised as incumbent not merely on the Church and the charitable, but on society as a whole.

It will no doubt be argued that there need be no unemployment problem in Kenya, for there is plenty of work for all, but this overlooks one important fact. Manual labourers are paid at a rate sufficient to support the labourer, but no account is taken of the subsistence of wife or children. In the case of the man who owns land, his wages provide the wherewithal that his land is incapable of producing in many cases - clothing, education for his children etc. But there is that growing class of landless Africans, particularly among the Kikuyu for whom the normal workman's wage is totally inadequate.

It is worthwhile considering what is the economic and social position of a landless African. He has probably received little if any education or training, owing to his parents' poverty; he cannot pay bride price for proper marriage by native law and custom for the same reason; if he is married, or cohabits, he cannot support his wife unless one or other of them carries on some legal or illegal trade; he cannot feed and bring up children, let alone educate them on a manual worker's pay.

What would be the reaction towards society of such a man. I suggest he would very probably join the ranks of the 'spivs' we are trying to control, and make crime his means of livelihood. He will in any case lose all pride in himself and will nurse a great bitterness towards those he considers have brought his troubles upon him - namely, the Europeans, who refuse to give him either land or a living wage.

An American book entitled *An Introduction to Social Science* for use by the armed forces states

:-

> Homeless men are typically individuals who for one reason or another lost their status. From the time the individual becomes aware of his loss of status he continues to deteriorate by degrees until he reaches the lowest stages.

If the bands of 'spivs' are, as I believe them to be, the younger members of the landless class, then special steps must be adopted to deal with them. I would strongly urge that too great a reliance on Police measures will only make matters worse; the lawless pauper will be put away for a time in jail, but will be compelled from economic pressure to revert to his original bad practices on release, but with an even more embittered outlook on life.

It may be that I am wrong in my assumption, but only a social survey or investigation can establish or refute the suggestions I have made. I consider that such a survey is of the utmost importance, since without it the proper remedies cannot be suggested.

Such an investigation could start with the interrogation of the Kikuyu in Nairobi and District jails and Detention Camps, followed by a check, at the individual's home, of the facts given by him.
Should it transpire that my suspicions are correct, then a solution to the problem may be difficult to find.
   (a) the provision of more land for the landless.
   (b) the raising of wages of labourers sufficient to provide for the wives and children of landless men.
   (c) the payment of old age pensions to landless elders.
   (d) the provision of special educational

facilities for the children of the landless.

All these remedies can be objected to for some reason or another and the most careful consideration will have to be given to them.

Perhaps lessons can be learned from history. It should be possible to avoid the direct or indirect subsidisation of wages from taxes, which was the burden of the Speenhamland Acts on which Professor Trevelyan comments as follows:-

> The moral effect was devastating on all concerned. The large farmers continued in their selfish refusal to raise wages, the independent classes staggered under the burden of the poor-rate, while idleness and crime increased among the pauperised labourer.

He also states that the original objective was the giving of a minimum wage in relation to the price of bread, which was in principle the true remedy, and continues:-

> If it had been adopted for Berkshire and for all England, it might have diverted our modern social history into happier channels.

Without going into the question of remedies further, which in any case will be one of the utmost difficulty, I would merely urge the importance of an investigation into the actual social status of the habitual criminals of today, with particular reference to the extent of the problem of the landless or semi-landless class. Unless this is done, the Government may find itself going blindly on with more and more repressive measures, as the problem becomes accentuated, when the proper course may be found to be, as in England, a remedying of the economic hardships of the working man.

* * * * * * * * *

2. This was shortly followed by the following memorandum:

Some Observations on the Growth of Unrest in Kenya

I have attempted to set out below the basic causes of the present unrest and how they have been exploited since the end of the war. I write them with some diffidence as I know that many others who are in close contact with African affairs may have come to the same conclusions. Nevertheless at this crucial time a different point of view may help those concerned in their efforts to find a just solution and I trust it may be of some value.

This memorandum contains my own personal conclusions, and I have a certain knowledge of the matter having watched the growth of unrest since 1945 when I was appointed Municipal Native Affairs Officer, Nairobi, and seen it mount to its climax while holding my present appointment as Commissioner for Community Development.

At the same time, I have attempted to express the African point of view, for in my experience he seldom analyses his sense of grievance and the causes of it, in a way understandable to many Europeans."

The Post War Period
At the end of the war large numbers of Kikuyu were discharged from the Army and were paid quite considerable sums in gratuities. The majority of those who had been recruited were batmen, drivers or labour corps, and in the immediate post-war period the opportunities for further employment in the first two fields were limited. At the same time, the conditions of employment in civilian life were not as a rule nearly so attractive as

they had been in the Forces.

A number of ex-servicemen were trained at the various centres, for fitting them for employment in industry, commerce and the Government service, but these could not meet the demand.

The ex-servicemen looked around for useful forms of investment of their gratuities. They were often prey to unscrupulous company promoters of their own tribe, and as a result their savings disappeared. Some invested, against the advice of Government officers in half derelict ex-army vehicles which were not road-worthy, and thus again their savings were dissipated. Others embarked on the building of shops. As a result, the trading centres were soon filled with them. Some have never been completed owing to funds running out, others have closed down because of excessive competition, and only a small proportion remain. Much money was wasted in this way.

Some tried to set up large wholesale trading businesses. Owing to inexperience, peculation by directors and staff, and over-ambition, these mostly failed.

Attempts were made to persuade traders to combine and purchase goods wholesale. Most of these co-operatives failed owing to the dishonesty of their officers. An attempt was made to place the Karatina Vegetable Factory on a permanent basis. The venture failed since the Kikuyu concerned refused to take advice or accept help in its running, and it had to be demolished, thus destroying a valuable export from a densely populated area.

The gratuities in one way or another, therefore, quickly disappeared and the ex-servicemen began to look around for other sources of income. Although the losses of savings could have been avoided if those concerned had not been so suspicious of the Government which was trying to help them, and if they had not been so addicted to cheating each other, they emerged from their experience merely bitter against the "powers that be" and refused to accept the fact that their wounds were self-inflicted.

Many, therefore, began to seek employment, but as I have noted, openings were few and rewards less than those to which they had grown accustomed. Although there was plenty of employment at the current wages, which however only took into account the needs of a single man without a family, few ex-servicemen would accept it. It should be noted that the wage structure is built up on the assumption that the family can obtain its livelihood from the land, and this brings me to my next series of observations.

The Land
It is probable that the war period tended to counteract or mask the economic hardship of increasing over-population in the Kikuyu areas. The increased earning power of servicemen, together with the good market for produce of all kinds to troops and prisoner-of-war camps in the Colony brought a wave of comparative prosperity to the Kikuyu.

It was probable that many of the young men who joined up were derived from the "muhoi" or tenant farmer class, which, as Mr Norman Humphrey notes in his "Kikuyu and the Land" published in 1945, are steadily being squeezed from their holdings. Little hardship was experienced by these men during the war as their families received regular remittances and could produce high priced vegetables, chickens and eggs from their diminishing plots of land.
After the war no such relief was forthcoming, but the population has continued to increase and the number surplus to the carrying capacity of the land is now greatly in excess of the figure

of 14,000 families given by Mr Norman Humphrey for South Nyeri District alone.

Those men who had become landless or semi-landless were, therefore, confronted with an inability to support their families if they were married, and if, as was usually the case, they were not trained to earn skilled wages, to support themselves.

There was one outlet however, namely migration to other areas, and no doubt many ex-servicemen embarked upon this. Emigration has, of course, been going on for some time. First of all it was to the European farms where many have settled as "squatters". Others have moved to the Forests and become resident labourers in the same way. Yet others began moving into South Nyanza and the districts adjacent to Kikuyu or Embu and Meru and later into the Kilimanjaro area of Tanganyika.

In most areas where they have migrated their hosts have found them at times awkward to handle. In Settled Areas and Forests they have often cultivated more land or herded more stock than that to which they were entitled. In African Areas they have sometimes refused to recognise the local chiefs and have tried to obtain recognition of their own.

As a result of this attitude, which can be attributed to a sense of not unnatural insecurity on the part of Kikuyu, their hosts have been increasingly reluctant to accept them, or support the policy of interpenetration encouraged by Government.

The insecurity of squatters on farms and in the Forests is real, since their agreements can be terminated by the land-owner at will, and those too old to work can only rely on his good will for continued residence and support. This is often given, but is by no means universal nor indeed compulsory.

At the same time the Kikuyu saw large areas of land in the European Highlands which were apparently not being usefully developed. He saw the Government making vigorous efforts to increase European settlement to take up the land which he so urgently desired. He saw European farmers given financial assistance and training. All this led to resentment.

Wages
Dissatisfaction with the level of wages began to be expressed. This affected all Africans, but was not serious except among those who had no land on which to support their families. Thus in the towns, the increase of the minimum wage to correspond with the rising cost of living met the needs of most labourers, but not the African who had little land and a family to support. It should be noted, however, that it is not only the Kikuyu who is short of the minimum land required to support a family; this also applies to certain tribes in North Nyanza and Ukambani.

In so far as squatters are concerned the wages are so low in many cases as to be insignificant. Where they could earn additional sums from the sale of produce, however, less dissatisfaction was felt, but there has been a tendency lately to reduce this source of income. Thus the man who has become accustomed to a higher standard of living, or is striving to achieve one for himself and his children, finds it increasingly difficult to do so. All Africans earnestly desire education for their children and this means money for fees; for those who cannot derive an adequate income from their land or are in the higher wage levels, this is virtually impossible to earn.

At the same time, while there was clearly great prosperity among the immigrant communities, the level of African wages as relating to the cost of living remained the same or even fell. This was particularly so in the farming areas, though it was offset by increased prices for produce where a sufficient quantity was permitted to be grown for sale.

There was, however, dissatisfaction that whereas in the Forest and African Areas a cess was charged on produce sold which was devoted to social services, no such provision existed on European farms.

There is one most important consideration that must not be overlooked. Whereas during the war there was the safety valve of the forces to provide a valuable source of income, in the peace that followed there was none. In South Africa and the Rhodesias there is always the opportunity of employment at good wages on the mines, and this compensates for other economic hardships such as land hunger. In some ways these territories to the south are in a stronger position than Kenya. In Uganda, of course, the African has the opportunity of earning a good income from cotton and coffee. In the Chagga country of Tanganyika coffee is also a lucrative crop. In Kenya recently the Nyanza maize and cotton have been very remunerative. In Kikuyu country only wattle provides an alternative to wages and this is often grown at the expense of food crops."

Housing
It is often claimed that the lack of housing is one of the chief causes of social unrest. While recognising the seriousness of the deficiency in the town, in my experience this is not the principal evil. Africans living in the towns seldom complain about the lack of housing though they do resent the low level of wages and the regulations relating to lawful occupation of housing. What they principally urge is the provision of land on long leases or freehold, on which they may be permitted to build their own

mud and wattle dwellings. The Kikuyu are those who have been most clamant for such a policy.

The advantages of such a scheme are that houses can be built quickly and cheaply, the occupants are not so subject to control and direction, and the house-owners have a source of income from tenants. The last named factor is of importance as many houses owned and built by Africans become a source of social security; detribalised elements can acquire such houses during their working life and support themselves from the rents in old age.

It must be remembered that Africans are used to primitive living conditions, and prefer to live in an over-crowded and unhygienic state so long as they can thereby economise and save money for such purposes as educating their children or buying stock and land. These are more important to them than comfortable housing and adequate food."

Education
While the hard core of Kikuyu with a grievance expanded with the increased pressure on the land, it was added to by the boys leaving the Primary Schools who were unsuccessful in obtaining the good jobs for which they imagined they were qualified. The number of openings for boys of this level of education has not kept pace with the increasing output of the schools.

At the time their fathers first sent them to school, boys were walking out of the Primary Schools into clerical jobs. Now the state of affairs is very different and the market is saturated.

At the same time such boys have no technical qualifications and have not reached the educational standard to qualify them for training in one of the Government trade schools. Some at great cost to their parents enter one of the secretarial colleges and emerge with a worthless certificate which is of little help to a large firm, but are often dissatisfied with the training they get and leave to obtain a job as a semi-skilled craftsman.

Many, however, finding that their education has been an apparent waste of time and money, become disillusioned and bitter and their parents share in their resentment. They join the ranks of the disgruntled.

It should be remembered that the Beecher Plan provides for an enormous increased output of this class of youth over the next few years, and the problem of their absorption into society will become increasingly difficult unless special measures are taken to achieve it.

The disgruntled group of ex-servicemen and disillusioned youth has turned its attention at times to the establishment of Independent Schools. Their work gives satisfaction to them as representing a means of achieving universal education, which they consider Government is resisting, not realising that cost and lack of teachers are the main obstacles. It also represents a source of income, since levies for the building of new schools have been made and seldom accounted for, and the fees are handled by the organising committee in the same haphazard way.

Opposition to the Beecher Plan, which rightly aspires to improving the quality of education rather than its quantity, is seen as a threat to the existence of the Independent Schools, and as an attempt to end the income derived by the organising committees.

Another cause of resentment is the fact that the ex-school boy is not permitted by Kikuyu custom to acquire land from his parents until he marries and thus cannot put such agricultural knowledge as he has acquired at school into practice. As marriage is often delayed, sometimes indefinitely, owing to the exorbitant bride-price obtaining at the present time, the young man sees little opportunity of becoming an agriculturalist and thus taking a respected place in society. Where also he is unable to marry according to accepted custom he feels himself an outcast of society and behaves as such.

Other Causes Of Resentment

The factors already mentioned are the basic causes of the resentment which is apparent today. There are, however, other reasons for the bitterness which has developed among the Kikuyu.

There are for instance the various forms of discrimination which are a barrier to the Kikuyu's economic and social aspirations. There is the legislation which restricts the planting of coffee and certain other cash crops; there is the fact that Africans are not permitted to acquire land in the White Highlands; there are the different wage scales which are applied to Europeans, Asians and Africans by Government; there are the restrictive covenants which prevent Africans living in the European areas in some municipalities; there is the opposition to his using the larger hotels.

Convincing reasons are often given for these restrictions, nevertheless it should be remembered that they do not all exist in the neighbouring territories of Uganda and Tanganyika and are a real cause of bitterness especially among the growing class of educated Africans.

"These restrictions have also the effect of emphasising, often unreasonably, the inferiority of the African in culture and ability. He is aware of his deficiencies, though he will seldom admit it. He is therefore prone to blame the European or Asian for his failure in business and employment. In fact, his failure is too often due to his lack of those moral standards which apply in Western society; as a result he falls a prey to greed and fails through dishonesty to make a success of his business or job. His realisation that he has not the background to aspire to conform to Western standards often leads to defeatism and that most dangerous disease the inferiority complex. This in turn leads him too frequently to release in drunkenness and betting. In the final resort he decides to revert to the primitive existence of his forefathers and this is apparent in the doctrine of Mau Mau. At the same time the young men have a yearning for power and recognition. This brings them into conflict with their own elders. The respects for parents which was intrinsic to primitive society has disappeared. The elders are often partly to blame, however, in refusing to recognise that the young men can contribute to the advancement of Society.

Finally, I think there is an undoubted sense of despair that the views of the African unofficial members on how to remove the basic causes described above so seldom, if ever, prevail. Doubtless their views are not always responsible, but the Kikuyu, rightly or wrongly, appear to have lost all faith in constitutional government as practised in Kenya and have decided that the Government and European unofficial members are allied against him.

Exploitation of Grievances
This is then the background, as I see it, to the growth of unrest over the last eight years. I will now attempt to suggest how this has been exploited during the same period.

Soon after the war Jomo Kenyatta arrived back in Kenya after fourteen years in Great Britain, where he had thoroughly absorbed Communist doctrines and even, it is rumoured, visited Russia. It was not long before unrest became apparent.

The Mombasa strike in 1947, organised by the Workers' Federation under the immediate direction of Cheege Kibachia from the same district as Jomo Kenyatta, achieved considerable success, and improved conditions of employment were introduced. But for the efforts of Europeans and Asians the work of the port would have come to a standstill.

Following upon this the Federation moved its headquarters to Nairobi and set about organising a general strike in the capital. This never materialised however, partly because an increased minimum wage had been brought into force about the same time, and a strike could not have been successful without picketing the Nyanza tribes, who were generally satisfied with the award. Jomo Kenyatta at a meeting of the Kenya African Union just before the General Strike was due to be called, gave instructions that it should not take place and it collapsed.

The Federation, however, provided a means by which the organisers could collect funds. Meetings continued even after the idea of a strike had been abandoned. They were attended by vast crowds and speakers stirred up feeling against Europeans. They concluded by passing round the hat and collected large sums, until the subscribers became disillusioned when the societies' officers were found to be using the funds for their own purposes.

Next came the campaign against certain strong chiefs in the Kiambu District. A strike was organised at the Uplands Bacon Factory which resulted in a riot and a number of Africans were shot.

Then the campaign was started among squatters in Rift Valley Province to encourage them to rise against their conditions of life. New members were being recruited all the time to join the K.A.U. and as usual the subscriptions were not accounted for. There is no doubt that they provided the income of the organisers of the campaign.

Next a fund was opened for the building of the Githunguri Training College of which Jomo Kenyatta is the Principal. Large amounts were collected and the building was started, but has not reached the first floor. There is little doubt that the subscriptions were devoted to the expenses of Jomo Kenyatta and his minions. The cost of running the College must be amply met from the high fees charged for an indifferent education in most primitive conditions. At the same time the drive to collect funds for the Independent Schools organisations continued.

It was again decided to call a general strike in Nairobi, and in fact, throughout the country. Owing to the subversive nature of meetings organised prior to it, and the danger that the people might become inflamed, strict control of meetings had to be imposed. The strike itself was a failure after the deportation of Makhan Singh and Fred Kubai and the introduction of legislation making it an offence to bring public services to a standstill.

Then came the campaign of vilification of the Government and Europeans generally on the subjects of the land and discrimination. This was the beginning of the organisation known as Mau Mau regarded by many as a revival of the Kikuyu Central Association under another title. Representatives of K.A.U. were sent to Great Britain to campaign for the resolution of these matters and to seek the support of Left-Wing politicians. Then finally came formation of Mau Mau with its forced oaths and its fees of Shs. 60/- a head. These again were never accounted for, but must have reached immense sums.

The pattern has been constant throughout, firstly an attempt to create chaos and to make Government and white settlement unworkable, and secondly to collect funds for the organisers who have vowed to accept no employment from the European. The collection of funds, of course, further depressed the standards of living of those employed. The organisers have based their campaign on experience gained in the past, and have finally come to the conclusion apparently, that the early attempts at general strikes and disorder have failed to achieve their object of redressing grievances, and nothing less than complete tribal solidarity enforced ruthlessly and followed by insurrection would be effective.

Accompanying this final phase has been a drive to persuade all Kikuyus that any measures introduced by the Government are worthless, whether they be patently beneficial social services or not. This trend has been apparent in the past in connection with the inoculation of stock or soil conservation measures. It is significant that recently the Mau Mau has taken over the enforcement of soil conservation measures itself, no doubt to indicate that self-government is the only effective solution. It has banned the drinking of European beer and has attempted, and in some cases succeeded, in abolishing European clothing.

All this while the crime wave has mounted, which may or may not be connected with the campaign. It cannot, however, be unrelated to social and economic hardship, and this view is endorsed by the Commissioner of Police.

Organisation Behind The Campaign

It is quite apparent that astute direction has been behind the promotion of these plans. It was no coincidence that Jomo Kenyatta arrived when he did, nor that the plan began to unfold so soon after his arrival. It has been supported throughout by Left-Wing politicians, in Great Britain and Kenya, the latter being for the most part Indians, but there are, I have no doubt, Europeans as well.

There is every reason for Communist Russia wishing to see Kenya, a bastion in the Commonwealth defence line, in a state of anarchy. Strategically it is an obvious area for communist activity. Where the ground was as fertile as it was, the work of creating disaffection was easy.

At the same time the history of our Colonial territories such as Palestine and the Gold Coast gave every reason for the organisers to believe that they would be successful. At any rate the Kikuyu could be inspired to fight for self-government on the Gold Coast lines if for no other reason than through fear of an extension of apartheid to Kenya.

There is little doubt that the methods of Malayan terrorists have been studied, as have those of the Sinn Feiners, and it remains to be seen whether the campaign is intended to follow the pattern there of destruction of crops and the murder of land-owners. It has already reached the stage of destroying buildings, cattle and pasture. The efforts made to create disaffection among students in Great Britain are well known, as is the support given by Left-wing politicians to the irresponsible African leaders.

Conclusion

This note is not intended to suggest remedies, but to emphasise what social and economic hardships exist and that they have been growing, particularly since the war. It is intended to stress that these hardships are liable to become greater as the number of half-educated youths multiply, and as more Kikuyu lose their jobs as a result of the unrest and more squatters have their agreements cancelled.

Whether the country can afford to finance large public works to provide employment, possibly compulsory, for the disaffected elements, or whether it is too late to do so is a matter for consideration. A suggestion along these lines was made by my predecessor, Mr P E W Williams in his pamphlet "Youth Camps". It was not accepted on grounds of expense. Whether the allocation of additional land, as has been done in South Africa and Tanganyika is a more practicable alternative is also for decision.

There are, however, certain facts which I think are incontrovertible. The first is that land hunger is acute among certain Kikuyu, and was so in 1945, when Mr Norman Humphrey produced his report on the Kikuyu Lands. The second is that wages and conditions of work are inadequate for this class of Kikuyu. The third is that security for Kikuyu in old age is lacking. The fourth is that with very little doubt communist influences are at work, and are taking the well known line of the Sinn Fein in the Irish troubles and exploiting this element.

It is interesting to note that Mr Norman Humphrey considered that Community Development represented the best hope of providing a solution when he wrote the report mentioned above, and he made suggestions as to how it might be implemented.

I would suggest, however, that if my observations are correct and a social survey establishes this fact, there is a strong argument for a large expansion of the welfare side of the Community Development Organisation. By this I mean that if it is decided to embark on large capital works or settlement schemes, with good conditions of service, commensurate with those of the armed forces during the war, then it will be essential that those in greatest need should be enabled to benefit from them. This will require investigation of individual cases of hardship and landlessness, with trained officers to undertake it.

The problem is similar to the removal of a cancer, certainly such is simple in the early stages of the disease, but localised treatment, though prolonged and expensive, can be effective even when the complaint is more advanced. If no treatment is undertaken the disease will inevitably spread through the entire system and be incurable.

I would point out that Mr Thompson has, with very limited resources, undertaken this kind of work in Fort Hall district, and the District Commissioner considers it invaluable. It is more fully described in my article "The Problem of Youth" which is to be published in Corona under the title of "The Young Kikuyu".

Every thinking person realises that the present measures to re-establish law and order can be no lasting answer, and, to carry my simile further, are more in the nature of injections of morphia to a diseased person. I would, therefore, urge that a cure along the lines suggested be given careful consideration by Government."

T G Askwith
Commissioner For Community Development
24 October 1952

* * * * * * * *

Remedies

3. And, finally the following was sent to the Chief Secretary in 1952:

CONFIDENTIAL
30 October 1952
The Chief Secretary
The Secretariat
NAIROBI

Thro' Chief Native Commissioner

1. Further to my memorandum CCD/1 dated 25 October 1952 on the Growth of Unrest in Kenya, I have had a discussion with two responsible Kikuyu members of the Jeanes School staff, Mr Owen the Senior Probation Officer and Mrs Kenny, also of the Probation Service, both of whom have had close contacts with the problem of crime in the course of their normal duties.

2. I put to them briefly and confidentially my interpretation of the causes of the present situation and invited their comments. They all endorsed my views as to the basic causes, and then made some suggestions as to how they could be remedied. I give them below for what they are worth.

3. The Land: All were convinced that the increasing shortage of land, coupled with recent squatter policy and the action of other African tribes to remove Kikuyu were the main causes of unrest. They did not consider that the allocation of more land was the only remedy, though settlement schemes on the lines of Makueni would be most helpful.

They considered that the restriction on squatter stock and of acreage under cultivation had led many Kikuyu to return to the reserves and further aggravate their present over-crowded state. They were convinced that if more generous terms were offered to squatters, a great move back to the farms would take place, and contentment restored though security in old age must be ensured.

They suggested that the policy of inter-penetration should also be encouraged.

With regard to land in the African areas, they thought that far more ought to be done to convince people of the importance and reasons for agrarian reform, and considered that Community Development methods should be more widely used.

4. Wages: All were convinced that if a generous increase in wages were introduced, more particularly in the towns, the main cause of unrest would disappear. They said that the good wages and prices of produce during the war prevented people from worrying about land shortage, in fact no one thought about it. It was only after the war that more land appeared to many Kikuyu to be the only remedy, since wages have barely kept pace with the increasing cost of living.

They considered that wages should be sufficient for the family and not merely the single man. They agreed that at the moment the one-third increase in wages recommended by Mr Mathu would act as a temporary expedient. They felt that educated Africans were bitter because they saw little hope that they would be able to reach the highest rungs of the ladder. Even though few might have the ability to reach them, the fact that a small number did so would act as a spur to the rest.

The narrowing of the gap between the salaries of Europeans, Asians and educated Africans would tend to break down social barriers and make co-operation and friendship easier to achieve. There must be wider opportunities for Africans in

Government, the trades and professions.

5. Housing: The prime need is for better housing and more owned by Africans, particularly for them to let out to lodgers. Such housing provides social security in old age.

6. Education: A more realistic approach to education was urged, so that boys leaving the primary schools might be equipped for life and not become disgruntled and join subversive organisations.

The need for more adult education in its widest sense was considered essential. A great deal of difficulty in introducing Government plans was due to insufficient explanation. This in turn was due to the fact that chiefs who had been given the task of carrying them out, were often uneducated and hardly understood them themselves. For this reason the African members thought that the whole system of chieftainship was becoming discredited, and urged that the older uneducated chiefs should be retired and more progressive younger men appointed in their place.

The hard-core of Mau Mau was not the ordinary labourer but the sophisticated and the semi-educated. These felt the various injustices, imagined and otherwise, most keenly and inflamed others to share their attitude.

7. Trade: One member thought that the prices of produce was another cause of unrest and felt they should be increased. The restriction on the movement of produce from the reserves had the effect of lowering the standard of living of those working in the towns. When Africans received food from home their wages went further, since they did not have to pay the high price of meal in the shops.

8. Government Policy: It was felt that a blue print of Government policy insofar as it related to Africans should be prepared. At present Africans saw no dawn on the horizon and this gave Mau Mau its appeal, for it made definite promises of land, even though this implied a return to the primitive. At present Africans had a sense of despair, for they had lost their faith that they would ever be permitted to rise to take leading positions in the country. Government assurances of advancement for Africans when not acted upon, led to distrust.

"It was considered that the approach to the African should be much more personal and that Africans should be employed wherever possible to undertake this work. Government and people had become too far removed from one another.

9. Political Prisoners: It was suggested by one member that the nomination of Jomo Kenyatta to the official side of Legislative Council would have a remarkably good effect! He considered that there was much to be gained by co-operating and working with him. A very large section of the African community, apart from the Kikuyu, looked to him as a leader and his deportation would not reduce Mau Mau activities. He thought that the devil you knew was better than the one you didn't.

It was considered that the after-care of political prisoners was important, though their influence on the rest of the Kikuyu would be very slight if the conditions of living were improved as recommended above.

10. Conclusions: Briefly the generally accepted remedies were, therefore, as follows:-
   (a) Settlement areas and interpenetration should be encouraged, and the conditions of squatters improved and stabilised.

(b) Wages should be increased, particularly in the towns, to correspond more nearly with the cost of living of a family.

(c) African-owned housing should be encouraged and helped.

(d) A more practical education for children and a wider education of adults on community development lines were essential and urgent.

(e) A statement by Government was required giving Africans hope of future advancement.

11. I enclose a copy of a memorandum I wrote in January 1950 on the subject. The trend of events has unfortunately been as I foretold at the time.

T G Askwith
Commissioner For Community Development

* * * * * * * * * *

The Royal Commission on Land and Population 1953-54, Report

It seems probable that these submissions eventually contributed to the establishment of the Royal Commission on Land and Population. I, therefore, include the following extracts from its report. They describe the administrative structure upon which it considered development schemes should be based, but made no mention of land-hunger.

Extract: Agrarian Administration

7. At first the peasants do not consider plans for education, health or improved agriculture as their own concern: these are things thrust upon them by an outside, though benevolent, power which protects them and to which they must submit. They do not at first consider that they must themselves make an effort to better their own

conditions with the new techniques which are being urged on them. Unless direct stimulus is brought to bear they do not respond. The desire to move from a communal society to western individual society grows slowly. this is the first stage, the stage in which the district commissioner and technical officer must persuade, cajole and if necessary impose. It is, however, a stage which has been passed through in the spheres of education and health until now the more progressive people clamour for the services which at first they were reluctant to accept. In agriculture, too, it has been passed in places where the immediate advantages of improvements have been demonstrated. Coffee-growing in the Chagga country and elsewhere which at first had to be imposed, is now developing of its own momentum and the people are eager for more. The same applies in some degree to cotton in Uganda and to other cash crops. But the less spectacular side of agrarian change which is even more important in the long run but which the advantages are less immediately obvious is still for the most part seen as a tiresome and unnecessary innovation by meddlesome outsiders.

8. This is the problem with which the administrations are now confronted. How can the need for change in such important matters as land tenure, cattle, and land use be accepted and recognised as essential by the people as a whole rather than as something thrust upon them by government? The objection is to teach the people not only to appreciate the need for those changes but to bring them about themselves; to employ their own technicians and advisory services; to regard the agrarian revolution as their own affair to be achieved by themselves with government assistance where they want it. This process has gone some way in education and health because the benefits are more immediately apparent. On the land results are slower and

less spectacular. A man can learn to read and write in a matter of weeks, but it takes him many years to improve his herd.

9. We believe that governments should now consider this as a long term problem as well as an immediate administrative question; that they should, in their training institutions, teach Africans to lead their own agrarian revolution.

Compulsion
10. There are those who hold that when some measure is considered necessary in the interests of better land usage, be it the consolidation of fragmented holdings, the re-distribution of population, soil conservation measures or the culling of stock, the need for reform is so urgent that it is the Government's duty to enforce it in the general interest by compulsion without more ado. They can point to instances where innovations have been introduced by compulsion in the past which have greatly benefited and, in the end, been welcomed by the people concerned. Outstanding instances already quoted were the introduction of cotton in Uganda and of coffee in Kilimanjaro. In the latter case, Sir Charles Dundas induced the Chagga to grow coffee against their wishes when he was their District Commissioner. He succeeded, and many years later a grateful tribe invited him to visit their country at their own expense to be feted and acclaimed as the founder of their property. But reliance on compulsion cannot achieve the widespread changes in land usage which we believe to be necessary. Apart from other considerations such as the obvious desirability of avoiding compulsion wherever possible, it would require an enforcement staff quite beyond the resources of the administrations and, except where the direct results are strikingly profitable, as in the cases cited, the effect would rarely last once sanctions were removed.

11. We have had much opportunity for study of different methods in different areas and for hearing the opinions of those who have had practical experience of the problem, and we are convinced that the best results can be achieved at this stage only by patient propaganda, including demonstrations, and by persuasion. Where the best results have been achieved, these are the methods employed, but their effectiveness varies with the quality and number of staff available and with the degree of continuity of posting and policy, as well as with the nature of the people and problems concerned. A robust approach by men of character and personality who are individually known to the people, and especially to their leaders whether of the new or old schools, is the key to success. The more Africans who can be trained for this work the better. Peasants are more likely to be converted to new land use and land tenure practices by men of their own race, but they must be well-trained men who can win the respect and trust of the people. Finally, where compulsion is unavoidable it should be exercised by the enforcement staffs of the administration, or of the local authorities and not by the extension staff, for once they have had to compel they may no longer be able to persuade.

Community Development
12. In recent years colonial policy has come to regard the raising of the standard of living of people in under-developed territories, including agrarian reform, as a two-way process; first, the encouragement and stimulation of local initiative rising from the individual, the family or the clan unit; and secondly, the introduction of advanced techniques, guidance and direction by teams of specialist officers through extension services. To this end governments have established community development organisations. We do not wish to consider their general objectives here, but we would point out that, to be successful,

all attempts to propagate new concepts of social behaviour must have a clear aim which is intended to be an answer to specific problems facing the individuals concerned. Vague projects of rural betterment in general, or attempts at 'social uplift', will simply lead to a dispersal of much well-meaning effort.

13. We believe that increasing provision should be made for the training of leaders and field staffs in methods of persuading people to take their own initiative in the better use of their land and in adapting themselves to modern living standards. The fullest possible use should be made of the public relations or information departments and of trained community development officers. These are specialists in the art of inducing people to adopt changes and they can contribute much by way of advice and by conducting propaganda through the media of literature, cinematography, demonstration teams and other techniques. The field work, however, must be an inter-departmental operation designed to achieve certain specified objects.

Provincial and District Teams
14. There are two main official agencies for improving rural living conditions, including better land use. These are the provincial and district teams and the local government bodies. It is now common practice in East Africa for the central governments to work through teams at provincial and district levels. The typical arrangement is for the District Commissioner to be chairman of the district team and for all the district heads of departments to be members, as well as representatives of the public of all races. Often members of local government bodies are also members of the team, and thus liaison is maintained between the two principal agencies for development.

15. While the organization described is typical,

it is by no means to be found everywhere. In smaller districts inter-departmental liaison is informal and this is usually quite satisfactory but there is often scope for more co-operation with local leaders of all races. It may be that the work of the team is mainly concerned with predominantly African areas, but even where this is so, it would be useful to bring leading and interested Europeans and Asians, including farmers and missionaries, into the teams. They will often have an intimate knowledge of the farming potential of particular areas and give much valuable advice. In some districts of Kenya especially non-officials have contributed much to the development of African areas but much more use should be made of them everywhere, because it is of fundamental importance that the people should play the fullest possible part in planning and stimulating development. We, therefore, recommend that, where possible, leading non-officials of all races should be invited and encouraged to sit together on district teams. In particular it is important that local government bodies should be represented at team meetings to procure co-ordination of effort.

Field Officers
24. We have stressed the importance of personal contact between individual officers and the people whom they serve. Instead of there being, for example, five departmental field officers all dealing with the whole of an area from five different angles, guided by district technical officers. It may be objected that one man cannot possibly be an expert in all aspects of development, but the repository of the specialized knowledge is the supervising trained technical officer whose duty it is to guide those who are in more intimate contact with the people in the villages. If the work required of the field officer of the kind we recommend is too specialised and difficult for him to learn, then it is certainly beyond anything the average African farmer can

at present be expected either to understand or carry out. Indeed the field officer should have the all-round qualities of the successful farmer. We obtained many views on this subject during our travels and, in the light of the evidence we received and of our own observations we recommend that governments, should gradually build up a field staff, where it does not already exist, on the lines we describe in the following paragraphs.

25. Below the district level it should not normally be necessary to employ highly trained technical officers except for special purposes, such as a veterinary officer for dealing with the outbreak of disease or an agricultural officer for doing research or experimental work. What is needed is a cadre of good field officers working for the district organisation. First, the district should be sub-divided into sub-areas, under assistant field officers. The size of the areas allocated to individuals must depend on such factors as the density of population, the staff available, and the nature of the problems. But it is better to have adequate staffs in the more important and limited areas than inadequate staffs spread too thinly on the ground.

26. This will be much more effective than the departmental system which has grown up in so many districts. A senior administrative officer who has had experience of both the departmental and the field officer systems summarises the advantages of the latter as follows:

>(a) The peasant has a better knowledge and understanding with the officer through whom all instructions emanate.

>(b) A better co-ordinated programme of work is achieved.

>(c) Many small desirable projects are achieved, which would otherwise be overlooked, because they are no

department's responsibility.

(d) The peasant can get a balanced understanding of the government's policy and so public relations are improved.

(e) A general balanced advance in economic development is achieved.

Apart from these advantages, a man who is concerned with every side of development is more likely to obtain a true picture of the needs of a rural community than one whose interest lies only in one aspect of them.

27. A field service of this kind, dealing with all aspects of agrarian development under the district team, will play a very important part and the qualities most needed for the work are those of character and leadership. Academic or technical qualifications will not matter so much. The conditions of service should be such as to attract good men of all races and to give them good prospects of advancement. There is no fear that the growth of non-government agencies will render the field officer redundant. For many years there will be more vacancies than suitable men to fill them. The field officers will be in the front line of progress and, if the service is to attract the right men, they must be able to reach a high level of remuneration in it. We envisage a service which would be built up gradually as suitable men become available, and no doubt it is one which many of the existing members of the departments will wish to join. For example the existing field officers (agriculture) of Tanganyika, instead of being 'field officers (agriculture)' should become 'field officers', and instead of confining themselves to agriculture they should concern themselves with all aspects of land use.

28. While it is on the expansion of an efficient field staff that the government must largely rely to maintain the drive for better land use, it will take time to build one up. The employment of unsuitable and inexperienced men may do more harm than good. A reliable African assistant agricultural officer attributed the disappointing progress of an agricultural development scheme in one area to inefficient and inadequately supervised field officers with untrained assistants. Such a service should attract some of the best men of all races, but it is mainly to the Africans that the government will have to look.

Field Assistants
Below technical staff officers working in the field there are at present field assistants employed by the departments and by the local government bodies. Their duties often include the enforcement of usage rules, a function which should be performed by agents of the rule-making authorities. They vary in quality and effectiveness, depending on their personal qualities and the adequacy of their training and supervision. We had evidence which indicated that while in some instances such men were doing very valuable work, others had not won the confidence of those among whom they worked and were, therefore, of little value. Men of little education or standing, unless they are working under close supervision of more senior staff, cannot be expected to exercise much influence in inducing peasants to change their ways of life, and most of them probably serve little purpose except perhaps in enforcing regulations. Those who should and in many instances do, exercise considerable influence are the men who have position in tribal society, such as chiefs, elders and leading farmers. These are the leaders who can, and do, profit by courses in natural resources training institutions. What the best agencies are at the

village level, however, depends largely on the social and political conditions in an area. In some, the formation of young farmer's clubs may prove a useful medium for propaganda, in others the traditional chiefs and elders, and in others again, co-operative societies. In any case the field staff must work in close collaboration with chiefs, elders and other leaders and obtain their confidence. They must never usurp their functions but always enlist their support. Where the co-operative movement is strong, the leaders and members of the societies can be particularly useful.

32. We have referred at some length to the importance of field officers because we believe that in this lies the best immediate hope of maintaining an effective instrument to achieve agrarian change in the field and because we believe that it is in the sphere that Africans will have an opportunity to play an important part in the process, provided that property training facilities are expanded. We emphasize that the work of the district teams and field staff must be complementary to that of the local authorities for in the last resort, all progress will depend upon it. We stress that, at the same time, non-government agencies should receive every encouragement.

Tasks Can Be Achieved
33. We were impressed by the fact that those officers who were in the best position to know the difficulties of accomplishing important changes were confident that they could be achieved within a few years, if the necessary high-quality staff and opportunity were available. The District commissioner, Kisii, in a memorandum prepared for us, after acknowledging the magnitude of the task of replacing traditional systems of land tenure and farming by 'a system of economic, demarcated smallholdings cultivated according to

the accepted principles of good husbandry, precluded from fragmentation and subdivision' wrote: 'given adequate funds and adequate staff, but above all given staff of the right calibre and determination, directed with energy and imagination and reinforced where necessary by the law, I believe the desired results could be achieved in a reasonably short time.' Similar optimism was expressed by other experienced officers.

Extension Work Among Women
34. It is just as important to obtain the confidence and co-operation of the women in the villages as that of the men. Women, indeed, play a major part in cultivation and all the efforts to teach the men the benefits of better farming may be frustrated if the women are not converted too. This is an aspect of extension work which presents peculiar difficulties, due partly to the backwardness of women's education and partly to the inferior status of women in many tribes. We were impressed by the success which had attended the efforts of the agricultural department of Kenya to employ local women of standing to instruct their neighbours in better methods of farming. Women of standing in a location are instructed in their own areas and are then employed to go from garden to garden giving advice. They do this while still living in their own homes. It is a method which might well be extended to all areas where the population is not too scattered. It is by personal instruction by someone she knows and looks up to that the woman with the hoe is most likely to accept changes in her time-honoured way of cultivating. Much can also be done through women's institutes and clubs, which at present often tend to neglect agriculture even though it fills such an important place in the lives of the women concerned. In devising new farming methods it must be remembered that unless the matter is properly explained to them

women cannot be expected to understand the necessity for changes which often give them more work to do and, at first, bring them little profit.

35. It is repeatedly stressed that there is great scope for the education of women in East Africa and for welfare work among them. In certain areas, such as the Kikuyu country, women have a very heavy burden of drudgery, and the division of labour between them and the men, however suited it may have been to past conditions, is now certainly weighted heavily against the women. Missions and welfare workers are doing much to help, but they are still hardly touching the fringe of the work which is urgently necessary if families are to be enlightened and progressive. There should ideally be at least one woman in each district organising welfare work among the women through women's clubs and women welfare assistants, and we recommend that the attention of local government bodies should be drawn to this need. Some of the more wealthy local government bodies should now be able to pay for the training and employment of women social workers. In some districts it should be possible to bring women into the district teams and also into the natural resources committees of the local government bodies, whether by co-option or otherwise. Witnesses with whom we discussed the matter stressed the need to raise the status of women and their importance in every sphere of family life, not least as the trainers of children.

36. Female education is making some headway now and plans are everywhere in training for its extension, but there is so much leeway to be made up that this work must be supplemented by mass education among adults. Instruction should include the teaching and demonstration of the benefits of improved methods of farming. It would be possible, for instance, to enlist some of the women to support campaigns for the consolidation

of fragmented holdings, as this would save them much tramping to and fro. We recommend that in each territory efforts should be made to obtain the services of a woman agriculturalist to pay special attention to organising the education of women in the basic principles and economics of agriculture, not least in the schools and teacher training colleges.

****

As we shall see in Part III, many of these suggestions were incorporated in the programme of Community Development and Adult Education.

Chapter Five

The Declaration of a State of Emergency

Returning to events in Kenya, one of the first things that Sir Evelyn Baring did on taking office as Governor in 1953 was to try and learn what was behind the unforeseen chaos he had inherited from his predecessor, Sir Philip Mitchell. He, therefore, appointed a small working party consisting of Dr Leakey, the well-known anthropologist and Kikuyu specialist, Mr S H Fazan, the former Secretary of the Land Commission referred to earlier, and myself. We held several meetings and took evidence from a number of leading Kikuyu, and recommended to His Excellency that everything possible should be done to remove all causes of injustice and racial discrimination. These were, in our view, in one way or another the basic causes of the revolt.

At the outset of the State of Emergency the responsibilities of the Department of Community Development were extended to cover rehabilitation as well. As Commissioner, was sent to Malaya were its State of Emergency was drawing to a successful conclusion to study the methods adopted there. I was very impressed by the view repeatedly emphasised by the Governor, General Sir Gerald Templer, that no success could be expected unless one won 'the hearts and minds of the people'. This caveat was emphasised in the report submitted to the Kenya Government in due course, and formed the basis of the recommendations for the introduction of a similar system of rehabilitation in Kenya. With certain modifications to take account of the atavistic nature of Mau Mau, and after widespread consultation with all concerned, the plan was accepted, and in due course, put into effect.

I was invited to address the African Affairs Committee of the Electors' Union the main organ of settler opinion in order that they should learn something of the thinking behind the expanded function of Community Development to which had been added the job of rehabilitation.

The Commissioner of Community Development and Rehabilitation's

address to the European Electors in September 1953:-

> The new department of Community Development and Rehabilitation has been instructed to organise rehabilitation measures for the 1,400 detainees I have mentioned, the 8 to 9,000 Mau Mau convicts in special prisons, the unpredictable number who have been repatriated from the settled area and require to be employed on development schemes in the Central Province - some put the figure as high as 15,000 - and the even larger number of waverers of all tribes throughout the Colony.
>
> I was sent to Malaya to study the methods employed there with considerable success in rehabilitating those detained during the Emergency. I have also read of the methods employed at Makronissos in Greece to convert Communists. While there are many points of similarity in Malaya and Kenya, the problem here is in many ways far more difficult to solve.
>
> In Malaya, however, the problem is seen as one of rehabilitation and re-settlement or re-employment, not rehabilitation alone. I feel myself that an even better description of the campaign would be re-education and re-settlement or re-employment, and this I am convinced is what is required in Kenya.
>
> What we are confronted with is a vast problem of displaced persons. 150,000 have gone back to the Kikuyu areas from one place or another, and accentuated the difficulties of that already over-populated area. A large proportion of those serving sentences in Prisons are also from the settled areas, and will have to be re-absorbed either in settlement areas or in employment on farms or in towns in the next three years. If they come out of jail with nowhere to live or no employment to go to, or are unable to support their families, then we shall have the germs of even greater unrest on our hands. If this point is not borne

in mind, and immediate steps taken to guard against the dangers, rehabilitation will be a waste of time, money and effort.

There are also a vast number of Africans who have been wilfully misled by an ill-informed or mendacious minority to accept the doctrine that they would be better off if Europeans were driven from the country. The campaign to discredit everything that the European has done to develop Kenya and to try to lead Africans towards civilisation has been going on for a long time. A whole generation of Kikuyu has been involved.

It is our task to re-educate these Africans and to convince them that our plans are better and hold promise of a brighter future than those of the Mau Mau. In Malaya the Government's aim is to win the hearts and minds of the people and convince them that it has a better plan than the Communists. It is being, I think, equally successful with the man in the street as with those in the Detention Camps, which numbered at one time more than 30,000.

One advantage which Malaya has over Kenya is that they have been able to repatriate about half the detainees to China. This was possible since they were not nationals and had not lived in the country very long. Many of those repatriated were what we refer to in Kenya as the hard core like those who were picked up in the original 'Jock Scott' operation. This course is naturally not open to us and we have got to take such action as we can to rehabilitate this hard core or render it innocuous. It is, however, the hardest nut to crack, and they are about as easy to convert as the confirmed Marxist.

In Malaya they have had to do what they could to win over those hard core who were nationals however. In some cases they have been successful through a process of individual interviews at which those concerned have become disillusioned with applied communism and given up their former allegiance.

They have concentrated chiefly, however, on those who were intimidated to join the movement or were simply misled into believing that communism would satisfy all their desires. These have proved satisfactory material and of 1,400 who have passed through rehabilitation centres, only 14 have subsequently come to the notice of the Police, and I would mention that the Police Force in Malaya is a highly developed and efficient organisation, and the names of most of the 6,000 in the jungle are known to it and much of their family history as well.

The basis of the rehabilitation process in Malaya is re-education in camps very like training colleges. They are taught a trade, agriculture, some elementary education and games. As in a school they are watched and guided individually, and when they leave after their six months course they seem to regard the centre as we would our old school. They subscribe towards new buildings, return for reunions and write large numbers of letters to the officer in charge to tell him how they are getting on. A lot of the success of these centres is due, I am convinced, to the sympathetic attention given to the ex-detainees by these officers. They are by the way officers of the Administration with a knowledge of Chinese or Malay as the case may be, and of their customs. Incidentally, they do not attempt any of this for the hard core.

As I have said, however, our problem is somewhat different, though I am sure we can apply many of the lessons learned in Malaya. The Chinese in Malaya are for the most part uneducated though sophisticated - the communist movement grew up and was fostered in the Independent Schools.

They are adept traders like the Kikuyu, they are very hard working unlike the younger Kikuyu, they are expert nursery gardeners, they are highly intelligent, they have a history of banditry and guerilla warfare. I leave you to draw your own conclusions.

Now, how is it proposed to try to tackle the problem in Kenya? As in Malaya, I feel that the first stage of rehabilitation or re-education must be hard work, and no one can be eligible for it until he has gone through the mill. Hard work there is regarded as an essential first step and I am convinced that the same thing applies here.

The second step is training in a trade and agriculture. The purpose of this might be described as occupational therapy, but also it is helping to fit the individual for re-settlement or re-employment.

"The third step which overlaps the second is re-education to ensure that he is better informed than when he came in. The fourth step which overlaps the third is the restoration of moral values. Amorality begets anarchy either individually or as a group. In Malaya or Mohamedanism which is an equally cohesive force, or Christianity for the few converts, provides the cement to build up the broken individual. It is equally important in Kenya to build up those who have become degraded in a similar way.

What the cohesive force should be in Kenya could occupy all our time, but I myself am convinced that the approach must be Christian since our whole system of Government is based on a Christian foundation. It must have a greater appeal to those concerned than the destructive nationalism of Mau Mau.

With regard to the first step - hard work - we are in the process of finding suitable employment for all concerned. At Manda it will probably be agricultural development of abandoned land near the camp; at Athi River the digging of a dam; in the Prisons it is sometimes bush clearing for the loyal tribes, quarrying or public works; in the work camps development schemes to open up new areas for settlement, and among the waverers work to improve the agricultural potentiality of the African areas. This latter is already going ahead through the efforts of the Administration as never before and is altering the face of many areas.

Next with regard to craft training. The co-operators at Manda and Athi River have already started classes. These will be stepped up in the near future. It is intended that as much as possible, craftsmen from among the detainees shall act as instructors for others. It is proposed that the crafts taught shall not compete with the existing trade schools, but should consist of rough carpentry and metal working using simple tools such as adzes which are cheap to buy and difficult to break. At the same time they will be appropriate for the myriad simple jobs required in African areas or possibly on farms, including fencing, the building of cattle sheds, poultry houses and runs, pig sties, bee hives, windows and doors and so forth for those who are allowed eventually to return home.

Agriculture will include bench terraces, market gardening, poultry keeping, pig keeping, composting and so forth. In Malaya fish farming was developed most usefully.

Next we come to general education or re-education. Here it is proposed to base the instruction on a little book I have written which you may or may not have seen, entitled The Story of Kenya's Progress. The book contains the meat of the syllabus given to African leaders at Jeanes School, and is an attempt not only to give informatin about the factors which contribute to Kenya's economic, social and political development, but to put them into a simple perspective and see them as a composite whole. We feel that only by getting these facts into proper perspective, and by appreciating their Christian foundation, can a person become a responsible citizen. Inadequate as it probably is, it will form a foundation upon which to work, in what I regard as the most vital aspect of rehabilitation.

Normal or formal education will be very sparingly given as it is perfectly possible to impart this informal education to illiterates. It is moreover impossible to do everything, and we cannot embark on a full blown formal education campaign when an informal one in public enlightenment and citizenship will meet the immediate needs.

I have no time to go into the proposed scheme of work which the book comprises, but it is designed to fill the vacuum of ignorance which has been found to exist and which has been filled with the falsehoods and false doctrines of political leaders over the past many years, and which has I am convinced led to a great extent to our present troubles. I suggest that those who are interested might read the booklet even though its subject matter is very elementary.

Finally we may come to the matter of spiritual rehabilitation, if I may call it that. Here I am sure the Churches and Christians generally have a big part to play. They have to win back these misguided people to a better attitude to life and society. In Malaya service to the community is stressed, and in the final process of rehabilitation to which the detainees are sent prior to release, they go out and work in the villages teaching carpentry, games and so forth. It is the Christians in Kenya who are the real power behind the Resistance. In Kenya I hope that we can show them the value of farmers', carpenters', builders' and other clubs as a means of helping others and themselves.

That is the programme we hope to introduce progressively in the Detention Camps, Prisons and Work Camps. Langata Prison has been selected for a pilot scheme. We would like to organise a similar campaign for those who are living at home - as we are doing now - though to a far too limited extent. This will involve the expansion of citizenship courses, farmer's clubs, women's clubs, carpentry and building clubs, village improvement schemes and so forth.

There is one interesting example of what has already started in the way of rehabilitation for youths who have deserted the terrorists in Nyeri. You may have read about it in the paper. They are being housed in an ex-Independent School, and the District Commissioner has organised carpentry classes, civics talks by himself and chiefs, and so forth, with most satisfactory results. The attitude of these young men has altered completely. The D.C. Nyeri and Fort Hall would like one such camp in each Division of their districts.

We have had similar experiences as a result of courses in Jeanes School. Senior African Civil Servants in particular have remarked that they never realise how much they needed British help at this stage of their development. They had no idea of the constructive nature of Government's plans and how difficult it was to implement them.

There is another aspect of rehabilitation which will shortly require attention and that is of the women. It is believed that at the present time they are keeping Mau Mau alive and D.C.s are making strenuous efforts to keep contacts with women to prevent further deterioration. In

Machakos District the D.C. regards the Women's Homecrafts movement valuable as a buffer to the infiltration of Mau Mau. The women have, of course, far less knowledge than the men and have been easily swayed by the Mau Mau leaders. Contacts with them have been most inadequate, but this is being rectified by the appointment of women Agricultural Assistants. Nevertheless, it is very likely that a detention camp for women will have to be set up, and that will require appropriate rehabilitation probably based on civics, homecrafts and agriculture.

Finally, a special Rehabilitation Centre as the last stage before release from a Detention Camp when all concerned are satisfied that such release would not endanger security may be required.

A similar pre-release centre for convicts will I think be even more necessary to fit them for re-absorption. It is to be hoped that those in work camps will be absorbed naturally in the new settlements they will be developing.

All this however will require staff, and staff what is more, of the highest calibre. It will also be necessary to train a number of Africans of a good educational standard and of the best character to undertake the civics instruction at the camps and prisons. Mr Bisset, who has long experience of this type of work in the Army Education Corps and at Jeanes School is at present working out a scheme of training. Apart from staff the costs will not be considerable however, but if the job is to be done properly it would be false economy to agree that any but the best men and Joseph Thomson should be entrusted with the task.

The priorities as I see them are that we must concentrate upon those who are to be released first, in other words, the 8-9000 in Prisons, and the other thousands who will be sent to work camps. It is by no means certain that any large proportion of those at Manda or Athi River will be considered safe to return to their homes as His Excellency the Governor indicated recently.

At the same time we cannot neglect the waverers living in the Reserves - a big job of mental rehabilitation still remains to be done there if we are to win back their allegiance and co-operation in our development plans. In this connection it may be difficult to say who are the waverers and who are the loyalists. Whatever happens I must not give the impression that all this re-education and training is to be given to those who have become involved with Mau Mau all along. Although it is not directly my province, the work that is being undertaken by the Mau Mau convicts is all to aid the state of the loyal tribes - stone-quarrying and dressing for African housing, the Mbagathi Airport, the Machakos road are helping the state; bush clearing and rice schemes in Nyanza are helping the loyal tribes. The work camps will be opening up country for loyal tribes too, and the communal labour in the reserves will be helping the loyalists.

However, I think re-education on a much wider scale is necessary for all Africans if we are going to maintain their co-operation in development plans, to increase the carrying capacity of the land and raise the general standard of living. It is not just a question of more formal school education which only affects the children. It is a matter of teaching the adults the things they ought to know and understand through every means in our power; through women's clubs, farmers' clubs, crafts clubs, information office material, libraries and literature.

All these means are being used and the remarkable thing is that the women's clubs and farmers' clubs have been little affected by the Emergency and are even expanding with an excellent effect on those concerned. A great deal still needs to be done, however, and officers, both male and female, European and African, with the necessary imagination and public spirit recruited for the task.

Chapter Six

The Rehabilitation Programme

A good many misconceptions have arisen regarding the process of separating the sheep from the goats so I propose to describe the 'Pipeline', as the progression from detention to ultimate release was referred to. At the bottom of the pipe were the Screening Teams, most of them on farms under the general control of the Police. Here either the entire labour force of a farm or part of it would be brought in for interrogation. Trusted headmen were usually given this task and by various methods decided who was loyal and who had taken an oath of allegiance to it, either willingly or not. These would be regarded as unreliable and might be sent off to one of the vast holding camps at Manyani or Mackinnon Road on the Mombasa railway line. One must appreciate that the farmers were terrified at the suddenness of the uprising and many expected a 'night of the long knives' which actually never materialised.

The two camps had been set up to receive the thousands rounded up in Nairobi in Operation Anvil. There the process of screening was continued and those who seemed to be simply pawns in the game were segregated and in due course transferred to one of the Work Camps, most of which were in the Mwea Plains in Embu District, but there were others such as Marigat near Lake Baringo where Jim Breckenridge, an ex-farmer, was the most enlightened and human commandant. It was at this stage that rehabilitation started. We were not responsible in any way for Manyani or Mackinnon road where most of the alleged ill-treatment of detainees seemed to have occurred.

While at the Work Camps detainees were encouraged, but never forced to make a clean breast of any Mau Mau associations they might have had and to take part in a ritual cleansing ceremony which seemed to lift a great load of guilt from their minds, for one has to remember they had often sworn to murder for the cause if required. They were then entitled to take part in the rehabilitation programme which was largely educational and therefore very attractive to those concerned, almost all of whom were, as one would expect, illiterate.

In due course, and if they continued to respond well, they would be recommended for release and would be transferred to their districts of origin or tribal area. The chief and headmen would decide whether to agree to a release or not.

When all the obviously co-operative detainees had been transferred from Manyani or Mackinnon Road a decision had to be reached with regard to the remainder, some of whom were fanatically opposed to any form of cleansing. These ultimately were destined for transfer to Hola for permanent exile.

The extension of the operation with the detention of another 70,000 detainees was never envisaged at the outset. It involved the isolation of the entire unemployed population of Nairobi and neighbouring areas and their distribution from two vast holding camps on the rail to Mombasa and thence to a score of camps where development work was available nearer the tribal areas. A further 10,000 were serving sentences in jail for Mau Mau offenses.

This expansion was the brain child of General Erskine. Although it was obviously devised for strategic reasons it actually operated as a relief operation. If my assessment that Mau Mau constituted a form of Spartacus uprising of the unemployed and landless Kikuyu is accepted then detention enabled them at least to be fed, sheltered and provided with useful and acceptable employment. If they had remained at large without means of support they would obviously have been forced to prey on their fellows, join the insurgents in the forests, or surge into the White Highlands as illicit squatters, or a combination of all three. Thus it is suggested that this period of detention constituted a similar state of affairs to that which operated during the last war, when a like number were syphoned off from the economy as recruits in the armed forces. In neither case, of course, was it intended to provide a relief from the pressure of population, but the result was the same and without it the stability of society would have been threatened.

The rehabilitation programme in the camps was in the hands of men and women chosen carefully for their integrity and humanity. A number were recruited by the Colonial Office in the UK. Others were Kenya residents, some of whom did excellent work in most trying circumstances.

An Advisory Committee consisting of unofficials, with a retired Provincial Commissioner as Chairman, and the Archbishop of Kenya as a member, visited the camps regularly to ensure that no abuses crept in. As has been mentioned, the CID had a special unit to supervise the whole operation. Finally, I and senior staff spent long periods touring the camps to supervise operations, in the company of Mr Beniah Ohanga, the first African Minister, to whom I was

Permanent Secretary. In view of the magnitude of the operation it is difficult to see what more could have been done to guide the process and prevent abuses of power.

In so far as the more junior members of the rehabilitation staff are concerned, all were recruited by the churches on our behalf, from men and women of the highest character. The Society of Friends and the Moral Rearmament Community also made valuable contributions

After long discussions with those who were well versed in Kikuyu lore, it was agreed by all concerned that the best approach to the problem would be by making Kikuyu elders available in all the detention camps to whom any detainee would have access to discuss his problem in relation to the oaths he had taken to support Mau Mau. Church elders were chosen for this duty not because they were Christians, as such, but because no true Christian would submit to the heathen rites evolved by the oath administrators.

It was agreed that the strongly superstitious nature of most Kikuyu would make them terrified of refusing to support the terrorist organisation and to guard its secrets. On the other hand, if an individual, by the very fact of being housed in a detention camp, secure from reprisals by a Mau Mau gang, felt confident enough to defy the Mau Mau, he should be ready to take part in a traditional cleansing ceremony, and by so doing, purify his soul of the evil rites he may have been forced to observe, and thus free himself of the obligation to keep its vows. No one, to my knowledge, disputed this approach though some have questioned the reliability of some of the confessions. However, it was the most promising process we could evolve in the circumstances.

The change of demeanour of those who had been persuaded to partake in a cleansing ceremony was so marked that one had little doubt that it had been a genuine psychological help to relieve them of their sense of guilt and shame for it must be remembered that the more advanced forms of oath were entirely contrary to Kikuyu lore and of the utmost bestiality. Those without African experience will, perhaps be unconvinced by this conclusion, but those who worked in the rehabilitation programme had no such doubts or they would have expressed them.

Oaths are, of course, as old as time and are practised for a wide variety of purposes. They are used in courts of law to counter perjury, by a wide variety of religions and cults to foster integrity, in natural assemblies to encourage loyalty, and so forth. The Kikuyu were unusual in providing for the reversal of an oath. The Mau Mau oath was partly to reinforce loyalty to a leader and a cause and partly to bind an individual to secrecy. They have been described in detail by other writers.

It has been suggested that not all Kikuyu by any means were in favour of the overthrow and destruction of the state, and only a few hoped to see the removal of Europeans and other foreigners. Many, therefore, were prepared to reverse the validity of their previous oath, particularly when it was applied under duress.

A minority however for one reason or another felt fanatically bound to fight to the bitter end for the objectives they espoused. These were mainly the forest fighters and what were referred to as the 'hard-core' in the detention camps. They seemed to have found that it maintained their morale to be re-oathed with increasingly degrading oaths in order to withstand the moral pressures confronting them to throw in the sponge. It was remarkable what powers of resistance were developed in this way, for to exist under onerous conditions for years at a time requires a high degree of fortitude.

So as the oaths became progressively repulsive, not only to Europeans but also in Kikuyu eyes, those concerned regarded themselves more and more as outcasts of society. This in fact was the object of their severity. There was to be no looking back or return to normal society until the battle was won.

Oathing continued in the holding camps, however vigilant the warders might be. One noticed when visiting those for the hard-core that their features were changing and this was very noticeable to the camp staff. The whites of their eyes began to turn yellow and narrow and to lose their normal expression. The staff referred to them as 'leopard eyes'. How this came about no one knew. The individuals were not sick but were obviously under some form of psychological stress. The assumption that it was due to the advanced oaths they had taken was inescapable.

The Kikuyu elders were of the opinion that such people were beyond the influence of any form of rehabilitation. Cleansing from the more basic oaths obviously gave a sense of psychological relief but we had to admit that there seemed to be no way of removing the utter fanaticism of those who had taken the more advanced pledges.

Naturally, such a vast programme involved a great recruitment problem and the quality of the commandants varied considerably. Most of them were human and understanding in spite of whatever prejudices they might have held. In one instance Josiah Mwangi Kariuki, in his book *Mau Mau Detainee* reports that the Camp Commandant even helped him to follow a British correspondence course in journalism while in detention. It was common practice to allow and even encourage detainees to decorate their sleeping quarters in their spare time. Some remarkable murals were achieved as a result. Although no actual educational programme was organised for those who gave no indication of their opposition to the violence of Mau Mau, no restriction was imposed on the detainees arranging literacy classes among themselves. What is more, MRA actually carried out a most comprehensive educational programme at the camp for well-educated detainees they staffed at Athi River.

For those who satisfied the elders that they were no longer supporters of Mau Mau, a literacy programme was available and, as has been mentioned earlier, one of the text books used as follow-up literature was Kenya's Progress, in the hope that as many people as possible would appreciate that there were better ways of solving political problems than by revolution. In fact, the majority of the African tribes continued along this path throughout the period of the Emergency, and were never involved in Mau Mau.

Another aspect of rehabilitation relating to the camp for juveniles at Wamumu will be described in Part III under the sub-heading entitled "Youth Centres".

With regard to the actual conflict itself Professor Robert Egerton has written an extremely comprehensive account in his book *Mau Mau*. This describes how a comparatively small number of men and women held out in the forests for some seven years with no weapons or military supplies apart from what they could steal or manufacture for themselves. They also had no outside support against the combined forces of the colony supplemented by three British battalions of infantry. The Mau Mau insurgents were only finally overcome by the defection of their own men and the operation of local SAS-type units. Peace was established in the tribal areas through the efforts of the greatly expanded Provincial Administration and its tribal police, known as the Home Guard. The nationalist leaders played no part in the struggle, being shut away for the whole period of the Emergency at the Athi River Camp under the ministrations of the MRA. Equally the vital unofficial 'Mau Mau Army Service Corps in Nairobi had been rendered helpless by its confinement in various detention camps until just before Independence.

The great bulk of the rest of the Kikuyu endured great physical hardship, including an enormous amount of labour in connection with earthworks to deny the terrorists access to supplies in the tribal areas, the vast villagisation programme and the terracing and land reform measures connected with the Swynnerton Plan, quite apart from mortality as a result of terrorist attacks. It was this community of what became known as 'loyalists' who not only suffered much but rightly benefited eventually from the improved economy made possible by the Swynnerton Plan.

On their release the nationalists stepped into positions of power and wealth when Independence was achieved. Many loyalists and politicians were also able to acquire land in the settled areas through various settlement schemes. So perhaps justice had been done in one way or another, but it was often extremely harsh, not least for the settlers themselves, although they were compensated by the purchase of their land.

One cannot help wondering, however, whether a settlement would ever have been achieved without Mau Mau. Would the various reforms have been achieved without it - the permission to grow coffee and tea in the tribal areas, for instance; permission for Africans to acquire land in the Highlands; the huge rice scheme in Embu and Marigat made possible by detainee labour, finally, even Independence itself?

But possibly the terrorists or "freedom fighters" as they might prefer to call themselves, suffered most and moralists will no doubt say that this was only right and proper. However, something would have to be done to enable these people to obtain a settled livelihood.

There are some aspects of Professor Egerton's account which might, I think, be given a rather different interpretation. He described, for instance, the somewhat comic titles and honours the Mau Mau leaders have given themselves and suggests that this was intended to impress people overseas. Such self-awarding of honours was not simply a Kenya phenomenon, however, and is noticeable throughout Africa. I suggest it can have another interpretation.

As Professor Egerton mentions, most of the volunteers were very young and inexperienced, with a sprinkling of men who had served in the Burma Campaign under similar conditions to the forest round Mount Kenya. These few experienced soldiers were trying to build up an army from scratch and, I suggest, paid the British a compliment by modelling it on our pattern as far as they could, hence the bugle calls and the emphasis on discipline and the ranking. But they apparently combined their fighting methods with certain traditional practices which they had learned from their elders. This explains their code of sexual ethics, the prohibition of alcohol and so forth. When we come to examine the revival of traditional communal organisations in the community development schemes, the same merging of European and African cultures will become apparent to the advantage of both.

So I suggest that far from indicating a reversion to savagery, this tendency to draw on the pattern of the past was an intelligent adaptation of traditional methods to the modern requirements of bush warfare. In any case, it proved eminently successful as is shown by the surprisingly low rate of casualties and the length of time the gangs were able to survive as a fighting force under the most arduous conditions.

Looked at in another way, this tendency of building on the pattern of the British Army, as well as reviving what was best in traditional culture, tends to support my contention that it is too easily assumed that Mau Mau aimed at wiping out all aspects of European civilization and reverting to a primitive way of life. It seems that their military wing was just as anxious to preserve such aspects of western culture as they had been able to absorb within the limits of their inadequate resources, as the better educated nationalists were concerned to preserve western institutions.

So Mau Mau was by no means simply destructive or atavistic as is maintained by some observers. This attitude was largely fostered by the settlers' press to gain the support of British and world opinion. The fact that there was no instance of the rape of a white woman throughout the Emergency is significant in the light of so many contemporary wars. The imitations of British Army ranks, decorations and camp disciplines should be recognised as a compliment rather than a rejection of western values.

After the Emergency was over one of the young officers, Geoff Griffin continued in youth work, and built up the Starehe Youth Centre in the slums of Nairobi for young vagrants and orphans. It acquired an international reputation and was run on similar lines to Wamumu. Later still after Independence he took charge of the Kenya Youth Service formed to provide employment in public works on disciplined lines for the streams of boys who still flooded into the towns in search of jobs.

To supplement these efforts to deal with juvenile unemployment, craft-training schemes were set up throughout the Kikuyu and neighbouring districts as part of the measures taken to extend rehabilitation to the rural areas. The idea was simple. Workshops were built by the boys themselves, in temporary materials, and they were then given instruction in the manufacture or repair of anything needed in the rural economy, from school desks and benches to beds and shoes. Everything made was sold or paid for by the local inhabitants, and so handymen were trained to serve the needs of the neighbourhood. The interesting point about this scheme, is, perhaps, that it seems to have predated the 'Intermediate Technology' project which has received such publicity since.

The final stage of the process was the acceptance of the detainees back in their tribal areas. It was natural that the Chiefs were cautious while terrorism was active on their doorstep. At the same time, it would have been dangerous to release large numbers of people into society with no means of support. This could be tantamount to inviting them to join the Mau Mau gangs operating in the nearby forests. So large numbers of detainees had to remain in the work camps engaged in productive development work opening up huge areas for the cultivation of rice. Until conditions in the country were such as to enable the detainees to be absorbed into an improved economy they must be kept usefully employed.

Many thousands became rehabilitated in the first year or two, and were engaged in the paddy-fields, and taking part in the literacy classes and other rehabilitation activities after work. Others joined them from the holding camps in a steady stream: 60,000 of the original 80,000 had been released after rehabilitation, leaving 20,000 retained in 1956.

It was at this stage that the Minister for African Affairs decided to introduce a new system to speed things up. On the arrival of new intakes from the holding camps, instead of simply mixing them with the rehabilitated detainees in the camps, in the hope that the latters' more responsible attitude would have a good effect n them, they were forced to conform to a punitive regime which is described in Charles Chenevix Trench's book *The Men who Ruled Kenya*.

I could not bring myself to agree to the use of force in this way since it was contrary to the whole principle of rehabilitation which had been accepted by government. There had, in fact, been incidents where detainees had been illegally assaulted and even killed in the past, so approval of the use of physical violence in any way, as an instrument of official policy was,I considered, fraught with danger for all concerned, not least the staff who were required to put it into effect, apart from being ineffective from a rehabilitation point of view.

I, therefore, officially advised against the adoption of such tactics. Soon after, I was relieved of my responsibilities in connection with rehabilitation, though not for community development. I feel convinced that the new policy led inevitably to what was referred to as the Hola Incident, when eleven detainees lost their lives.

Apart from this I had always maintained that Mau Mau was the result of destitution among what was probably a comparatively small section of the Kikuyu tribe who were landless. It was, therefore, vital to maintain them in the work camps until such time as they could be provided with a reasonable livelihood, or land. There was no point in trying to speed up the process.

The European farms which had previously provided support for so many of the detainees and their parents were becoming increasingly unreliable as a source of employment on their release. One cannot simply blame their owners. Their needs for labour fluctuated wildly, as did their income and they were legally entitled to employ who they wished.

The agricultural reforms which were undertaken in the tribal areas during the Emergency mainly benefited those with land, and so those without it were still unprovided for. In my view, only when their settlement on farms acquired from Europeans was put into effect in 1962 was a beginning made to solve the original cause of the revolt: 7,500 families were so settled in that year. It is significant that after that no further mention of Mau Mau was made. Apart from sporadic outbreaks of unrest their needs had at last been recognised even though not completely satisfied. Thousands later took the law into their hands and flooded into the highlands and settled as illegal squatters.

Those who belittle the programmes of education and recreation organised in the work camps overlook the salient fact that no outbreaks of violence or unrest occurred in the camps during the Emergency, apart from the time when the detainees were killed at Hola. One can only hope that the inmates also obtained something of value from their time in detention even though it was no picnic.

What is not generally appreciated is that the detention camps - alias work camps - were, in fact, labour lines for the huge irrigation schemes near by, which were being developed for the ultimate benefit of the inhabitants of the particular tribal area in which they were situated. The people of Embu would be the main beneficiaries, but the scheme at Marigat would serve the area near Baringo and so on. It would not have been difficult for anyone to escape if they had wanted to, but presumably they were too well-treated and fed to make the idea attractive.

It seems that it was the former detainees, most of them simply unemployed, who continued to be the principal sufferers from the Mau Mau conflict. They went into it landless and came out in much the same state, except for what they had been able to acquire when the white settlers began to leave. Few can have benefited from the Swynnerton Plan. They therefore remained as a potential source of unrest even when Independence was achieved. They started as unemployed and finished as such. Only the loyalists seem to have benefitted from the reforms.

The fundamental need of the detainees, as I have emphasised all along was more land. This was the holy grail at the end of the long trail back to freedom. Unless some assurance could be given that this dream would be realised rehabilitation of the landless was unrealistic. But no such guarantee could be given for political reasons. It did not make any difference whether the rehabilitation process operated on a voluntary basis as insisted upon in my original plan or forcibly, as introduced when I was relieved of responsibility. The key to successful rehabilitation had to be peaceful reabsorption, resettlement and employment, not simply docile behaviour in the work camps themselves.

Moving forward in time, Frank Furedi in *The Mau Mau War in Perspective* reveals how resettlement in 1970 in the settled areas was impossible: 'landless Africans simply had nowhere to go...mass unemployment, around 28%, had a demoralising impact on the population...[and] a demographic explosion combined with mass repatriation meant that between 1969 and 1979 the population of Nakuru District rose from 290, 863 to 522,333'. He also mentions how the Federation of the Kenya Peoples' Union and later its successor, the Nakuru Freedom Fighters' Association suggest a resurgence of Mau Mau itself.

I will refrain from commenting on the Hola affair as it has been dealt with by so many writers except to mention that there was another reason why I emphasised the importance of relying on persuasion rather than force. If an individual showed by his attitude that he was not prepared to give way to moral persuasion it would be futile to resort to force. This was confirmed in the Hola incident where it had apparently been decided to force the detainees to comply with an order to hoe the land and if they refused, to make them go through the motions of so doing. Accordingly a warder was attached to each detainee and they jointly took hold of the hoe. The warder then forced the detainee to go through the motions of hoeing, apparently in the belief that by so doing some spell of resistance would then be broken and the detainee would, like some automaton, continue to hoe of his own accord. When this reaction failed to materialise the warders seem to have lost their self control in frustration and caused the resulting mayhem.

The theory that some magic lay behind the mere performance of work seems to have arisen from the original policy document which I had prepared at the outset of rehabilitation, when the value of constructive work as an antidote to monotony and boredom was emphasised. The equally important concomitant that such work would be voluntary and so in accordance with the Geneva Convention seems to have been overlooked.

Every Englishman knows you can take a horse to water but you cannot make him drink.

I am only concerned here in a re-examination of those events which have been inadequately reported in order that a fair assessment of their importance may be made. All that need be said is that the subsequent Committee of Enquiry set up by the Colonial Office under the chairmanship of Mr R D Fearn, a British Prison Commissioner, advised on the rejection of the system introduced after my removal from office, and the restoration of the original policy to use persuasion rather than force in the rehabilitation process. Rehabilitation by force is, after all, surely a contradiction in terms as was found time and time again even by some of the most brutal officers.

As has been reported elsewhere, the effect of the report was an almost indecent scramble to dismantle the whole apparatus and release the remaining detainees, including the hard-core, en bloc. It was fortunate that this was not accompanied by any unfortunate consequences, for most of them had no means of survival until their eventual re-settlement in the highlands took place.

It has been suggested that it was hopelessly idealistic to imagine that the hearts of men and women could be changed as a result of rehabilitation measures. One would be compelled to agree that this would be true if such measures had not been linked with political, social and economic reforms which were only finally achieved after Independence.

It is well known that there was no ill-will towards Britain after Independence. A Kenya settler actually continued as Minister of Agriculture for some years. Other Europeans stayed and continued working alongside indigenous colleagues. Kenya became one of Britain's most popular holiday resorts and its coffee its favourite beverage. But the best legacy was the good will enjoyed by all sections of the community.

There is a postscript which should be added to complete the picture. After the Emergency was over a large Memorial Church was built at Muranga in the centre of the Kikuyu country to commemorate the deaths of the thousands of Christians who had lost their lives in the conflict. The vast majority, of course, died at the hands of their fellow tribesmen. A feature of the post-Mau Mau period is the remarkable religious revival which took place. Unlike Britain, the churches were packed on Sundays. It was as if all were delighted to see the end of atavism which marked the previous grisly period.

Chapter Seven

Promoting Local Leadership

Jeanes School had a long and interesting history and has been associated with many generations of leading Africans in Kenya. Not least among them was the late Tom Mboya who was trained there for three years as a Health Officer and became the President of the Students Council

It started in 1925 to provide a special form of training for village teachers who were destined to become leaders in their own communities in various rural spheres. They were not merely trained as teachers but as Agricultural and Health instructors and as stimulators of progress in many directions. As such their role was not very different from that of the Community Development Assistants who were trained in later years. Their wives also received instruction in homecrafts and were trained to play a complementary role to their husbands among the women of the countryside.

The Jeanes School was closed down at the start of the Second World War and was taken over as a training centre for the Army. After the war it continued for four years as a civil reabsorption organisation at which ex-servicemen were given training to equip them for their return to civil life.

When this scheme came to an end in 1949 it became the main adult education centre for the colony and the nucleus first of the Social Welfare Organisation and the Department of Community Development. As such it continued and grew substantially until eventually the wheel turned a half circle once more and part of it was taken over for the new Administrative Staff College where Africans were to be trained to take the place of British District Officers and District Commissioners. The essentially Community Development training centre was retained however, while the adult education wing disappeared.

During the twelve years that the training centre existed however, it played a significant part in training many thousands of African men and women from all walks of life in a variety of subjects including agriculture, animal husbandry, health, co-operative development, social work, citizenship, trade unionism, sport and youth work to name only a few.

The training centres became so popular that the African District Councils of Nyanza Province put up half the cost of establishing a similar training centre for that province and similar small centres were built at Embu and Meru. At the same time the demands on the women's homecrafts section became so great that no less than twelve other centres were constructed in districts throughout the length and breadth of Kenya and financed by the African District Councils themselves. The system of training progressive farmers proved so successful that the Ministry of Agriculture adopted it for introduction in all its Farm Institutes of which some half dozen were set up.

Finally it pioneered, together with its sister establishment in Nyanza Province, the method of training African leaders of all kinds in the principles and practices of community development. It is this aspect of its work that will be described here, but before passing to that, one should mention that the work of enlightenment in local government, and the problems of development in a democratic society, which had been undertaken as a major part of the function of the adult education wing, together with the enlightenment given in agricultural and health matters, undoubtedly paved the way to the more ready acceptance of community development.

There was in fact the remarkable instance, which has been referred to in the chapter on the Kalenjin, of a group of farmers from a remote and backward area who after attending an agricultural course during which they were also taught the techniques of community development, returned home and without any official help or guidance successfully launched a community development scheme themselves.

Jeanes School was conveniently situated seven miles from Nairobi on the edge of the Kiambu District in rural surroundings. On the other side lay the fields of the Veterinary Department and beyond it one of the first African Schools to be opened by the Church Missionary Society in the Kikuyu country.

All the courses were residential and this made it possible to provide much more thorough and intensive training than if the trainees had to come in daily. It was also well equipped. Half the land was taken up by the school farm, which resembled a small holding with similar conditions to what might be found in an advanced African farm. There was also a visual aid room for the showing of films.

Over the years the old Army huts were gradually replaced by modern stone dormitories and in the Community Development wing there was a large number of cottages, which were usually occupied by the women students or husbands when accompanied by their wives. A good tuition block was also constructed in this area and a double storeyed block of dormitories for single girls and women.

In the centre of the compound were the playing fields where potential Olympic Athletes and international footballers were trained. The track was one of the finest in East Africa. There were plenty of trees, flowering shrubs and lush grass which made the place pleasant to work in.

One of the objectives was to make the atmosphere friendly and as informal as possible. Courses usually ended with a tea party at which speeches of good wishes and thanks were made. Those who attended were given a certificate and were allowed to buy a pocket badge which one often saw being proudly worn throughout the length and breadth of the Colony. In fact to let it be known that one came from Jeanes School was to ensure an enthusiastic welcome. Reminiscences of experiences at the school in former years would be the general topic of conversation and reminded one of a school reunion. To many of course this would have been the first and only time they had attended such an institution and what they had learned and seen was often a revelation to them.

The courses which had the greatest influence on community development were, of course, primarily those for community development assistants, progressive farmers, leaders such as Chiefs and members of local government and women being trained to develop clubs. It may be of interest to describe each in turn.

Progressive Farmers

This was the course which was pioneered by the Agricultural Instructor in 1950 and which eventually became the pattern of training for all the Farm Institutes set up by the Ministry of Agriculture which is a sufficient commendation in itself.

The idea behind the course was that if one concentrated on the progressive farmers they would be the most likely people to benefit from the training and at the same time provide an example of good farming for their neighbours. The first assumption was proved to be correct, for the trainees certainly put into practice what they had learned during the course. The second was not always fulfilled, particularly if the farmers were singled out for special assistance by the Agricultural Officer. This would put them rather apart from their neighbours and give them advantages which others did not enjoy. However when they became members of groups they were invaluable in convincing the others of the value of the new methods being recommended.

The course invariably lasted for five weeks which was found to be the most convenient period; not too short to complete the syllabus, not too long for the farmers to be away from their homes or to lose interest.

Instruction was given partly in the class room and partly on the school farm. All the members did actual work on the farm and so by degrees it was developed and improved by their labour. They were selected from the same area or District by the Agricultural Field Officer concerned, who also played a part in planning the curriculum of the course. It was this officer who followed up on the course and ensured that the farmers were putting what they had learned into practice.

The course was therefore tailor-made for the area from which the farmers came and was suitable for the conditions which prevailed there.

Demonstrations were given of simple farm implements, pesticides and seeds as well as improved agricultural practices. Animal husbandry was of course an important subject.

It was the objective of the school farm to provide a demonstration of all aspects of farming so that they would be available for whatever course of training would be required. There were, therefore, demonstrations of dairy farming, poultry keeping, horticulture, pig keeping, coffee farming, afforestation, vegetable growing and so forth. The farm provided a living example of rotational agriculture and pasture control. The school dining hall was supplied to a considerable extent by the produce grown on the farm. Therefore all the demonstrations were severely practical.

No attempt was made to make the farm into an actual smallholding, since all these aspects would have been beyond the capacity of an individual farmer unless he employed labourers. At the same time the trainees got an insight into group work by working together in the farm.

The farmers would make visits to neighbouring European and progressive African farms to see how good farming methods worked out in practice. The hosts were always most hospitable to the trainees and the visits were much appreciated.

Community Development Assistants (men)

The basis upon which so much community development was based was the Community Development Assistant. These were employed by the African District Councils with funds derived from the local people.

In the early years before the concept of community development became clarified, the role of these officers was somewhat obscure. They were expected by their Councils to take charge of community halls and as such to be the motive force behind an adult education drive including the organisation of adult literacy courses.

As time went on they became increasingly organisers of recreation, which implied as a rule football and athletics, until the concept of group work became more fully understood. Then they became an essential element in this true community development and many played an important role. An example has been given of the Community Development Assistant who did such good work in Nandi District. Others in Elgon Nyanza did equally well. On the other hand they played little part in Machakos or Kitui and at the time the Central Nyanza scheme was launched all had been discharged by the local authority as an economy measure.

One cannot avoid the conclusion therefore that whereas many did good work in the field of community development, the other field staff such as Agricultural and Health Assistants could do so equally well when they had been properly orientated. The role of the Community Development Assistant seemed to be more in those fields not covered by any other officer such as the promotion of youth centres, sport and so forth.

The most effective catalyst in community development proved to be the community Development Officer making use of the existing technical field staff and traditional leaders for the implementation of the programmes. This will be further considered in the chapter dealing with the subject.

The course of training for Community Development Assistants lasted for one year but was later extended to eighteen months. During part of this time they were undergoing technical instruction at the school in fields of community development and adult education techniques; the organisation of recreation, agriculture, animal husbandry and health. Part of the time was in field work in the school - building, carpentry, agriculture etc. A third of the time was spent doing field work in camps in some district in connection with a community development scheme.

The result of the training was for the most part good. Some of the trainees as has been mentioned did excellent work, other were promoted and became Chiefs, Community Development Officers and even District Officers. The groundwork was therefore obviously valuable and the majority no doubt were equipped to become leaders in their communities.

The field training in particular gave the trainees an entirely different outlook. The experience of doing hard manual work was not only a revelation to them but enabled them to appreciate the physical problems which confront villagers.

Community Development Assistants (women)
This also was a one year course and the women were trained primarily in homecrafts with the emphasis on matters concerning the rearing of children and the care of the house. At the same time they were given instruction in practical agriculture and animal husbandry.

The results were excellent and the products were in great demand. There was excessive competition for places on the course and this became so acute that no less than fourteen other District Training Centres for women had to be opened to meet the demand. These were as a rule simple in construction and accommodated thirty to fifty women at one time. Jeanes School itself had accommodation for seventy. The District Training Centres organised shortened courses of three months' duration. About 1,500 women received some kind of training annually therefore.

Primarily they were trained to become instructors to womens' groups similar to Womens' Institutions in the United Kingdom. Sometimes they had their own meeting houses, sometimes they used some community centres.

They were supervised by women Community Development Officers in the districts and there were as many of these as there were male officers.

The more imaginative Community Development Officers saw the contribution that these womens' groups would make in the promotion of the community development. As time went on therefore one saw more and more of the clubs meeting in each others' homesteads to carry out group work on their own. At the same time the members of the clubs were invariably also members of the working community development groups and did good work in convincing the other members of the value of the work they were undertaking.

The training given at Jeanes School was gradually broadened to meet the community development need while the more domestic science aspect became less emphasised. Of course both sides were equally important, but it was felt that if these highly trained women were to make their maximum impact their influence must be felt beyond the sphere of the womens' clubs.

Chiefs and Leaders
This was basically a citizenship course to enable those in responsible positions to become more aware of the problems of government and the workings of democracy. The economics of development were given a prominent place. The principles and practices of community development were of course included as a part of each course.

As in the case of the farmers' courses, the members used to pay visits to factories, the Parliament Buildings, centres of local government, the railway and so forth in order to get an insight into the mechanics of developing a modern state both democratically and economically.

There is no doubt that the courses were stimulating and at the same time sobering for some of the members. There was plenty of time for discussion and the answering of questions. Some of the questions were revealing, such as that which queried why the government did not increase the wealth of the country by printing more notes. The economic consequences of such a policy had not been appreciated. The importance of stimulating exports if imports were required also needed emphasis.

All in all the leaders of the rural community undoubtedly returned more enlightened if somewhat over-awed by the complexities of the modern state.

Community Development Officers
It will have been noticed that the emphasis of training was upon the subordinate staff and leaders while little was done to train the Community Development Officers themselves who were the lynchpin of the whole structure.

This was an unfortunate state of affairs which it was hoped to remedy. The reason for it was that the officers were so urgently needed in the field that time could not be spared to give them a proper course.

Instead, on first appointment they were given a few talks and then sent to a district where community development was well established to see for themselves how it was organised in the field. After a few weeks they were posted to their districts. They were then visited once or twice a year so that their work could be evaluated and advice given as to how they could improve it.

Annually too, a conference of all officers was arranged at Jeanes School where they could discuss their problems and learn from each others' experiences. That this sketchy system produced such remarkable results in many cases is a tribute to the quality of the officers themselves, their keenness and imaginative enterprise.

Each officer was required to send in monthly reports and extracts were circulated to their colleagues in a bulletin.

So the training of the officers had to be confined to on-the-job training and bitter experience, while policy papers were circulated to them, which they had to apply to their own conditions.

Group Leaders

Whereas the first group leaders from Machakos District were trained at Jeanes School, thereafter no more work of this kind was done there for the simple reason that true community development could not be organized among the neighbouring Kikuyu during the early years of the Emergency.

However, the sister centre at Maseno in Central Nyanza embarked on a major programme of such training to support and expand the community development projects there. They were remarkably successful as were those for Chiefs and Headmen. The main purpose of the courses which were residential as at Lower Kabete, but of only ten days duration was to inculcate the need for consolidation and farm planning and to indicate how this could be achieved through community development methods.

Understanding being an essential pre-requisite for any community development scheme if the people are to truly desire the fulfilment of the project, the training aspect was of paramount importance. It was partly as a result of this work that the scheme was so successful.

The principal of the training centre who had previously distinguished himself at the parent organization, did a remarkable job, and the centre became the training ground for the field officer of the district, but more particularly of the Agricultural Officer.

The same system was afterwards adopted at the Farm Institute in the neighbouring district of North Nyanza. In Nyeri District the Farm Institute was also used for the training of group leaders in the development of consolidated holdings. In Baringo ad hoc arrangements were made at the local Secondary School during holidays while in Embu a fully fledged Community Development Training Centre was set up not merely for the training of leaders but of women leaders of clubs.

Orientation

The problem of converting officers from District Commissioners to technical field staff to the ideas of community development is not only the most important but usually the most difficult task.

These officers have usually had many years of practical experience and have made great advances in their respective fields. To suggest that greater and more rapid progress could be made by radically different methods is sometimes regarded as almost insulting and one can appreciate this attitude.

When community development was first suggested the usual answer was that it had been practised for many years and there was really nothing novel about it. But in fact of course there was all the difference between a programme where the people had contributed to self-help activities under the direction of chiefs and headmen and doing the same thing under their own leaders and through group work.

Men of action are seldom prepared to accept a new theoretical approach without serious misgivings and who can blame them. If on the other hand it is possible to show them an example of community development in action there is a greater likelihood of their giving it a trial. Many still argued however that the idea might work in another district and in other circumstances but would not do so in their own areas. It should be realized, however, that this attitude is by no means confined to countries under colonial rule. Identical attitudes are to be found in the Middle East and Asian countries operating with similar administrative patterns.

The examples have shown that even where the administration found itself confronted by a complete impasse and a refusal by the people to co-operate they have been prepared to give community development a trial.

So the crucial need in the process of orientation is to provide the required object lesson. In Kenya however this was by no means easy for, as has been pointed out, the magic formula itself had not been discovered in the early stages. Various processes had been developed and certain principles had been found to be sound, such as the limitation of the projects to a small area in the first instance, the emphasis on practical instruction and so forth. But the vital spark to vitalize the programme had not been found until the idea of group work was tried in Machakos. Even then the discovery was almost fortuitous for no one really knew that the idea had its source in the peoples' traditions and would prove to be such a powerful force in so many different areas and among tribes with widely different cultures.

One can only date the spread of community development therefore from this discovery. The work during the preceding years had been valuable in many ways, but exploratory like the early stages of a laboratory experiment. After that it was a matter of application and adaptation on a wider scale and in varying conditions.

But communications were poor and particularly bad between officers. They seldom visited each others districts except on transfer and the success achieved in Machakos might well have been regarded as a method which happened to be particularly suitable for that area, but which would not be applicable elsewhere.

However at this stage the Fairy Godmother of American aid came to the rescue and made it possible to engage Community Development Officers once more. There was no time to give them any training. In any case they arrived in dribs and drabs and any course would have had to be repeated several times. So after each officer had been told about the experience of community development work in Kenya and given literature and reports to study, he was sent off to Machakos to see for himself how the scheme worked. He was then packed off to his district with the Departments' best wishes to try and introduce similar projects there.

The District Commissioners were of course ready to give them every assistance, whether they were convinced of the validity of their idea or not. The idea had been discussed with them and they had agreed in principle to see how things worked out. Ultimatley it was the Community Development Officers themselves who had to work out their own salvation. I paid as frequent visits as I could to give them tips and advice, to smooth out, if I could, such difficulties as might have arisen in discussion with the District Commissioner and technical officers.

The first Community Development Officer, an African, went to Kitui where in similar conditions to Machakos the seed germinated quickly. The next went to Nandi where the problem took longer to solve. Another to Baringo and so on. Each officer launched a pilot scheme which in itself was an object lesson for the other officers at the station. As time went on, as the examples have indicated, Machakos ceased to be the only source of inspiration. If the initial objective of the scheme was to be housing, then Kitui paved the way, if land consolidation, Central Nyanza and so on.

So experience showed that the best method of orientation was not any course of training or seminar or conference, although these helped to prepare the soil for the planting of the seed, but the establishment of pilot areas of Community Development Officers who had themselves been orientated by personal experiences of an existing project.

The most effective method of orientation was, therefore, a system of cross-fertilization. The basic stock was the same in all cases but the strain varied according to the soil in which it was planted.

However in this context another experience in orientation may be of interest. The writer just before leaving Kenya was invited to visit Nyasaland (now Malawi) to undertake an orientation tour of all the Provinces preparatory to the introduction of community development in the country.

The government was confronted by similar difficulties to those which had been experienced in certain of the Districts described. The African population for political reasons had adopted a generally obstructive and uncooperative attitude and little progress could be made with development schemes. It was thought that if the ball was thrown to them, which is the fundamental concept of community development, then progress might be restored.

But of course in this case, orientation along the lines found effective in Kenya was quite impossible, though visits to various districts in Kenya were later arranged for senior government officers and African leaders to enable them to see community development in action there. Instead I visited each Provincial Headquarters in turn and with the aid of coloured slides of group and training activities showed how community development was promoted. General discussion with acute questioning from experienced field officers followed. Finally proposals were made for the setting up of a Community Development organization.

The officer appointed to take charge of the Department later went on a study tour of East and West Africa to gain first hand knowledge, which again emphasizes the importance of personal experience in orientation. Reports indicate that community development has got off to a good start in the territory.

The next point that must be made is that not unnaturally experienced administrators and technical officers do not like being lectured at. It is not always possible to avoid a certain amount of this, but as soon as possible the discussion stage should be reached. The best approach was therefore found to be the organisation of conferences, the various aspects of community development being introduced by a speaker. The best advocate was usually a fellow officer who had had first-hand practical experience of the process. In this way the participants themselves found themselves working out the programme for themselves, though they needed tactful guidance in this and advice as to how to avoid pitfalls.

The conference agenda would be framed to consider and solve certain stated problems. Each of these problems would indicate the contribution community development could make and constructive conclusions were usually arrived at. The important thing was that the conclusions had been arrived at by the participants themselves and therefore carried conviction. They had also been reached in the light of practical experience and not of theory. This aspect will be referred to later when the training of field staff in techniques is discussed.

But if administrative and field officers require orientation so of course do the subordinate field staff and group leaders. Again the same principle was found to apply which expressed simply is, 'seeing is believing'. Accordingly after the initial discussions with the group in the pilot area and the selection of its leaders, they would set forth with the supporting field staff to see community development in action in some other appropriate area. This uniting of group leaders and junior field staff was found to be especially valuable as a camaraderie was built up between them. It was especially important where previously there had been animosity between them.

On their return home a period was allowed for the leaders to explain to the groups what they had seen. This was the only way of convincing them. They would get a clear picture from their own leaders whom they knew and trusted. The group would then discuss among themselves how the experience of the other area could be applied in their own, for adaptation and modifications would have to be made to suit local conditions and the type of programme.

At the same time the junior field staff would discuss their experiences with their colleagues. The new approach dictated by the introduction of group work and the altered role of the technical officer from a directive to an advisory one would be the subject of long argument.

The next stage would be reached when the group and the official staff would again come together for final discussions. The would provide the final stage of orientation of all concerned before the actual programme was planned.

In all of them the Community Development Officer would be involved, not asserting himself but ready to point out the aspects which would be appreciated and studied.

Looking farther ahead there was the need, if it could possibly be arranged, to orientate the senior officers of government, the Directors of Departments, the Provincial Commissioners and so forth. These officers were often on tour and it was again a matter of trying to arrange for them to see community development in action in the course of their crowded itinerary.

Then again, there was the need to orientate those in training in all departments in community development. If they could complete their courses not only with the technical knowledge they required but the social understanding of applying it through community development methods, then more allies would be made. Unfortunately such a task required more staff than was available to the department, but the position will no doubt be rectified in due course.

Techniques

No hard and fast rule can be laid down for the promotion of community development schemes, though certain broad principles have been found to apply. But there is an infinite variety of techniques which have been found useful in different circumstances when it comes to implementation. Some of these could be evolved in the light of recorded experience, in various countries. Many emerged from the experience and experiments of the Community Development Officers themselves and it was amazing what ingenuity they employed.

A number of these techniques revolved round the fundamental problem of how to enlighten country people regarding the ways and means of bringing about an improvement in their way of life. The content of such a programme will be dealt with in the Community Education section but the implementation or interpretation to the population at large is a question of technique.

In the first place it was manifestly impossible to enlighten the entire population at the same time. Certain mass media were certainly developing which were making their influence increasingly felt, such as the radio and the newspaper, but not everyone had a radio and not everyone could read. The achievements of the first Community Development Officers in these fields have been described.

When it came to explaining the purpose behind some particular new method of cultivation, land holding, health precaution or animal husbandry which was to form the focus of some project, it was found best to concentrate on the leaders. They would in turn pass on the knowledge to the group.

But prior to the introduction of group work other leaders had been given a variety of courses at the Jeanes School as has been explained. Among the most important of these, so far as rural development was concerned were of course the progressive farmers. They not only sometimes became the foundation members of groups, as in the case of Baringo, but also provided active demonstrations of better farming which in due course the group tried to emulate.

This raises an important point. For many years various experiments had been made to persuade the mass of peasant cultivators to introduce new methods of agriculture. Demonstration farms were established but it was found that few people even living adjacent to them adopted the improved practices. They argued that the government with all its resources and money could undoubtedly produce better results than they could, but it was beyond their capabilities to do so. It would also involve too much labour and only the wealthy farmers could afford to employ such labour. It was probably the problem of labour which was the deciding factor and this was not overcome by the mass of the peasantry until the adoption of group work.

Then the Agriculture Department arranged to settle a few progressive farmers in small holdings at these centres for an entire year to guide them through the right processes. This again did not prove successful.

Eventually the department adopted the system pioneered at Jeanes School of short courses for progressive farmers from selected districts to teach them new techniques, but not to expect them to become farmers on the Western pattern living by the sale of their produce.

Another way of spreading ideas through leaders was by means of womens' clubs. This will be described later but they definitely set new standards which others tried to emulate when group work started. We must recognise however, the great work done by the missions in this field long before community development was thought of. Around every Christian mission is to be found a village of the faithful adherents. Their houses and gardens are usually of a much higher standard than others in the neighbourhood and are an indication of the civilizing influence of the missions. It will be remembered that it was a church group which formed the jumping off place for the Central Nyanza Scheme. So again we see the influence of progressive elements of the rural population.

Another factor was that of travel. The opportunity to do so was opened up with the abolition of tribal welfare. At the same time, however it was usually the young men who availed themselves of the chance. Many leading people from certain districts had hardly seen anything of the rest of the country and the progress being made in other districts.

The organization of educational tours therefore acted as a great stimulus. This was not something which had been stated by Community Development, but the opportunity for chiefs, herdsmen, district councillors, teachers and other influential people to attend courses at the Jeanes School gave new impetus to the idea. They went home with a determination to improve conditions in their own areas. The building of the road in Baringo was a case in point. This was directly the result of a course attended by the Chief and the enthusiasm he managed to pass on to his people.

The expressed intention behind all this leadership training was to persuade them to pass on what they had learned and start some activity. The results were often encouraging.

Another technique which has been referred to is that of the film. In the early days almost the entire machinery of the Information Services was geared to the adult education drive in support of community development. As time went on unfortunately they tended to become more informational and less educational, more geared to explaining government policy than preparing the way for community development.

The radio however, although going through the same phase gradually became more educational and played a valuable role in this field.

With the assistance of funds from UNICEF each Community Development Officer was provided with a 35mm camera and encouraged to take transparencies of his schemes. These were projected in other areas and were most effective in passing on new ideas where educational tours were difficult.

Again the Mobile Cinemas tended to be used almost entirely for recreational purposes. At one time a start was made not only to make educational films but to exhibit them in a way which would help to induce the people to adopt new ideas. This meant that they had to be shown to selected audiences, explained carefully, and discussions and questions on them encouraged. They would probably have to be shown two or three times until the lesson went home as the tempo was usually too quick for untutored minds. This is a defect not shared by the slide projector which was therefore found more effective as an educational medium. It gave as much time as was required for explanation, and the movement did not distract attention from the basic lessons to be taught.

Another technique which proved exceptionally stimulating and which was undertaken by all departments and was not even pioneered by the community development was the District Show. Here exhibits of every kind were arranged, competitions for agricultural produce and livestock organized and various demonstrations staged. They also had their entertainment side with bands performing and dances. Enormous crowds collected and people obviously learned much from the exhibits and competitions.

The first Community Development Officers also developed the use of glove puppets. They were used partly for entertainment but more often for education in health and civic virtues. They always collected large and enraptured crowds. On one occasion at an Agricultural Show, as soon as a show was announced over the loud speaker the crowds used to desert the stands and crowd around the community development exhibit where the performance was to take place.

Acting was also used particularly by the womens' clubs. Again like the puppets the plays sometimes were for fun, sometimes for education and sometimes they held a moral. They were always most popular and gave scope for the African's natural dramatic ability. Sometimes they were performed in the open air, sometimes in halls and community centres.

Choral singing formed a part of the curriculum of community development courses at the Jeanes School as did drama and the making and use of puppets. Eventually a specialist officer was engaged to promote these part-cultural, part-educational activities. The enormous enjoyment that the performers and audiences derived was reward in itself, but at the same time they definitely played a part in moulding public opinion. One lady Community Development Officer who had been a missionary before her appointment, had pioneered the use of puppets in Kenya. She had used them with great success to encourage literacy and as part of a health education drive. The women seemed to regard the puppets as almost human and used to shake them by the hand at the end of the performance.

Community Education

The task of teaching new methods of agriculture and animal husbandry is the province of agricultural extension and the instilling of knowledge of health and hygiene the concern of health education.

The departments concerned were fully aware of the need to increase knowledge in all these fields and had comprehensive programmes to achieve it. Their efforts, as has been mentioned, were supplemented by the Jeanes School, the womens Homecrafts Training Centres and the womens clubs.

There was another field of equal importance to rural development which was the main concern of the Community Development Department. This was in the field of Community or, as it is sometimes call, Social Education.

From the early days of the Jeanes School, in its capacity as the Adult Education Centre for the Colony, one of the principal activities was to enlighten leaders about the working of the government, local government, the basic problems of marketing and trade, the function of co-operative societies, the importance of communication and such like subjects. These opened the eyes of people, whose horizons were naturally limited, to the requirements of the modern state. The subject matter was either simple or more advanced according to the educational level of the students.

But another group of subjects of equal importance to rural development concerned social problems. There was naturally consideration of the relationship of group work and community development, but there were also studies of the social impact of education, marriage customs and dowry, inheritance of land and fragmentation.

A solution to these and similar problems could not be achieved by legislation but only by a change of public opinion. This in turn could only be brought about by an appreciation of the fact that a failure to find solutions would inhibit progress; finally that only the people could work out solutions while understanding the measures taken in other countries in similar circumstances.

One way to direct attention to these questions was through the organization of debates. These became a regular feature at Jeanes School and were keenly fought. It was interesting to note from the results how public opinion was changing, often through the influence of the more educated elements.

The classes were also so organized that at least half the time was spent in discussions, questions and answers. The members therefore contributed as much as they received, for a greater understanding of their mentality and social problems was obtained in this way. This helped the teaching staff to frame the syllabus to the best advantage.

The demand for such citizenship courses exceeded the supply and so in a number of districts special local ones were held. Certain members of the staff used to assist District Commissioners to organize courses making use of the Community Centre or school or whatever building was available.

The various technical officers used to deal with their plans for the district which would be discussed. The District Commissioner would probably deal with local government, the problem of law and order and so forth. The Jeanes School lecturers would deal with the wider issues and social problems.

They were popular and considered valuable by the District staffs. One feature of them was often a Brains Trust. The idea was that the participants would be asked to write down any question on things which were worrying them. They would be put in a box and then distributed to a panel of the District Commissioner, technical officers and the Jeanes School Lecturers, who would attempt to answer them. No doubt many matters were elucidated in this way which might otherwise not have been explained.

A further extension of this idea took place from Jeanes School, Maseno where courses were organized for leaders at locational or parish headquarters. The leaders were in this way encouraged to think out their problems in co-operation with more sophisticated minds. At the same time officers obtained a clearer understanding of the attitudes and mentality of the leaders of the rural communities.

Sometimes problems were posed for the participants to work out such as "What would happen if there was no police force?" or "What would be the result of the government doubling the number of pound notes in circulation?" or "What would happen if there was no railway or roads?"

Women's Emancipation

The contribution that women can make to the success of community development is not always appreciated. Since the benefits of more abundant food, better water supplies and improved housing, affect her as much as if not more than her husband, her interest in anything which can bring these advantages is understandable.

At first the work among women in Kenya which was initiated by the Community Development organization was primarily a social welfare activity, with no direct connection with community development in the strict sense of the term. It came about somewhat fortuitously in the following way.

During the period when the Jeanes School was operating as the Ex-

Servicemens' Training Centre a number of wives of students were accommodated with their husbands in cottages on the compound. Not wishing to waste the opportunity of providing them with some domestic instruction, a training scheme was started. While their children attended a model school, they learned how to cook, make clothes and acquire a general knowledge of homecrafts.

When the Training Centre was taken over by the Social Welfare Organization, as it was then called, it was decided to continue this excellent work. But the number of married students grew fewer and the facilities available could not be fully utilized, so it was decided to accept other women for training.

The training was of a high standard and became very popular and demand soon exceeded the places available and the problems of deciding who to accept became more and more difficult. So much thought was given to the best way of getting full value from the training centre.

It was eventually decided to accept candidates from Districts, on a quota basis. But merely to do this would serve no long term purpose, so it was decided to try and build up a chain of womens' clubs through which those trained at the centre could pass on their knowledge.

This scheme was discussed with the trainees and welcomed and it was agreed to form an Association to serve as an umbrella for the fledgling clubs. The women decided to call it *Maendeleo ya Wanawake* or 'Womens Progress'. So a movement which was eventually to number over a thousand clubs and probably thirty thousand members was born. The clubs became a symbol of emancipation for women, whose life was often a drudgery. It stimulated them to find and even to build club rooms, to make uniforms for themselves and to organize a wide range of activities including singing and acting plays in addition to learning to sew and care for their children.

Of course it was sewing and dressmaking that was the chief attraction. Treating this as the basic 'felt-need' in community development parlance, the other activities, such as agriculture and health, were gradually added to the programme.

The clubs usually met once a week and the instructors who had been trained at Jeanes School, were soon employed by the African District Councils, and visited them in turn. It soon became obvious that the Jeanes School could never meet the demand however, and so the African District Councils were encouraged to set up their own training centres. They were given a small grant by the government and provided with a Supervisor, though in some cases the Councils even employed their own. The District Training Centres were often simple affairs, as they had to be built on a shoe string budget, but they developed a real character of their own. What they lacked in amenities, they made up for in cleanliness, neat flower beds and a happy atmosphere. They sprang up at the rate of about two a year until there were eventually fourteen of them. In fact all the major districts established their own centres.

The Jeanes School then concentrated on training women for supervisory work, while the district ones produced the instructors. What was remarkable however was the way that husbands or parents were prepared to meet quite heavy fees for board and lodging. Later UNICEF gave valuable assistance to relieve them of this burden but in the early days the African District Councils could only afford to pay for the training. However this did not deter the women and every Centre had its waiting list.

While the Jeanes School arranged a years' course, the District Centres were usually three month ones. The Jeanes School course was much more advanced and as time went on the students were better and better educated. All were literate and many in fact spoke English.

Finally the Jeanes School adapted its training to fit in with the community development programmes which have been described already.

But to return to the village clubs. The first attraction, as has been mentioned, was that of sewing and dressmaking and this led to their providing themselves with uniforms of their own design. One of the most colourful sights was to see an assembly of some dozen or more clubs sitting in groups like a patchwork quilt at the opening of some new Community Centre or waiting their turn to sing at some festival.

Their meetings were almost always partly for the purpose of singing and this seemed to give them an emotional release and joy which was quite affecting.

For centuries they had toiled in skins or drab clothing, but now they had the opportunity at little expense to deck themselves out and satisfy their unexpressed and possibly unappreciated desire for colour.

This led to an arrangement whereby bolts of materials were bought at wholesale prices and sold to the members to make up into dresses. People coming back to a district a year or two after the formation of these clubs, often remarked how the whole character of the people seemed to have changed by their acquisition of bright colours.

The change in the women was in fact much deeper than some people realized. From being the most conservative element in the society they acquired new standards of living and brought pressure to bear on their husbands to help them to satisfy their new wants. Thus the readiness and even desire to change their way of life may very well have come more from the women than from the husbands.

In another way too they were changing and in one district the Maendeleo members even had the courage to denounce the witches who had dominated their lives for so long. This was an even more significant change than that of their clothes and it soon spread to women who were not members of clubs. This in turn broke the bonds which bound them to reactionary conservatism, and may well have been a factor which made the introduction of various community development schemes acceptable.

The force which lay behind this movement cannot therefore be under-rated. Their influence was recognised by the terrorists during the Mau Mau and the Kikuyu clubs often met with some trepidation and membership dropped considerably.

It was always a struggle however to wean the clubs from their programmes of embroidery. First of all however their activities were widened by the introduction of instruction in child care. Then came cooking for the child and family and finally growing better food for them. So through the mothers natural concern for the child and its welfare they learned to appreciate the other agricultural and health reforms which had to be taken in their interest.

Finally the stage was reached where clubs began to meet in each others' homesteads and instead of just sitting under a tree and sewing or singing, they began to help the housewife to improve her home and garden. In this way they became involved in their own special form of group work, plastering the house, sweeping the compound, planting vegetables and the like.

All sorts of ways were evolved to stimulate interest in club work, not that there was any great problem in doing this at first, but after a time the members felt that they had learned all they could from their instructresses. Then it was the time to organize competitions between the clubs.

Annual sewing and handicraft contests were organized, first on a District and then on a Colony wide basis. Similarly choral and drama festivals were arranged. This meant that the instructresses would need more training so refresher courses had to be started.

The drive for all this came largely from the women Community Development Officers who were most devoted and indefatigable. Most large Districts had such an officer and they usually worked under most trying conditions with very limited resources.

They always had the whole-hearted support of the husbands and the other Government Officers who recognised the excellent work they were doing. This no doubt compensated for the very hard work involved in driving thousands of miles a year over hot and dusty or cold and muddy roads, visiting clubs and supervising their activities.

Others were of course in charge of the Training Centres. Sometimes they even had to combine both functions, but no one knew quite how they managed to do it. If the male Community Development Officers deserve every praise, so did the ladies. The Training Centres became a great asset for every station. The trainees would often cater for tea parties arranged for chiefs and other important people, on ceremonial occasions. One centre included a tanning and leather making course, another pottery. There was always scope for imagination and enterprise on the part of the Supervisor, who seemed to gain much satisfaction from her most exacting task.

Youth Centres

It was mentioned before that some of the most successful community development schemes were started as a result of crises of one kind or another. The Youth Centre movement like that for the women may be regarded as falling more within the social welfare or educational fields than in that of community development. But it is difficult to draw the line. If the criterion is that it should arise out of a felt need of the people and be largely undertaken by them themselves then the Youth Centres, must be classed as community development. However, it is not very important. The main point is that they were set up on the initiative of Community Development Officers and as an experiment in the solution of a grave social problem.

The immediate crisis in this case was Mau Mau but the problem went deeper than that, and would be found among the youth of almost all the varied tribes of Kenya. It went back to a defect in the educational system, a defect, it should be recognised, which is by no means confined to emerging countries but which is present even in advanced ones.

Put simply, it was the problem of the boy who leaves his Primary School and cannot gain a place in a Secondary School. In Kenya as in many other African countries such boys feel that they are entitled to something better than a job as a mere manual labourer. Their parents who have scraped and saved for school fees usually feel the same way about it. Added to which there are not always even sufficient vacancies in menial tasks for all the school leavers and the Primary Education does not qualify them for anything very skilled.

So every year more and more boys leave school in a disgruntled state of mind, look for jobs, fail to find them and join the ranks of the unemployed, the youth wings of political parties, juvenile delinquents, and even at times, criminals. They are disillusioned with life in the rural areas, it is dull hard work and unrewarding. In any case while their fathers are alive they have no land to cultivate. They feel that their schooling has been a waste of time and indeed many thoughtful people agreed with them and even came to the conclusion that those who never went to school were often less discontented than those who had. No particular aspirations had been awakened in their souls and they were prepared to take a job when cash was required, to share the work of their father's farm and to loaf around the shops and the coffee houses for the rest of the time. The pattern of life was not very different in fact, to that of millions of others in all parts of the world.

Yet other thoughtful people argued that it should be possible to provide some other form of craft training, perhaps on apprenticeship lines, for such boys, as is the practice in other countries, and thereby fit them for work which would satisfy them and was needed by the country. Surely in a developing country there would always be need of craftsmen either working full-time or part-time. In any case every farmer would be a better one if he was at the same time a handyman.

The germ of the idea came from an imaginative Community Development Officer working in the Machakos District even before the launching of the first Pilot Project described earlier. In one of the periodic economy drives, his services had to be dispensed with and he was transferred to the Information Services from which he moved on to work with one of the daily papers on which he did outstanding work. Such are the effects of economy measures. It is usually those working in the social fields who are regarded as expendable, but as time goes by it becomes apparent that their work contributed indirectly to the economy of the country more than many technicians whose services were retained. This is just such a case in point.

This Community Development Officer as early as 1950 and well before the Mau Mau uprising, became aware of the problem of school leavers in the district. As is usually the case he had very slender financial resources. In fact it was seldom that Community Officers had much in the way of funds. They had to achieve results the hard way, but in so doing their projects were often more realistic and firmly based than schemes which cost a great deal more.

In this case he found an old grass roofed dormitory, which had been used as a labour camp in the past. It was at the time unused and unwanted and very dilapidated. He got permission from the District Commissioner to make use of it as an experimental training centre run on apprenticeship lines.

The idea was simple. A trained carpenter would be persuaded to start a school in this building. The boys would live there and provide their own food and clothing, but would pay no fees. The instructor would be assisted by an initial issue of tools and he would train the boys to produce articles for sale on the local market. He would buy his own wood, nails and so forth and make a livelihood if he could.

There was a ready response to the scheme and it soon built up a demand for its products. It was followed by a similar training scheme for tin smiths and finally a third for garage mechanics and this proved to be the most successful of all. The boys had to indenture themselves for two years and at the end of that time were given a certificate by the instructor. They found no difficulty in finding employment at the completion of their training as handymen on farms or as employees of other craftsmen. The mechanics were quickly absorbed in garages in Nairobi and other towns.

There were of course certain formalities to be overcome but both Education and Labour Departments looked on the scheme with a kindly eye and in fact shut their eyes to many of its inevitable deficiencies. The living accommodation, for instance, was not luxurious, but neither were the homes from which the boys came. The articles produced were often crude but they were also cheap and there was a keen demand for them from those who could afford no better.

But it must be realised that before the day of the technical colleges and the trade schools, all craftsmen in more advanced countries gained their skill in this way, and who can say that craftsmanship was not of a very high order indeed in the Middle Ages? There were some indeed who asserted that it was ridiculous to hope to make a craftsman of a boy with only four or five years of schooling behind him. This might be true if one is aiming at producing cabinet makers but the great demand in emerging countries is for simple carpenters, tinsmiths, builders, bicycle repairers and so forth, either working on their own account or for others.

So it was clear that the training centre was fulfilling a real need and moreover the soundness of its conception was born out by the fact that it continued to function and even expand when the Community Development Officer was axed. Indeed the garage mechanics instructor even rented for himself a plot in the light industrial area of the town and became completely independent of government aid or support.

The success of the various sections depended partly on the teaching ability of the instructor and partly on his business sense. He had to market his commodity, though government orders were channelled to him whenever possible. As a result some trades prospered more than others and the garage mechanics school was the most successful as a result of a combination of teaching ability and business acumen. In this section the traders used to bring their lorries for repair and the Police became so confident in its efficiency that they used to send vehicles to it when found to have faulty brakes or lights.

It was not until a real crisis arose however, as mentioned earlier, that the powers-that-be could be persuaded to take note of this successful experiment. It came about in this way.

As the security forces began to gain the upper hand over Mau Mau they realized that many of the terrorists were men with the same background as the disgruntled youths who could not find places in the Secondary Schools. The more educated ones took to politics and were often highly nationalistic but were seldom violent. It was obvious that unless these embittered school-leavers could be fitted into society and made satisfied with their life, they would be a constant source of trouble.

The Ministry of Community Development therefore suggested the setting up of Youth Centres on the Machakos model. It was the Nyeri District which first tackled the problem on a wide scale and this has already been referred to in the chapter dealing with the District. The other Kikuyu Districts of Kiambu and Fort Hall followed suit.

They proved immensely popular and the African District Councils voted considerable sums for the employment of Community Development Assistants to supervise them. For these were much bigger centres than those in Machakos where there were never more than a hundred trainees all together. These new centres often had a membership four or fives times that number. Their membership was also mixed, boys and girls.

They began to deal with the problems of juvenile delinquency and vagrancy too. Nairobi had, of course, become the Mecca of the type of youth for whom the centres were opened. Instead, therefore, of merely repatriating them to their homes when they were caught wandering round the city without any means of support, they were absorbed into a Youth Centre, either in the town or in their district of origin.

The objective of the Machakos scheme was simply and solely to teach a trade. That of the Kikuyu centres was much more than this. They attempted to alter the outlook of the boys and girls; to make life fun, with games and gymnastics; to make them proud of their centre by the formation of bands. The instruments were often home made, but well wishers sometimes presented bugles which were greatly prized. A major success was in persuading local communities to actually donate the land on which the centres were built. They were constructed through self-help methods with men freely giving their time to make and erect the roof-trusses and the women coming in teams to plaster the walls and floors. Penny whistles which usually cost a shilling made a very satisfactory noise.

The boys began to make uniforms for themselves and to acquire a pride in their appearance. At this point we must digress a little to show how their new outlook came about.

When the big round up of 'passive-wing' members of Mau Mau took place, a large number of youths of the type described above were caught in the net. They found themselves in one of the vast dreary detention camps which were established near the railway line between Mombasa and Nairobi. It was virtually a desert and there was little for the boys to do.

It was at this stage that a young Kenyan European, not much older than some of his charges, was sent down to hold the fort until a special camp could be set up for them. He had virtually nothing but his own personality and keenness to help him, but in a short time he had so enthused the young Kikuyu that they were joining in games drill and gymnastics with the utmost vigour. To such an extent in fact that they began to fall sick. The camp doctor diagnosed over-exertion in a hot climate and he increased their diet to counteract it. There was then no more trouble. A simple form of education was also organised to keep the boys occupied during the day and their morale reach new heights.

In due course a camp was obtained for the boys up country and with great enthusiasm and with their young mentor they left, a thousand strong in a special train.

The new camp was placed in the charge of a former officer of the Kings African Rifles, Major Gardner, who was assisted by two other young European Kenyans, Roger Owles and Geoff Griffin, and a retired Missionary, Mr Dennis, seventy years old but as active as a man half that age. These four were thus the core of the staff of the only camp to be administered entirely by the Ministry of Community Development. In the other camps the Ministry only provided the rehabilitation staff. They consisted, therefore, of a man of mature age with many years of experience of dealing with African troops and a great sympathy towards them; two young Britishers born and bred in Kenya, the one a son of a farmer and the other of a retired police officer; and the veteran missionary who was a highly trained craftsman.

This team established one of the most remarkable rehabilitation centres in Kenya. The boys were quickly engaged in building their own school and levelling their playing fields. Two churches, one for Protestants and the other for Catholics, were constructed. A small farm was set up and the main compound itself became a model of neatness. Flowers were planted around the dormitories, which were merely what became known as 'A' frame huts - long corrugated iron structures with the roofs coming down nearly to the ground.

Each hut was put in the charge of a leader and the whole camp was run on the lines of a somewhat disciplined Public School. There was no doubt that the boys thrived on the system however. Many of them had never been to school in their lives, although the majority had spent a year or two in a Primary School. Many had a very bad record and in due course even admitted to serious offenses in the past. But they were all treated alike and given the opportunity to expiate their crimes.

They not only took a great pride in their appearance but in their dormitories too which they decorated with a variety of clay figures and ornamentation. All kinds of pictures of soldiers and animals appeared painted on the clay buttresses in local earth pigments.

A band was established which in due course used to go and play at sports meetings in the neighbourhood. Their football team also played matches against local sides.

Then the commandant began to interest employers in Nairobi and on farms in the boys and persuade them to employ them when the time came for their release. There was no shortage of applicants as many had visited the camp and seen the smart, alert squads marching to work or play. They had also heard stories of how the boys had responded to this rehabilitation programme. On one occasion for instance a couple of them decided to run home. Within a short time a group of their friends had chased them and brought them back. There was, of course, no barbed wire at the camp, that was one of the first things to be pulled down.

So the time came when approval was given to the release of the first group of boys to approved employers. They were an immediate success and in fact had such a good influence on the rest of the labour force that the employers asked for more.

So it was that after a year or two, the thousand young men, as they had become by then, found themselves back in the world from which they had been outcast. Although they had mostly been taught the rudiments of a trade, it was not this that made them so sought after, but their character and trustworthiness. No one had expected that former Mau Mau thugs would compete with the normal school leaver for the best jobs. But so it was and people began to think that perhaps something of the orderly disciplined training of Wamumu, which was the name of the camp, might be incorporated in the system adopted at the Youth Centres.

So it was that the Centres in the Kikuyu Districts combined something of the experience of the apprentice schools of Machakos and something of the Wamumu system. It proved to be an excellent combination and in a short while other Districts which had not been affected by Mau Mau, but had a similar youth problem, began to follow suit. All over the country centres began to spring up. Each District seemed to develop its own particularly characteristic form of centre reflecting the individual ideas of the Community Development Officer or the needs of the District. Even Machakos itself began a big drive to build centres of which it had been the original exponent. They stretched all along its northern border and began to attract the loafers from the trading centres and to give them an objective in life.

The movement became so big that an association was formed on a Colony-wide basis to enable ideas to be interchanged and funds from charitable sources to be allocated fairly. For by this time a number of well-wishers such as the Dulverton Trust had become impressed with the work being done and made most generous donations. But the bulk of the funds still came from the boys themselves in cash and labour and from their District Councils, so they can be said to have been well founded on a basis of self-help and thus be regarded as a community development scheme.

An interesting footnote was provided by the continuing interest of the independent government of Kenya in this movement. Its value as an antidote to the somewhat unruly and uncontrollable Youth Wings of the political parties was no doubt appreciated.

The side line of these youth centres was their pioneering work in the development of new crafts. Some centres became small scale factories, tanning and processing leather. In one District the boys contracted themselves as building teams to construct houses. In another they made curios for sale to tourists. There seemed no end to the original ideas which could be developed.

Possibly the most satisfying activity was started by the original pioneering district of Machakos from which so much good has come. One cannot help feeling that the charming character of the people must have something to do with this constantly recurring characteristic. The centres set aside one day a week to go out and undertake some work of social value, such as the building of a house for a poor man or the construction of a school, without payment for their labour needless to say. It is the development of a social conscience which one hopes will be the lasting value of community development work, the idea of working not merely for mutual advantage but for the common good. Social service when based on common good-will is so infinitely preferable, as well as so much more effective, to that provided by a government body or voluntary agency. It is something which has grown from the initiative of the people and in accordance with their wishes, instead of being based on some alien idea with somewhat artificial standards.

Sport and Recreation

One of the besetting sins of civilization is boredom. The more security, the more leisure there is and the more the majority of the people are obsessed by it. The old days may have been harder, more uncomfortable, more dangerous, but they weren't boring. There probably wasn't enough time to be bored. It appears to be the problem of the age and leads to juvenile delinquency, drunkenness, vice, cranks and crime. The same symptoms became apparent in Kenya. Tribal life had probably been a grim period of history patterned with famines, disease and wars. With the coming of Pax Britannica, some did not know what to do with their new plenty, their new health, their new security.

For this reason and partly, no doubt, on account of the traditional British love of sport, it had been the practice for many years for the Administration to organize it in the districts and urban areas. It usually fell to the junior District Officers to do this, and since one of the qualities looked for at the time of his selection was often prowess at some form of sport, he was well equipped to do so. An account of the various competitions which were started would fill a book. They ranged from football leagues, athletic meetings and marathons, to canoe, sailing and swimming races.

Thousands attended these various contests either as competitors or spectators.

The young men became just as ardent football fans as the British. They became just as enthusiastic about track events. Outstanding athletes became heroes.

Not that the idea was particularly new. Most tribes had some traditional pastime. Some were keen on wrestling, others on chasing and hunting buck, others with standing-jumping. All were keen on dancing; with some tribes it took the form of a repetitive shuffle, but with others, like the Wakamba, it involved the most remarkable gymnastic leaps and somersaults; other tribes exhibited incredible powers of endurance, dancing continuously throughout the heat of the day.

But as with most things, the poor Administrative Officer became more and more immersed in paper and bureaucratic activities, and he was glad, when Community Development Officers were first appointed, for their assistance in organizing sport. So it became one of their principal activities.

At the same time when the Ex-Servicemens' Training School became once more the Adult Education Centre of Jeanes School, the Physical Training Officer came over to the new institution. He began by organizing sport for those attending courses and then special athletic and football course for the whole Colony were started. He later became the Colony Sports Officer and used to visit Districts to arrange special training course there.

Thus while the Community Development Officers took charge at the District level, the Colony Sports Officer concentrated on the territorial one. He trained the athletes and footballers for competitions with other African countries and later for their participation in the Commonwealth and Olympic Games, where they gave an excellent account of themselves.

The Commissioner for Community Development became responsible for the promotion of sport.

Steps were taken to encourage unofficial sporting organisations to accept the responsibility of directing football and athletics competitions as between Districts and Provinces as well as internationally. This evolution from sport being an officially sponsored activity to a voluntary amateur concern was successfully achieved by stages.

It was here that one of the most difficult problems had to be overcome. How to merge the various racial groups into one overriding governing body for each sport. That this was achieved is a measure of the increasing racial harmony which was being established and the good sense and tolerance of all concerned.

It had its awkward periods, however, and it took time to get everyone accustomed to the idea.

An inter-racial athletics association was formed at a fairly early stage. One for football took longer. Interest flourished in rugby, hockey, basketball and volley ball, and a number of minor games.

But this promotion of sport on an inter-racial basis no doubt contributed to an easing of the inevitable tensions which are unavoidable in a mixed society. The teams for the Commonwealth and Olympic Games were always inter-racial in character and this occurred eventually in the case of inter-territorial football competitions.

So whereas the promotion of sport was regarded as one way of breaking down racial barriers, creating a climate of good-will and thereby helping to build up a sense of community in the Colony, strangely enough it was far more difficult to break down the animosities which existed between the different tribes. At one time matches between tribal teams began to take on the characteristics of inter-tribal warfare, at any rate among the spectators. Before one important fixture in Nairobi between teams of two of the largest tribes, information was received that the spectators were preparing to go to the stadium armed and ready to do battle either during or after the match.

The leaders of the two tribes were called together and persuaded to co-operate in disarming the crowds before the match. They accordingly worked their way quietly among the crowds removing sticks, knobkerries, knives, even axes and metal headed staves. The armoury filled a lorry which was driven out of harms way. The spectators were taken unawares and dumbfounded, and were reduced to verbal invective during the match which passed off comparatively uneventfully. Unfortunately those who had come determined to fight were not to be outdone and on leaving the ground resorted to stone throwing on the grand scale. Many were injured on either side. As a result before the next match all available labour was instructed to remove every stone lying round the ground to reduce the ammunition available. Then with the judicious interpenetration of tribal elders the crowds were persuaded to return home, without resorting to blood-shed.

Another incident of a somewhat different kind occurred in Nairobi on the occasion of V.E. Day in celebration of the final end of the war. It was decided to encourage the people to celebrate on a large open field adjacent to the African housing estates. Barrels of beer and carcases of meat were distributed to the various tribal leaders in proportion to their numbers resident in the town. Unfortunately though each tribal group was allocated distributing centres, which were separated as widely as possible, some of them inevitably received their rations of beer and meat before others. When those who had been served first had consumed their allocation, they broke into a dance and then had the bright idea of sharing the beer being distributed to other tribal groups. They trotted over singing and leaping and fell upon the nearest of their rivals. Then all hell broke loose and a general holocaust ensued. Blood flowed, but fortunately no one was seriously injured, and in no time tribal groups were pursuing each other all over the field and back to the housing estates.

We had to admit at the post mortem that the form the celebration took was undoubtedly an unwise one, even though the people had obviously enjoyed their set-to. It showed how close to the surface tribal animosities lay and how easily they could be inflamed. This experience is not directly connected with the promotion of sport, unless one includes dancing and possible inter-tribal warfare in that category, but it did bring home the fact that sport does not necessarily promote peace and good-will.

Attempts were then made to encourage mixed tribal teams sponsored by firms and government departments in the towns, for of course the same problems did not exist in the country areas where all the inhabitants were members of the same tribe. Even the visit of a team from another area did not cause trouble, as this usually arose among the spectators, who in the rural areas were almost all resident there.

These mixed tribal leagues enjoyed a fair success but never drew the crowds like a clash between tribal teams. The inescapable conclusion was that feelings were far more bitter between tribes than between races and if sport was to soften them, it would have to be very carefully and firmly directed.

On the whole the standards of play and sportsmanship among the actual contestants was much higher than is often the case in more advanced countries. An element of professionalism inevitably crept in and the idea of racing for a medal or a cup was bewildering for athletes. Among footballers however the symbol of the cup was of great importance and the winning team would usually chair the captain holding it in a triumphant dance round the ground after the presentation. The women would ululate and the men would stamp and sing and the supporters of the losing side would slink away in utter dejection.

It may be wondered what all this has to do with training, but in Britain the promotion of team games has always been regarded as a form of education or training for citizenship in itself. The training of the athletes in techniques and the instilling of the ideas of physical fitness and preparation, played a big part in the work of both the Colony Sports Officer and Community Development Officers. Many District Commissioners felt that this was one of the most important roles they could play. In fact it was difficult to persuade them that the promotion of community development itself was their primary function, however desirable and worth-while sport might be.

A feature of sport was the way that both officials and unofficials devoted hours of their spare time in helping in the training of athletes and the encouragement of football clubs. The high standard reached is due as much to their efforts as to the members of the Community Development Department.

If there is one heritage of the brief period of British rule in Kenya as in other colonial territories it is probably that of sport. We must hope that the amateur spirit which is the essential ingredient of the best of British sport will be the element which survives, but experience in the world at large makes one doubtful whether this happy outcome will be realised.

Chapter Eight

Restoring Fertility To The Countryside Through Self-help

This section of experiences and observations of community development in Kenya is written at a time when the effectiveness of the system as a means of raising the standards of living of peasant peoples is being questioned. Most books on the subject start off with a definition of community development. It is not proposed to do so in this case, but to let the examples speak for themselves. At the same time, it is proposed to suggest some guiding principles which have been found to govern the successful promotion of community development in Kenya, in the hope and belief that they may prove valid for other parts of the world.

The emerging countries are no longer concerned with the content of these two ideologies of capitalism and communism. Their overriding interest is to catch up the more advanced countries in their standards of living. They are therefore prepared to study the methods adopted by any other country to see if they can assist them to attain their objectives, although they are likely eventually to choose their own course.

At the same time, it must be recognised that this has been precisely the objective of the much-abused colonial powers during their period of trusteeship. It is now the concern of all the more prosperous nations. The United Nations itself launched a Development Decade, and more funds and technical assistance are being provided to assist the underdeveloped areas of the world to improve their ways of life.

Britain has done as much as any colonial power to bring its wards to the stage of stable self-government. It has also pioneered in many fields methods to promote their economic and social well being. It has made a major contribution in the field of community development, not only in the evolution of this highly democratic concept, but in its successful introduction.

To understand what this contribution is, it is necessary to go back to the period of the last World War, to the time when Britain and the Commonwealth were fighting for their very existence. Even then, considerable thought was being given to the problem of preparing colonial peoples to assume the responsibilities of self-government. The problem was most acute in Africa where the influence of western thought and ideas had been so much shorter than in the vast Asiatic countries. In the latter, advanced systems of government based on sound educational institutions and a stable economy had been established. In all these countries there was inevitably an undercurrent of inter-communal, inter-religious, inter-tribal unrest which had been masked by the existence of a firm government, but will take many decades to die out and be replaced by tolerant democratic attitudes.

Now it was in Enugu in the forties that a certain District Commissioner, Mr E R Chadwick, who was serving in the Eastern Region of Nigeria, succeeded in stimulating the villagers to tackle their own development problems in a remarkable way. An adult literacy campaign had been launched in the area on a large scale and the people became avid for further progress. When it was suggested that they might build schools, health centres, drinking fountains, and roads in return for material assistance from the government in the form of roofing materials, cement and so forth, they responded readily. In fact, they responded too readily and there were difficulties at the start. The film 'Daybreak in Udi' provides a vivid picture of how the initial difficulties were overcome.

But unfortunately the people in their enthusiasm built so many schools that the supply of teachers could not keep pace. The same occurred with Health Centres. Each village linked itself by a road to the highways instead of joining the various villages and thereby shortening the mileage. As a result they were physically unable to maintain the roads.

But there was no doubt that this method of stimulating the people to undertake their own development had been outstandingly successful, and it was made the subject of special study at one of the Summer Conferences which were held annually at Cambridge University for officers of the Colonial Civil Service while on leave. At this Conference, certain principles were laid down for the wider application of the idea as a guide to other Colonial territories, and shortly afterwards attempts were made to introduce community development, which was the name adopted at the Conference, in most of them.

The main principles accepted were that firstly, adult literacy provided the stimulus upon which the element of self-reliance could be built; that the formation of village councils provided the organisational framework; that the system of grants-in-aid gave the necessary support and that a programme of adult education created the climate of understanding necessary to win the willing co-operation of the people.

Subsequently, UNESCO made a special study of the process, which it termed Fundamental Education, and published a valuable monograph with this title. Various American Universities began to study the system and the Ford Foundation based a substantial programme in India upon it. The United Nations opened a section to provide technical assistance to countries wishing to introduce community development.

The various schemes met with varying degrees of success. In some areas they never got beyond the stage of adult literacy and social education schemes. In others, they provided an intensification of the ideas of agricultural extension and health education. Possibly only in Ghana were these projects characterised by the wave of popular enthusiasm which had been such a feature of the Nigerian experiment.

As time went on, some of the community development campaigns even became as bureaucratic as the institutions they had tried to humanise. A jargon and mystique was developed, and it became a subject of special study in the rather rarefied atmosphere of university. In some countries, the adoption of community development, in name if not in spirit, offered a way of impressing world opinion with their liberal policies, while all the time maintaining the status quo ante.

So, unfortunately, in many parts of the world, the philanthropic nations have tended to become disillusioned with the response of the emerging countries to the community development idea. The countries themselves have even at times looked over their shoulders to the alternative programmes being organised in the communist countries. Recent experience and past failures of the system of collective farms in Russia has not, however, gone unnoticed by them.

A wave of disillusion and despair seems to have swept not only the emerging countries but their well-wishers in the more advanced areas of the world. All ask themselves how the bonds of apathy and fatalism could be broken in peasant communities. They came to the conclusion that community development was a brave idea in theory, but did not work out in practice. They seem to have failed to remember that it had worked in West Africa. It was argued that this was a flash in the pan and the method was probably only suitable for tribal societies. They commented too that even in West Africa it had never got beyond tackling the physical problems of building schools, roads and prestige projects.

It is suggested, however, and this has been borne out by the Kenya experience, that the basis of the original community development schemes in Western Nigeria has never been correctly analysed. It seems more than likely that the catalysing effect of adult literacy was, in fact, less important than the possibly unconscious revival of a traditional system of mutual cooperation, which had lain dormant to a lesser or greater extent after the introduction of a western form of government. It was found in Kenya that an almost universal practice existed in the past of corporate effort, not only to provide for community needs, but to assist individuals to undertake tasks which were beyond their separate capacities. Thus, the whole village community would assist in providing for its defence, various kinship groups would assist each other to clear forest for cultivation, harvest crops, build houses, and so forth. Was not the campaign to provide village services in Nigeria a revival of this very system? More significantly, could not the revival be expanded to provide for an even wider range of activities which could promote the economic and social progress of rural communities? This, at any rate in Kenya, was found to be the case, as the following examples will show.

It seemed simply a failure to appreciate what had provided the initial spark in the pioneering community development schemes, namely the resuscitation of the age-old concept of mutual assistance, and not the various processes which had become accepted as the necessary prerequisites, which led its protagonists along the long trails through the wilderness. It was the almost fortuitous discovery of the source of the energy-producing molecules which led to the establishment of community development as a living force over broad areas of Kenya. In so doing, it was demonstrated how the system could overcome social problems which had been too great for the normal processes of government to solve. It established a continuing and self-motivating force, working independently but in partnership with the existing official agencies.

What perhaps is of greater interest is that subsequent study and experience has shown that the concept of traditional corporate effort is by no means confined to Africa, or to tribal societies. It exists in as divergent societies as Afghanistan and Turkey, and has been reported from Indonesia and Mexico. Moreover, in these countries, it has also been shown to be capable of revival and adaptation to modern conditions.

The experience gained in Kenya may not therefore be merely of local or academic interest, but of significance on a much wider scale in helping to solve the problems of development in the emerging countries. It is in this hope that the following account has been written.

Early Experiments

When the Department of Community Development was established in 1950 it inherited a structure which had grown partly out of a civil reabsorption organisation set up after the war and partly out of a social welfare scheme. The first was formed to assist ex-servicemen to return to civil life with some training. The second was really a misnomer; it aimed largely at building up an adult education, recreational and cultural organisation through the establishment of social centres in the rural areas. It was hoped that these would make the country more stimulating to live in and the towns less of a magnet. It was hoped also that they would form the centres of enlightenment through adult literary classes, the establishment of libraries and so forth which would assist in a raising of the standards of life of the country people.

Unfortunately the centres did not prove to be the attraction it was hoped they would be, nor did the acquisition of literacy by adults become such a draw as was expected.

It was necessary to rethink the whole policy of rural development and try to find a way which would galvanize the people to action to improve the countryside.

In West Africa, it was true a widespread literacy drive seemed to have provided the desired spur, but the same magic did not appear to operate in Kenya. Large classes would enrol and gradually dwindle away as the middle aged or elderly pupils found the course too arduous.

So it was decided to try and emulate some of the outstanding development schemes which had followed in the wake of the literacy campaigns in West Africa, without relying on the stimulation, real or imagined, of literacy. In the event, it was found in Kenya that an incentive to development could be injected without the preliminary of a literacy drive, but many failures and partial successes had to be chalked up before the magic formula was discovered.

First of all, a conference of the nine officers, whose work in the civil reabsorption field was drawing to a close and who were finding the task of injecting life into the rural areas through the agency of social centres somewhat disheartening, was held. A study of community development in other parts of the world was undertaken and the officers were encouraged to return to their districts and experiment in the introduction of self-help schemes along the approved lines.

These schemes were successful as far as they went, and were only terminated by the fall of the economic axe which decapitated all the officers at one blow. During the short time that they were developing these schemes much useful experience was gained, and the officers must be given credit for the progress they achieved, and sympathy for being cut down in their prime. The real key to success was not found till later, but it probably would not have been discovered but for their pioneering work. At the same time, it might have been found earlier if they had been allowed to continue in their task.

A few examples will be given of experiments made in certain districts where these officers operated, and it will be seen how some of the ideas developed and eventually bore belated fruit in the successful fulfilment of community development in these and other areas. The examples are varied and express the individual qualities of the Community Development Officers themselves as well as the requirements of the different Districts.

The first successful experiment to be described took place in the Machakos District. The Community Development Officer, Charles Hayes, among many other things, cooperated with the Agricultural Officer to organize what were known as Farmers Days. This was really an applied 'extension' activity and the people collected at a selected homestead from the surrounding area to see a variety of demonstrations. There would be demonstrations of poultry keeping, vegetable growing, latrine building, child care and so forth. There would be posters and talks, and they proved very popular. It will be noticed later that this focal point idea was incorporated in the first introduction of group work in this District at a later stage. The Farmers Days' combined with other agricultural extension activities and the farmers' courses organised at the Jeanes School, Kabete, which will be described later, undoubtedly contributed to an improvement in agricultural techniques. They did not however, nor was it expected that they would, make an impact on the major problem of the District, soil erosion.

The second experiment took place in Central Nyanza District, the scene of another successful community development campaign some years later. A small area known as the Manyassi Valley which was situated in the middle of the district was chosen.

First of all the basic problems were investigated and analysed. The Manyassi Valley is a shallow depression running down to Lake Victoria. Previously there had been much sleeping sickness in the area. The fly which carried it had however been got rid of by the clearing of the bush. It is poor country and the soil is for the most part sandy. It was found that as a result many of the able-bodied men were out of the district at work for long periods since the land would not produce enough to maintain more than a subsistence economy.

The methods of agriculture and animal husbandry were primitive, the villages were dirty and the inhabitants were for the most part illiterate. Soil erosion was another problem which had been accelerated by the constant weeding required in the cultivation of cotton.

The District Team studied the results of the survey and decided to begin by concentrating on teaching the people to construct enclosures for cattle. The object was to persuade the people to change their traditional practice of tethering the cattle in the village which resulted in the manure being scattered and thus encouraged the breeding of flies and consequently the spread of disease. At the same time the manure was not used as a fertiliser for the fields to increase the humus in the poor soil. The construction of cattle sheds would make it possible to produce compost which could be spread on the fields periodically.

It was also decided to encourage the people to plant live wash-stope using a local aloe to reduce soil erosion.

A scheme of rotational grazing was drawn up to enable areas to be rested in turn and allow the pasture to recover.

Other measures which were planned were the construction of outside kitchens and improved stoves raised off the ground to replace the traditional three stones which are such a danger to children. Other proposals were the building of latrines and the improvement of water supplies.

It was decided however not to embark on too many improvement measures at the same time owing to the limited labour supply and the difficulty the people would find in absorbing many new ideas at once.

The basic principle of the scheme was to concentrate as many field staff as could be spared in the area to conduct an educational programme and guide the people in making the necessary improvements.

A team consisting of two Community Development Assistants and Agricultural, Veterinary and Health Field Officers was therefore formed and posted to the area to work under the Community Development Officer. The only material assistance proposed was the provision of nails for the construction of the cattle enclosures. A campaign was then launched to explain to the people the purpose of the scheme. This was supported by material prepared by the Information Service.

When the people had fully understood the ideas and given their support to them the scheme was put into operation. A demonstration cattle enclosure was constructed in one of the homesteads by the owner himself. Lines for wash-stops were laid out. A model kitchen was built.

The inhabitants came to watch and returned to their villages to put into practice what they had learned. No homestead was obliged to introduce the improvements but many did so. A spirit of rivalry and competition grew up and by the end of the year thirty enclosures and many improved kitchens had been built. Some miles of live wash-stops had been planted.

Some remarkable instances of cooperation occurred which were in fact a prelude to the active programme of group work which was to develop later. The possibilities of getting work done this way had not at this stage been appreciated however.

One village was inhabited by an old man and his two old wives whose children were out at work. They were physically incapable of constructing a cattle enclosure.

Without any prompting from the community development team however, and in fact without its knowledge, the neighbours cut the poles required and erected the enclosure for the old people so that they might benefit like everyone else.

Even more remarkable was the schemes' influence on the surrounding area. Over one hundred cattle enclosures were put up without any material assistance from the government or prompting from the development team. This was the result of the example of the benefits derived in the valley from the innovations and a general awakening of initiative.

In order to give a greater impetus to the spread of the campaign a film and film strips were made by the Information Service. A field course was organized by the staff of the Jeanes School in the valley and in the villages themselves to implant more firmly the lessons to be learned and to broaden the people's appreciation of local social and economic problems.

Plans were then made to organize a course at the Jeanes School itself for farmers and leaders from the whole lake area to spread the ideas even further.

The concentration of field staff in the area and the emphasis on education and training had been justified by the almost automatic extension of activity through the initiative of the people themselves. The spirit of community development had in fact been instilled.

Expenditure on the scheme was very low too for nails were only provided in the initial demonstration area. No additional staff were employed who were not already working in the wider area of operations. They were concentrated in Manyassi to begin with and then returned to their normal stations.

It was at this stage that the economy axe fell and the Community Development Officers' services had to be dispensed with. The scheme was put in the charge of an Agricultural Officer but the momentum slackened as its wider implications of an attack on backwardness in a variety of fields through the initiative of the people, and supported by campaigns to spread understanding of the problems and their solution, tended to be lost sight of.

Another community development scheme was launched in the neighbouring district of North Nyanza at a place called Malaha, at the beginning of 1952.

This scheme was a disappointment as it did not have the snowball effect which occurred at Manyassi. In retrospect, the reasons for this are clear but it provided a useful object lesson of what to avoid when introducing community development. In this case too much material assistance was given and as a result the initiative and self-reliance of the people was not promoted. It therefore petered out. It is true that here also the post of Community Development Officer was abolished but this was not the real reason for the failure of the project.

Malaha, was like Manyassi, a poor area. There were few trees and the soil was sour. Here too an investigation of the needs of the area was made and a plan of campaign drawn up by the District Team. It was more comprehensive than that at Manyassi but in the same way a large team of technical field staff was concentrated to teach the people the value of the improvements suggested.

The programme was divided into three parts, village improvement, public health and agricultural development. The village improvement plan involved the rebuilding or repair of houses, the cleaning of compounds, the building of improved food stores, cattle enclosures and poultry houses. In connection with public health it was planned to build a dispensary, improve the interior conditions of houses and eliminate rat infestation. The agricultural improvement measures included soil conservation, crop rotation, the introduction of new crops such as rice, and the planting of trees.

In view of the treeless character of the countryside, building poles had to be transported by lorry to the area and generous help was given in the provision of nails and tree seedlings.

The results in the area were impressive. 210 homesteads were repaired or rebuilt and plastered inside and out. 100 latrines were built, 8 fountains were made, 40,000 trees were planted as wind breaks and farm boundaries, and 6 cattle enclosures were constructed. A great impetus was given to the work of leaving filter strips to reduce erosion in the fields and of planting banana and citrus orchards. At the same time a considerable area of bush was cleared for pasture.

A scheme which had not been envisaged when the programme was first planned was the establishment of an ambitious communal rice planting scheme. This involved clearing fifteen acres of swamp land. About 3300 man/days of voluntary labour were put in over a period of four months. The people decided to devote the profits of the scheme to constructing a dispensary. A nursery for a variety of trees and plants was also established.

In spite of this encouraging start the momentum was not maintained. Expansion outside the original area failed to take place since the people in the surrounding homesteads expected the same level of assistance as had been provided in the pilot area.

Nevertheless many of the activities undertaken were later carried out on a wide scale when the idea of voluntary group-work was introduced. The innovations had become accepted even though the people in other areas were not prepared to introduce them at that stage.

It is probable that if they had joined together they would have expanded the project. In fact, later they did precisely this and the area was fully developed in this way.

But another interesting thing happened. The people of the original area also lost interest and allowed much of the improvements to fall into disuse. A kind of apathy seemed to set in. A post mortem put it down to the fact that they had been spoiled and an insufficient contribution had been expected of them from the start. That community development spirit which was so noticeable in later schemes was certainly lacking.

Therefore, although a great deal of material improvements were made by the efforts of the people, the scheme was not considered a success. The seed had sprouted but withered away in the stony ground of the people's apathy.

In another part of the district the unhappy people suffered another disappointment but for an entirely different reason. One community living on the far side of a river wished to obtain access to the main road for the export of its crops. Without being prompted by anyone whatsoever but imbued with the idea of self-help which had been preached, they got together to build a bridge. They cut down huge eucalyptus trees and dragged them with their oxen to the river bank. They hauled them across with chains at the river's narrowest place and fitted cross members. They laid a surface and cut access roads to either side, and for the first time were able to drive their carts and lorries from their fields to the market.

Unfortunately, that year the rains were heavier than usual and the river rose to the level of the bridge. It swished around the timbers and scoured away the bank beneath them. The great logs slid into the muddy torrent and in a matter of minutes the work of weeks was undone. It was a great tragedy for these patient and hard working people.

The post mortem revealed a different cause of death in this case. The people had built the bridge in the wrong place where the bank was unstable and constantly being undercut. If only they had asked for the advice of the engineer this need never have happened and all those weeks of labour would not have been wasted.

To their credit the people decided to try again, this time in a place chosen by an expert and to a design provided by him. They even got some cement to reinforce the abutments. What is more the nearby womens' club came in and carried all the sand and stone for the concrete as their contribution leaving the work of dragging the tree trunks to the men.

This time the bridge held and gave encouragement to others to follow the example of the pioneers. The lesson in this case was not too much material assistance but too little technical advice. This was found to be one of the classic principles upon which community development should be based and it will be further discussed in Part III.

A similar failure occurred in the Baringo District, inhabited by a branch of the Kalenjin tribe. The most densely populated area of the district lies along a ridge of hills running down the centre of the Rift Valley at this point. One road passes along the crest and feeder roads joining it like ribs. In one area the people felt that it would be a great advantage if they could join two of the ribs together half way down the slopes of the ridge. This meant crossing a deep valley.

The people were not deterred by the different terrain and worked for months cutting a ledge up each side of the valley. They built a bridge over the river which in this case held, but they had made another mistake. The gradient of the approach road was too steep for a fully loaded lorry to climb, particularly in wet weather.

It was a great disappointment to all concerned, but they refused to be beaten and cut a new road which had this time been properly aligned by the road foreman. If only they had asked his advice in the first place they would have been spared many weeks of labour. The opening day was a great occasion and this time the lorry laden with cheering villagers climbed the slope without difficulty.

The Chief who had led this project throughout and who incidentally had attended the first course for Chiefs at Jeanes School in 1950 touchingly presented a locally made table to the Commissioner for Community Development who performed the opening ceremony. It seems more than likely that the course had stimulated the Chief to lead this campaign. One felt however that it was he who should have received the prize. It was a great achievement to start again after the first disappointment and to complete the work successfully.

There was at this time no Community Development staff whatsoever in the District and the initiative came entirely from the Chief and his people. Similar examples of such enterprise by these people will be described later where they again embarked on community development on their own as a result of a Jeanes School course.

One of the principal contributions of these early experiments was the development of adult education techniques. The radio was in its infancy in Kenya but each Social Centre was provided with one. Most community Development Officers were responsible for the publication of a weekly or monthly district Newspaper. They thus paved the way to a considerable extent for the introduction of an adult education campaign.

Although most Community Development Officers organised adult literacy classes, there were for the most part disappointing in so far as their popular appeal was concerned. Probably the support they gave merely in the production of the newspapers, in the selling of publications of the East African Literature Bureau, under Charles Richards, which did such excellent work in the production of books in the vernacular, and in the building up of libraries all provided an incentive to the people either to learn to read or to develop this ability after leaving school.

In addition to this they did valuable work in assisting in the production of films used to introduce community development projects. An outstanding example of this took place in Fort Hall District where a film was produced to explain how bracken could be eradicated. This was the forerunner of a most successful campaign involving hundreds of the inhabitants of the highland areas, which, but for the removal of the Community Development Officer from his post and the outbreak of Mau Mau, might well have developed into the first really successful community development campaign.

They experimented with the production of slides which were in many ways more effective as an educational medium than the films, since they could be produced more cheaply and therefore more plentifully and could be given a local slant. Being in colour and depicting local people they were also more convincing to the inhabitants of the area.

These officers prepared programmes for the radio and arranged for local speakers. They evolved a powerful force for the introduction of new ideas which was to prove of the greatest value at a later stage.

One of the officers even set a traditional drinking song to new words which extolled the virtue of planting trees, this being one of the current campaigns. The children sang the song on their way back from school much to the astonishment of their parent. No doubt it helped to din in by slow degrees the importance of building up rural resources of fuel and building timber.

Following up this appreciation of the importance of adult education in its broadest sense and not merely in its relation to literacy, they made the initial effort to introduce projects by a campaign of enlightenment. By so doing they initiated the junior field staff in the need to explain why they were trying to introduce new methods. The Community Development Assistants who had been trained at the Department's main training centre at Jeanes School, helped the technical staff to adopt the same methods.

Another major activity of these first officers was the encouragement of sport and recreation. This was more of a welfare activity, and not directly connected with community development, but there is no doubt that it fulfilled a important social role which will be discussed in a separate section. Allied with the Colony Sports Officer based on the Jeanes School they assisted in the raising of the standards of athletics and football to international and even Olympic levels. At the same time, by relieving boredom, the besetting problem of modern society, they contributed to a more contented community.

So possibly the principal achievements of these pioneers of community development were the demonstration of the value of concentrating on pilot areas in the initial stages, the importance of preliminary adult education campaigns, and the promotion of the social and cultural aspects of village life.

Their experiences and the resulting knowledge was of great value to their successors. If they had not suffered from the axe it is more likely that they would have achieved the break-through to community development through group work years before it eventually was achieved.

A distinction must be made between what might be called aided self-help schemes, which had been organised by various technical departments for many years, and those which relied on the organisation of the people themselves. Springs had been protected through the aided self-help principle for some time.

It was the accepted way of building Primary Schools also in most parts of Kenya. As a rule the initiative lay with the government and the distinction will become clearer when the various examples of community development have been given. The aided self-help schemes have been of great value undoubtedly, but the community development projects based on group work have been much wider in scope and have developed the initiative and self-reliance of the people as a whole.

Machakos

The district of Machakos has already been referred to. To appreciate the problem of introducing community development one must understand the special problems of this area.

At the time that the first really successful campaign was launched here in 1953 the country and its people were in a terrible state. Large areas of the lowlands were so eroded that almost desert conditions existed. The land lay red and bare, dotted with thorn trees and such scrub as had resisted the onslaught of the goats. Higher up the hills gully erosion had set in and the rain had scoured great clefts. Only on the actual summits a few sparse trees survived and the land was fairly fertile.

The district is bounded by the vast Maasai plains to the south which through poor rainfall is only suitable for pasture. To the west European farmers have established dairy farms and sisal plantations under similar climatic conditions.

To the north stretches the Kitui District similar in character to Machakos, and to the east a huge almost water-less desert inhabited only by wild animals and poachers.

Since the introduction of British rule and all that entailed in the reduction of disease of both humans and livestock, the removal of the fear of famine and the abolition of tribal warfare the population had increased threefold. The number of cattle sheep and goats no longer decimated periodically by sickness or the raids of the Maasai had also multiplied enormously.

The pressure on the land had therefore become excessive. The people, used to nature preserving a balance, could not appreciate that it was within their power to control their own destiny. They attributed their difficulties to the climate or to British rule itself. They could not see that only through the preservation of their heritage could they hope to survive.

The government saw the problem all too clearly. Only by limiting the numbers of stock and disposing of the balance and by undertaking large scale soil conservation measures could the crisis be passed. But it was another matter to convince the people of the remedy. Livestock possessed an almost religious significance. The larger the herds owned by an individual the wealthier he was considered to be, even though their quality might be of the lowest. The idea of slaughtering livestock even in times of famine was repugnant to them.

Soil conservation was something entirely new and the labour involved in digging ridges across the hill sides was regarded as so arduous as to be out of the question. In the view of the Wakamba who are the inhabitants of the district, the remedy was for the government to dispossess the European farmers on their borders even though their land was not so good as their own and though they depended upon them for employment to earn any extra money they might need.

A campaign to induce the people to reduce their herds ended in a protest march on Government House in Nairobi. An offer of help with machinery to dig contour ridges was equally vigorously opposed. The government was in an impasse. The land continued year by year to deteriorate, poverty increased as a result and with it, unrest.

It was at this stage that it was decided to try a community development approach to solve the problem. As will be seen in succeeding accounts community development was frequently resorted to at times of crisis, and it is gratifying to relate that in most cases it saved the day.

The government decided to post its more able field officers to the district and to carry out a widespread campaign of enlightenment to convince the people of the necessity of soil conservation and persuade them to accept the assistance of machinery to undertake it. In due course the people became convinced and accepted the offer of assistance but the Government felt that their self-reliance and industry would be seriously undermined if they grew too accustomed to the idea that all their problems might be solved by expensive large scale operations. It was considered essential that side by side with this rescue operation a self-help campaign in other directions should be organised.

The District Commissioner therefore planned a homestead improvement campaign similar to those in the Central and North Nyanza Districts which have already been described.

Discussions were held with the Department of Community Development which at the time was sorely depleted as a result of economy cuts and could do little more than offer the services of its training centre at Jeanes School near Nairobi. It had no Community Development Officer to assist with the organisation of the project. It had little in the way of funds. It could give some training, however, and a plan was worked out with John Nottingham the young District Officer who had been put in charge of the campaign.

One homestead was chosen for the sowing of the seed. All the field staff from the area together with an African Administrative Officer, John Malinda who was relieved of all his other official duties and was chosen as leader came to Jeanes School for a course of training.

The plan was simple. The objective was to persuade the neighbours of this particular homestead to assemble on a given day and tackle the many jobs which the householder wanted to carry out, but which he found difficult to do unaided. They would re-plaster and repair his house, build him a cattle shed, paddock and cultivate his vegetable garden, build him a lavatory and clean up his compound. Each member of the team would be there to show the villagers how to carry out each of these tasks.

Next the heads of the different homesteads in the area were brought in for a course at Jeanes School and the plan was discussed with them and the reasons for it. The reasons for the various improvements were explained and it was pointed out that they could only be carried out quickly and effectively by a group of people working together.

It will be noticed that no mention was made of the problems of conservation or of reducing stock, since both these issues were somewhat explosive at the time. It will also be seen that it had a number of points of similarity with the Farmers Days' already described. The leaders were asked to return home and discuss this plan with their people and if it appealed to them to let the Administrative Officer know and fix a day with him for giving the homestead its face-lift.

In a short time the villagers sent word that they wished to undertake the work and a day was fixed. All the field staff assembled together with the staff of Jeanes School who had been concerned with the course. It was a lovely sunny day and the villagers collected from all sides. Some brought tools, some poles, some thatching grass as they had been detailed to do by their leaders. They sang as they walked along the foot paths carrying their loads, for the Wakamba are great singers and even greater dancers, and however hard life may be they are irrepressibly cheerful.

Within a short time they were all engaged in their allotted tasks under the guidance of the field staff. A great hubbub reigned and sounds of singing came from every side. The women roared with laughter as they puddled the clay and slapped it on the walls, getting spattered all over in the process. The men hacked away with their pangas and lashed the poles together to make fences or frameworks for buildings. A group of youths wielded their hoes in time to the rhythm of a traditional working song.

The sun swung across the sky but the workers did not seem to notice its blaze. The water carriers were however kept busy quenching their thirst and the girls joked together as they strode along the path from the spring, the water glistening on their cheeks as it splashed out of the earthenware jars balanced on their heads.

A group of old men sat in the shade of a cork bark tree and took snuff. There was no doubt they approved of the way the young men were working instead of hanging round the market place.

As the sun began to sink into reddening banks of cloud and the hills turned first indigo and then purple, the tired men and women began to collect in the compound now weeded and swept. They looked around at the house with its new thatch, its new large windows and its smooth walls, at the cow shed which the cattle on their return from pasture were nosing suspiciously, at the neat fences round the vegetable garden. It was a transformation.

They squatted in a great wedge round their leaders, the women grouped themselves behind. They were asked if they wished to do the same work in another village. There was a murmur of approval. Obviously everyone wished his own homestead would be the next on the list. A discussion followed as to who would be the lucky man and when. Then they shouted in satisfaction of their achievement, straightened themselves and move off in twos and threes first to wash and drink at the well and then to find their way in the gathering darkness to their homes among the maize fields, to eat and talk awhile of the things they had achieved together and then to stretch exhausted on their hide beds and drift into sleep in the rosy glow of the fire.

That is how it started and it was soon to spread like a grass fire throughout the District. Efforts were made to slow down the expansion so that proper guidance could be given but this proved impossible. Difficulties arose. In some areas the people found they had insufficient tools for all the jobs and had to be lent them, but as time went on they subscribed together and bought their own.

Homestead after homestead was refurbished. Not only the able bodied benefitted, but also widows and old people who could only give moral support to the campaign, until the time came when all the homesteads had been given a new look. But in the first area something else had happened. When all the homesteads had been modernised it was suggested that now was the time to extend their horizons and tackle their fields. But why not ridge them instead of merely cultivating them together. The government staff would mark out the lines of the ridges and the villagers would do the work. The suggestion was accepted readily. Here then was the solution. The opposition to the idea of soil conservation was no doubt due to a number of causes, but an important one was the almost insurmountable difficulty of carrying out the work as individuals.

The leaders then began to work out a corporate system of work which spread with variations far and wide. First of all they would pool their teams of oxen which would plough along the lines marked out by the Agricultural assistants for the contour ridges. They would be followed by a long line of men hoeing together in time to a song which would be sung by a special leader, usually decorated with feathers and waving a fly whisk. In their wake would come another line of women and girls with shovels who would throw the loosened earth into a bank. Meanwhile a reserve team of men and girls would wait and accompany the song leaders and when the workers got tired would take their place. So the work went on continuously up and down the field steadily and inexorably and at remarkable speed.

If the soil control work took place about the time of the rains other helpers would follow, planting grass along the banks to bind the soil together.

During the next two years, hundreds of miles of ridges were dug and the face of the countryside was transformed. Not only did the country look different but the yields of crops began to improve again and some of the villagers even noticed that springs which used to dry up during the dry weather now flowed all the year round once more. The ridges no doubt acted as a sponge and retained the water underground.

What was more important was that the attitude of the people also changed. Their previous reluctance to dispose of surplus stock and concentrate on quality rather than quantity changed and overstocking ceased to be the overriding problem which it used to be.

But the people were not ready to stop there. They went on to dig dams to build coffee factories and to plant trees on an ever increasing scale. Even youth clubs and youth training centres were established in the same way in due course.

An interesting aspect of the campaign was that the communal effort was never called community development though it is a classic example of it. It was known by the traditional tribal name of *Mwethya*. This feature became common in other areas later. *Mwethya* was a customary tribal method of helping your neighbour to harvest, to break new land and to build a new house. Its application was limited to such basic tasks, which were the principal ones confronting the people in a subsistence economy. Its revival in a modern guise, tackling work which was never envisaged in earlier days, indicates the value, which has also been experienced in other parts of the world, of basing community development on traditional methods of co-operative effort.

A big difference between the revived form of *Mwethya* and its predecessor was however that the homestead benefitting was never required to provide food and drink for the labourers. This meant that the mutual assistance was extended to poor and rich alike and in this way more uniform development took place. After all if one field is not protected when others are, many fields can be damaged by erosion from this one gap.

Another important characteristic of this giant communal effort was that it was never regarded as government work. The District Commissioner stated that he never interfered with its operation or timetable. The technical staff were there to help when required and were of course always in demand, but the organisation of the groups lay with the peoples' own leaders.

Similarly it was the groups themselves who dealt with any backsliders or non-cooperators. From those who refused to work a goat might be taken and slaughtered for the rest. In this way an urge for rural development based upon the democratic organisations of the people themselves was built up, which gave a reality and foundation to the more sophisticated organs of local government which were growing at higher levels.

It has been mentioned that when the scheme of homestead improvement started the groups were lent wheel barrows, picks and shovels. The movement expanded so rapidly however that the people decided to purchase the tools they needed in wholesale quantities. This they sometimes financed themselves or got the money from their parish councils. The energy they put into the work was a great strain on the implements and they had to be replaced frequently.

Kitui

Across the border of Machakos to the North East lies the District of Kitui inhabited also by the Wakamba. The area has little in common with its neighbour however. The population is not so numerous or so dense and they have not been troubled by erosion to the same extent.

The people chiefly suffer from shortage of water, both for stock and humans. In the dry weather it was not unusual for the women to have to queue for six hours for their turn to draw a gourd of muddy water.

But erosion threatened the area in parts. So when the Community Development system pioneered in Machakos was introduced into the District, it was welcomed with amazing demonstrations of enthusiasm. The women in particular often responded in a surprising way. Owing to the absence of large numbers of young men, either serving in the Army or Police or working on farms or in the towns, many of the groups were almost entirely composed of women. Many of them used to provide themselves with identical dresses, and it was a remarkable sight to see some forty women all dressed alike, swing their hoes and shovels as one women.

On one occasion, in addition to the uniformed group of women there was another group dressed in a variety of ex-army clothing. On closer inspection however, it was found that this group was also in fact composed of women. Their discovery led to great hilarity and they were apparently having a dig at some of the idle young men of the neighbourhood who had failed to come out and work.

There is also a strong Mission element in the district and the members of groups in the more strongly Christian areas apparently felt it was not seemly to sing the traditional African songs. On one occasion there was therefore one group at one end of a field singing lustily and working with great energy, while at the other there was another much more subdued one chanting some form of hymn, which they could not keep in time with their swinging hoes. The contrast in the results achieved and the enjoyment derived from the two methods was painfully apparent.

The Wakamba as has been mentioned are a martial tribe and a very large proportion of the Kings African Rifles and the Kenya Police were at the time members of it. The spirit had permeated their whole life and it had a special influence on *Mwethya* in the Kitui District. The various groups, in addition to appointing their own song leaders, who were naturally mostly women, and group leaders, also evolved a system of joint group leaders. These leaders would call together a number of groups at certain times when the efforts of one group were not enough, as for instance for the construction of an earth dam. They were usually uniformed with different coloured sashes to indicate their responsibility and had a mock body guard of soldiers with dummy rifles. It was the sense of fun combined with remarkable organizational ability which made the Wakamba such a charming and rewarding people to work among.

As in Machakos an important aspect of community development in Kitui District was in connection with housing. The District was however more backward in this respect and most of the houses were merely of mud and wattle and in some cases simply of grass. The *Mwethya* groups, therefore evolved a different system. On one day they would come to a village and make the sun dried bricks for which they supplied their own moulds incidentally. This was, in fact, a feature of all such work, that virtually the only assistance the people obtained from the Government was in the form of guidance and technical advice, little material help being given. On another day, they returned and built the house with the bricks and completed the roof and thatch. In this way, thousands of new homes were provided.

Naturally the groups undertook a great deal of cultivation, and an incident which occurred will indicate the way that all were enabled to benefit from the communal effort.

Early one morning, after visiting a group weeding a garden, a crippled woman was passed, struggling along the path towards the workers. When we asked her why she was going there, for she obviously could not work, she said that if she attended and just joined in the singing, another day they would come and cultivate her garden for her. Similarly a large proportion of the houses built were for those away serving in the army or at work. Idle wasters were, on the other hand, never helped, and the group was often at a loss how to deal with them. They eventually decided to ostracise them as they did in former days, but naturally this is not such a dire penalty as it must have been in the times of inter-tribal warfare.

The results of the work on soil conservation in the District were the subject of a special report by the Agricultural Officer, who commented that never before had such a vast mileage of contour ridges been completed in one year. It was treble the previous record.

One of the concerns of the groups was to ensure that no member got an unfair advantage from *Mwethya*. They worked out an interesting method with the advice of the Community Development Officer, who was Titus Meatki, the first African Field Officer, posted to the District by the Department of Community Development. Each female member of the group was entitled to one day's work from the group, taken in rotation. It must be born in mind that some men had more than one wife, and therefore they contributed more to *Mwethya* and were entitled to more in return. Then a timetable was drawn up by picking the names of each member of the group from a hat and working accordingly in rotation. Group activities were also undertaken in connection with roads though not on such a wide scale, as the District was already fairly well served.

A further activity was the spreading of manure on the fields. The number of stock in parts of the district was considerable, but the manure often lay unused in the homesteads, where it was sometimes used as a tobacco patch. The chief obstacle to its use as a fertiliser was the physical difficulty, without an adequate number of carts, of transporting it to the fields. Through *Mwethya* however the entire contents of a cattle enclosure were carried to the fields in a few hours.

The way this drive for progress developed the initiative and inventiveness of the people can be illustrated by innumerable incidents. For instance, there was the group working in arid tsetse fly country, infested with snakes and the home of elephant and rhinoceros, who had set up their own little dressing station under a tree where the workers could have their cuts and bruises attended to. The nurse was neatly dressed and wore a spotless white apron and cap.

There was, it is true, an element of window dressing in this but it revealed the competitive spirit which lay behind so much of this activity. One group would vie with the another, not only in the amount of work achieved but in the originality of the way it did it. They also competed in the degree of sophistication they could include in their programmes.

For instance another group had made arrangements for water to be carried up from the spring for the workers. Not content with this, however, they insisted on boiling it first and then keeping it in a large drum over which had been spread a clean white cloth. This idea was probably suggested by the members of one of the women's clubs which were so widespread in the District. The women learned hygiene and sanitation as well as needlework in the clubs which will be described more fully later.

A number of groups had found a way of making the old men useful. They would often be seen squatting under a tree sharpening the blunted hoes or picks and fitting new handles when they became broken. This small incident is an indication of the vigour which the workers put into their efforts. Some observers have commented that these groups were nothing more than an elaboration of the traditional dances. It is true that the people did get an enormous amount of fun out of their work, but do not let us delude ourselves that for that reason it wasnot really hard work. Work is no less work whether or not it is done to music. It is true that when a visitor came to admire the efforts of a group they would often entertain him for a time by spinning their spades in their hands or by doing a pirouette or two before going on with their digging. This might be called exhibitionism, and so it was, but a very charming way of showing off their team spirit and their excellent drill.

In one area the people had even gone so far as to organize a competition in group organization. A cup had been bought and presented by a local trader and keenness to win it became intense. Marks were given, not only for the quality and quantity of work achieved by the groups, but also for its variety. Marks were also given for inventiveness and originality.

The winning group had taken a leaf out of the Agricultural Extension book and organised demonstrations of various kinds in the homesteads where they were working. There was a compost heap, a few hens being sprayed with insecticide and a seed bed for vegetables. Under a tree a few old men who were too old to work were sitting in front of a blackboard and being taught to read. Near by a group of women were being given a demonstration in bathing a baby. Some older women were learning to knit. There was even a demonstration of pottery made by members of the group. Some of the younger women were plastering the house while in the distance could be heard the rhythmic songs of the workers in the field and the cries of the ploughmen urging on their teams of oxen.

The runners-up had even erected booths in the homestead in one of which a barber was giving hair cuts to workers during their rest period. In another a hospital dresser was giving a demonstration of first aid.

It all showed how quickly the people had snatched at new ideas. They had gleaned them from all sides, from the programmes of the women's clubs, from the demonstrations conducted during the Farmers' Days and of course from their own fertile imagination.

When one visited the groups at work or at play, if one prefers to think of it in that way, one could not help feeling how important was the stimulus element in any programme. More important than material aid by far was the value of praise and encouragement. Competition between groups was important, but the leaders were also eager to learn how their efforts compared with those in other parts of the territory hundreds of miles away. To feel that they were contributing by their example or experiment to the success of people in other areas delighted them.

Of course, the group efforts were often inefficient or wasteful, but the leaders were always eager for suggestions as to how they could improve their programme. There was the group that was building a cattle crush for the inoculation of stock. The women were walking in a long line from the river bed and back collecting stones. Each carried one stone on her head. A system of trays to be carried by two people might have been more efficient in the absence of wheel-barrows or even the loan of an ox cart or two. Nevertheless the work was done and it only cost the local government a few bags of cement and the services of a mason.

Another scheme was the construction of tobacco-curing barns which sprang up at great speed once the people started to help each other to build them. Prior to that, it was only the rich who could afford them. This resulted in a general improvement in the quality of tobacco produced and therefore an increase in the income of the cultivators.

One of the results of this programme was that the Agricultural Assistants who had previously made themselves so unpopular, became the friends of the people. They had now become, in fact, Agricultural Extension Workers instead of enforcers of farming regulations. Their effectiveness also increased, but at the same time they had to ensure that they were able to explain convincingly the reason for the introduction of new agricultural practices and not merely rely on their authority to achieve results. It no doubt opened their eyes, and those of their superiors, to the value of the educational approach, and the fostering of good human relations.

The fact that the Wakamba have a long military tradition has been mentioned, but their introduction of buglers to the community development programme came as a surprise at first. It was however entirely sensible and logical. In a number of areas these men, using horns instead of bugles, used to tour the homesteads before dawn to wake up the inhabitants and ensure that they reported for work in good time so that the maximum amount might be achieved before the sun made further work impossible. The groups would therefore operate from about 6 am to 11 am or noon but they often had a long walk home after their day's labour and then the women would have to prepare and cook the evening meal and do their other household duties.

The problem of the small children whom the mothers could not leave at home was overcome in an original way. Creches were set up at the homestead of operations looked after by one of the grandmothers. At times a rope was slung over a branch of a tree for the children to swing on and while their mothers were at work in the fields they would play or sleep in the shade.

Sometimes the group work took on a political slant, as for instance the occasion when three large groups, each about fifty strong and dressed in their separate uniforms, descended upon the house of the member of Legislative Council. In less than no time they had terraced his farm while he sat indoors in rather embarrassed detachment.

As was to be expected with these exuberant people the completion of some project was often celebrated with a dance. Troupes would assemble from every side, the men with lion skin headdresses and ostrich feathers on their elbows, the girls in dark glasses and a brief skirt each with a police whistle in her mouth to mark the rhythm. They would stamp and somersault in the rising dust hemmed in by an eager crowd. The drummers would pound out an accompaniment which reverberated softly in the hills and the glow of sunset would gleam upon their sweating bodies.

It was a fitting conclusion to a task which itself had cost them much toil and sweat but had also brought its own happiness and satisfaction.

Central Nyanza
Central Nyanza is the country of the Luo. They live in the flat plains bordering

the shore in circular homesteads hedged in by euphorbia twenty feet high. When the British first made their appearance in this baking fever-stricken land, the Luo lived in large fortified villages constantly at war with their neighbours, always on the defensive against the marauding Kalenjin who inhabited the highlands above them.

With the establishment of law and order in the land and the retention of the hill tribes within their own boundaries, the Luo like other tribes began to move out of their fortified encampments and build homes for themselves in the hinterland. The population increased, the fields extended, the sandy soil began to lose its fertility as crop followed crop, season after season. As each father died his land was divided among all his sons until each might find himself the possessor of twenty fragments scattered over an area of three miles or more. The wants of these younger men increased. They were quicker to see the value of bicycles, smart clothing and more than anything else, education for their children. The tiring soil was unable to produce the money with which to buy these desirable benefits. So they set off to the sisal estates where their magnificent physiques enabled them to earn good money, to the towns, even to the docks at Mombasa five hundred miles away.

In their absence their wives struggled to cultivate the land, to herd the cattle and feed the children, while waiting for relations to bring back the earnings of their absent husbands. There seemed no worth-while future in spite of the fact that the rainfall was plentiful and in many parts the soil was rich and capable of copious harvests of maize, millet, cotton and groundnuts. The cattle too were among the best to be found in the territory.

The men, separated from their native land and often their families sometimes became a prey to disaffection. Whom could they blame for their difficulties but the colonial power which was governing the land?

But the government, and particularly the Agricultural Officers had for years been struggling to teach the people to develop its potential. New cash crops had been introduced, cotton, ground nuts and maize. More often than not they increased the problems of soil erosion. They tried to persuade the people to adopt soil conservation measures and the use of manure. There were too few hands, and they mostly female ones, to undertake the work.

An air of frustration and defeatism began to permeate the official and African spirit. Added to this the oppression of heat and disease inhibited the local population from making the great efforts required to remedy the situation.

It was at this stage that the Agricultural Officers became convinced that only through a widespread programme of consolidation and subsequent farm planning could the people be enabled to wring from their soil the harvest which would enable them to prosper in their own lands and on their own farms.

But how was the social revolution to be brought about - a revolution every bit as drastic as the enclosures effected in England.

It happened that about 1955 some successful experiments in land enclosure and farm planning known after their originator as the Swynnerton Plan had been undertaken in Kikuyu country. The government had launched a giant land consolidation project to cover the whole area. This campaign began to show considerable promise and parties of Luo leaders were taken to see the progress being made.

These Luo leaders came from a rich area of the District which had been selected for the pilot scheme. Large sums of money were expended on installing water supplies and access roads. Committees similar to those set up in the Kikuyu Districts to share out the land were established and considerable numbers of technical staff were posted to the area to demarcate and survey the holdings and plan their development.

The achievement of their objectives would have brought undoubted advantages to the farmers. They would in the first place have obtained a firm title to their land which would have enabled them to use it as security for loans; they and their wives would have been saved the toil of walking from one small plot to another to eke a subsistence from the soil; they would have been able to farm their land as an economic unit with a proper rotation of crops; manure from their cow sheds would have been close at hand for spreading in the fields; their cattle would have been able to pasture in well-kept paddocks secure from infection from their neighbours' herds.

But the process of exchanging the land of hundreds of farmers in an equitable way was an immense problem. Land disputes going back for generations complicated the issue. Distrust was felt about the reliability of the land distribution committee set up by the Government in the Kikuyu Districts.

All this led to a reluctance on the part of the Luo to adopt the scheme however logical and valuable it might appear. There were also problems of the pasture which was used by tribesmen from other parts in the area being consolidated; moreover some of the owners of the alien stock were men of political power. There was therefore opposition from the start and eventually all technical staff had to be removed and the scheme virtually abandoned.

It was at this stage that discussions were held with the District Commissioner to see if something could be salvaged from the wreck by adopting a community development approach. It was agreed to give it a trial and a plan of campaign was prepared.

As in the case of Machakos, it was decided to select one small area from which to make a start. A Community Development Officer, Bill Sturruck, with an African District Officer as his partner, were charged with the task of persuading the inhabitants to carry out land consolidation themselves under the guidance of the Agricultural Extension Officer.

Talks were held with the villagers and in a surprisingly short time a group not only approved of the idea of land consolidation but had agreed to carry out the work themselves. They were prepared to accept the advice of the technical officers regarding the lay-out of access roads and in due course would welcome guidance regarding the agricultural lay-out of their new holdings. They intended to undertake the land exchanges entirely by themselves and to arrange the planting of boundary hedges by the group.

Shortly after work began the area was rapidly consolidated and hedged. The layout of the holdings was then undertaken and as soon as the most suitable site for the home was indicated the group constructed a homestead complete with auxiliary buildings.

Very soon the idea caught on in neighbouring areas and the campaign began to spread throughout the district. The Community Development Officer in fact returned to the area where the original scheme had collapsed and revived interest using the new methods. The people then agreed to co-operate and the area was in time consolidated.

But the programme did not stop short at land consolidation and farm planning. On completion of the phase the people turned their attention to other forms of development. One of these was the provision of clean water supplies. These consisted of a fountain for the drawing of drinking water direct from the spring, below that was a washing slab for laundering, below that again a cattle trough and at the bottom a fish pond.

Since these installations were built entirely by the people with cement supplied by the local authority, the villagers took a personal interest in their proper maintenance. They have as a result been well looked after.

As in Kitui, the people also undertook the manuring of the fields in the new holdings by co-operative effort with remarkable results. The yield of the crops increased considerably. As in the Wakamba Districts it was also found that a traditional form of corporate effort had existed in the past, but had dried out as a result of the introduction of a money economy and a western form of government. The system was not difficult to revive, adapt to modern needs and expand.

There were some interesting features of this campaign. One was the composition of the initial group. It consisted of a strong Christian community which numbered among its members a retired Sergeant Major of Tribal Police as well as being the home of the present chief. This community not only had a high standard of living, but a strong social sense. It therefore was quick to appreciate the advantage of consolidation and was in a position to co-operate to achieve it. The example having once been given of the effectiveness of the community development approach other areas were ready to follow along the same lines.

Another feature was the virulent political campaign which was mounted in opposition to the first unsuccessful project. This opposition entirely disappeared when community development methods were adopted.

A third feature was the low cost of the campaign. Few specialists were required as the work of survey and registration had been left to a later stage when consolidation was completed. A further feature was the way that all members of the community including Chiefs and other important residents took part in the actual planting of hedges. All seemed to take a pride in their joint efforts and achievement.

Another important aspect of the campaign was the contribution made to its success by special training courses for group leaders, technical staff, Chiefs and Headmen. This is described in another chapter.

An interesting development was the establishment of a nursery for coffee trees by the people themselves for the supply of seedlings to newly consolidated holdings. The original seeds only were supplied by the Agricultural Department from which thousands of seedlings were propagated.

An important feature of this programme was the fact that no Community Development Assistants or Village Level Workers, as they are termed in some parts of the world, were employed. The core of the Community Development Team consisted of two men, one a Scotsman who was the Community Development Officer, the other an African who was, like the organizer in

Machakos, an Administrative Officer. The Administrative Officer, it should be remembered, was working as a Community Development Officer and no longer relied in any way on his rank or authority.

The advantage of this partnership approach was that the Community Development Officer proper was in a good position to ensure effective liaison with the District team, which was mostly composed of expatriate officers. The African who was also a native of the Province, if not of the actual district, was able to obtain the confidence of the people.

With them the Agricultural and Health Assistants resident in the area worked. Moreover they worked as a team. When guidance was needed in agricultural matters the Health Assistants helped to give instruction in the new methods. Similarly when health problems were the order of the day, such as the protection of springs, the Agricultural Assistants lent a hand.

It goes without saying that enforcement never played any part in the programme. Everything was achieved through the group leaders who wielded such authority over the groups as was required, while the technical staff acted as advisors.

The impression should not be gained that this was a rapid process. Selling the idea of land consolidation in an area which happened to be close to the home of its principal political opponent was not easy. Once this had been achieved progress was more rapid.

Then in a district of this size with a population approaching half a million, other centres of operation had to be opened from which the new ideas could spread. But the Community Development staff was limited to one man and therefore other field officers had to be trained in the community development approach.

Technical Officers were invited to see the progress of work in the pilot area and the subordinate field staff underwent courses of instruction at a nearby community development training centre. The Chiefs and headmen attended similar courses. When a new area was chosen it would then be the Agricultural Officer and his staff, assisted by the District Officer, who would have to launch the community development scheme. It is gratifying that they actually did undertake this work in the right way. There is nothing that succeeds like success, even though it may often prove a bitter pill to admit that one's previous methods were not the right ones.

One of the principal achievements of the Community Development Officer was the way he exercised his tact among officers who had been brought up in the authoritarian approach, and won them over to the indirect community development method. His African partner achieved remarkable success in undertaking a similar exercise among Chiefs, headmen and subordinate field staff.

Another feature of the programme was the inclusion of house building. Many houses had to be resited in the consolidated holdings. Moreover, now that the farmers had obtained security and a planned farm they felt prepared to make capital improvements which they would not otherwise have been so anxious to do. In addition to the houses which were built by the groups, cow-sheds and improved stores were erected in the homesteads. Paddocks were fenced or hedged and the whole countryside began to take on a new appearance. From a jumble of huts nestling among fields of maize and millet reached by narrow footpaths, houses more in the European style began to appear alongside grassy tracks, the farms laid out in an orderly way behind them. Gardens of flowers were laid out in front and the people seemed to have entered a new era.

What was more important, however, was an air of peace and co-operation, not only between the people themselves, but between them and the Government officers who were working to assist them in their development.

While this group work was in progress another scheme of land consolidation was being attempted in another part of the district. This was not the original project which had failed, but one which appeared to show promise of success. It was, however, not organised by the Community Development Officer.

The scheme was one of land enclosure and the government had built a most expensive water tank as its contribution to the scheme. Now this water supply had no direct connection with the land enclosure scheme. The people regarded it therefore as a kind of reward or bribe for doing the work of enclosure.

When the time came to try and extend the project to neighbouring areas, the people asked what they would get if they did so. They pointed out that they needed a school, even though their existing one as not full, and of course a water tank. When the government said that it could not afford to provide tanks for all areas, the people politely said that they therefore were not prepared to undertake the heavy work of land enclosure.

This indicated that the people were not convinced of the value of the scheme.

It should be remembered that land enclosure is a simple operation compared with land consolidation. No exchange of holdings are involved, merely the planting of hedges round existing ones. So if they were not prepared to do this, obviously there was something radically wrong with the whole project. The faults lay firstly in a misapplication of the grant-in-aid system, the provision of a service which was interpreted as a reward. The villagers argued that there must be some catch in the scheme if the government felt it necessary to spend so much on a tank. Secondly, there had obviously been a failure on the part of the government to convince the people of the value of enclosure.

Thirdly, democratically formed groups had not been established. But instances of failure, if the causes of failure are correctly analysed are as valuable in the evolution of community development principles and practices as of success.

Elgon Nyanza

On the borders of Uganda and to the North of Central Nyanza lies the wide fertile plateau of Elgon Nyanza. The rainfall is good and the land rich, but until recent years it had, for the most part, been pastoral country.

Once, however, it was discovered how suitable it was for the production of maize the acreage increased year by year. Ploughs began to appear and ever larger fields were brought under cultivation. so great were the inroads made in the former pasture that the children began to suffer from malnutrition, not from a shortage of food but from an excess of maize meal and a deficiency of milk, which used to form a major protein of their diet. The economy of the area had changed so rapidly that mouthers had not sufficient time or knowledge to adapt their feeding methods for their children.

It was then found that the area was most suitable for the growing of coffee and the wealth, in terms of money, of the people increased still further.

A problem then arose not of material wealth but of labour to undertake the agricultural work involved. Tractors began to appear, but few could afford such luxuries. Ox ploughs were in general use but were not suitable for such operations as planting and weeding. These still had to depend on hand labour.

Labour was also short for the construction or repair of houses and for the building of tracks down which carts could travel with the ever-growing volume of produce.

Amid all this there was, strangely enough, unrest which revealed itself in the growth of a semi-religious sect known as *Dini Ya Msambwa*. Its origins could not be traced to economic dissatisfaction for the District was increasing in wealth at a remarkable speed.

Perhaps it was the suddenness of the transition or the unevenness of the acquisition of the new prosperity which provided the breeding ground. Nevertheless, at one time it assumed grave proportions and exhibited alarming symptoms of fanaticism.

It was in 1955 that the Community Development Officer was posted to the District and began to develop the idea of communal group work which had however been initiated by a number of Community Development Assistants. The idea had been quickly adopted, and in a comparatively short time became an accepted part of the fabric of society. It did not suffer from the set-backs reported in Kitui and was extraordinarily broad-based. The groups grew almost of their own volition over wide areas and undertook a variety of activities.

An important side of their work was multiple weeding of crops. The Agricultural Officer had recommended this practice to increase yields and before the introduction of community development methods certain farmers engaged additional labour to undertake it. They found, however, that their increased income did not cover the cost of the additional labour they had to employ. They therefore abandoned the practice. With the introduction of communal work they obtained the full advantage of the increased yields.

It was the practice for musicians to accompany the workers to the fields and they were often to be seen encouraging them, blowing horns, ringing bells and singing. A considerable amount of house building and house improvement was carried out through community groups.

An original innovation made in this district was in connection with line planting of maize which is one of the major export crops of the area. The inhabitants had been converted to this method of cultivation but it was obviously difficult for individuals to carry it out quickly at the first onset of the rains, which moreover it was imperative to do. They therefore evolved a system of doing it in groups while at the same time manuring the field economically.

While two of the team held each end of the spacing line another would scoop the holes for the seed. He or she would be followed by another who would place a handful of manure in the holes while another followed to plant the seed. In this way field after field was rapidly and efficiently planted and the resulting yields were most impressive.

A visit to one area where this method had been adopted provided an interesting contrast to another farmer who had planted in the traditional way. His crop was extremely disappointing and he owed this to the fact that he had not joined the group, thereby benefitting from their joint efforts. He had decided to join at the next planting season.

As in other areas, the selection by the troops of their leaders was interesting. Almost invariably they were quiet unassuming men or women. The importance of the influence of women in society was emphasized by the fact that they did, in fact, sometimes choose women leaders. It was not therefore the most assertive people who were chosen as leaders. The groups wanted people they could trust to apportion the work fairly; they must have tact too as well as organizing ability. There seemed to be no regular practice with regard to age either. Sometimes the leaders were older people, sometimes quite young men. Quite clearly however it was their personal characteristics which influenced the choice rather than any status they might enjoy in society.

In many areas tree plantations were established by groups, and this is of some significance. Although in this part of the country it was not the general practice to use dung as fuel, nevertheless building timber was often scarce. In the earlier and somewhat unsuccessful community development scheme, already described, it had been found necessary to transport poles for many miles to enable the people to build cattle sheds.

In the present scheme however the groups were persuaded to see the value of building cattle sheds. Traditionally it was the custom to keep the cattle out-of-doors in a thorn enclosure at night. During the day the dung dried up and blew about the homestead. It also lost much of its value as a fertilizer. By erecting a roof over the cattle they would not only keep their condition better, given protection from the keen night air, but would at the same time bulk good quality manure. At the appropriate time this could be carried to the fields.

Again however the problem of construction arose and this was accentuated by the shortage of timber. Group effort again solved the problem: while some cut and brought poles others did the same with thatching grass and the buildings were usually erected in a couple of days. This bulking of manure combined with the line planting mentioned earlier undoubtedly contributed greatly to the yields of the farmers and raised their standards of living.

One noticeable feature of community development in Elgon Nyanza was that the groups were small ones. They were in fact family groups consisting of various brothers and their wives and sometimes their children and parents. They had a great pride of achievement and were very anxious to show visitors what they had accomplished. When one was touring the district it was extremely difficult to avoid being dragged from one group to the next and one's itinerary got very behindhand at the end of a long day. Each group wished to show off either what it was doing or what it had achieved. It was this eagerness for appreciation and praise that gave the people such great charm.

This satisfying progress must also be viewed against the history of considerable unrest in the past. Though no claim is made that community development had in itself removed this feeling of dissatisfaction, it can at any rate be claimed that during the time that the campaign was in progress no sign of unrest was apparent. The people were all involved in a great drive for rural improvement through their own efforts and were obviously very appreciative of the fact that their ability to overcome problems by their own efforts had been recognised and appreciated.

One episode is worth recalling in this context. A certain Chief had become imbued with a great desire to improve the condition of his area. He had launched a campaign of pasture improvement by the removal of brush wood and the fencing of paddocks, with live hedges. Unfortunately he had been unable to carry the people with him in this project. It was found out on inquiry that he had tried to achieve his objective through the force of his own personality instead of persuading the land owners to undertake it through group work. He had failed to convince the people of he necessity of fencing their land. As a result although hedges were planted they were constantly breached by cattle and the object of the scheme was defeated. If the people had seen the point of the scheme they would have made the hedges impenetrable and enlisted the help of their neighbours to effect this if beyond their individual powers.

This was an example of officialdom which by failing to win the willing support of the people and showing them how to solve a problem through mutual co-operation also failed in its own objective.

Elgon Nyanza provided as stimulating an example of community development as anywhere in Kenya. Groups started of their own volition much as they did in Kitui until the authorities had no idea how many existed or what they were doing. The people showed a great variety of approach if not the humorous originality of the Wakamba. They indicated their ability to adapt their traditional methods to modern needs as in the case of row planting and spot manuring of maize. In another instance one group started a brick works for the supply of a new trading centre. With the earnings from this they paid all the taxes of the members of the group for the ensuing year, a magnificent example of enterprise.

But it was the people's pride in their homes which provided the most satisfying experience for the visitor. These newly built, repaired homesteads, shaded by trees, surrounded by cropped grass and ornamented by flowers which glowed against the whitewashed walls, often created an atmosphere which anyone would envy. One felt how fortunate were the families who lived in such delightful surroundings.

The Kalenjin

In the highland of Kenya living cheek by jowl with the European settlers live a group of similar peoples of nilo-hamitic origin known as the Kalenjin. They are akin to the Maasai and often similar in appearance. Like them they are traditionally pastoralists but in more recent times have also become agriculturalists. They inhabit the belts of forest and grass land bordering a part of the former Maasai grazing areas now occupied by European farmers.

They are extremely athletic people who have for years not only produced the Colony's outstanding Olympic competitors but also the cream of the army. Numbers also serve in the police. In earlier days one of their amusements was to chase antelope to a standstill and they were often to be seen vying with each other in standing jumps of great height.

Their country is rich agriculturally but for the most part neglected. They are highly intelligent people and expert stock men but preferred to employ neighbouring tribes to cultivate their land till recently. They also for many years scorned education and as a result got left badly behind in the march of progress, for what it is worth. Some might say they were equally happy in their traditional state.

However, the time came when money values began to assume an importance among them and the earnings of their sons in the armed forces and police proved inadequate to pay for all their requirements. Development of their rich and fertile land became as important as elsewhere. Community Development had to be adapted to their particular needs in the special circumstances of their environment.

The largest district of this tribe was Nandi, next door to Central Nyanza. The part chosen for the first pilot project was situated in fact right on the Central Nyanza border at the foot of a steep escarpment. We felt that if community development worked here it would work anywhere.

It was unfavourable from the point of view of its geographical position as well as the social state of the people. Torrential rains were common and the water cascaded down from the hills above, leaving destruction in its wake. Great gullies had formed and the grazing on which the people depended for their cattle was in danger of disappearing. Added to this it was a malarial area being low lying. The Nandi were not used to the disease and it was unknown in the highlands which were their normal home. Finally, the people lived in the pernicious vicinity of the sugar plantations. With their illicit gin factories, drunkenness had become a major social problem and gave rise to frequent assaults and murders.

The whole area had an atmosphere of degradation and decay and being remote from the administrative headquarters of the District had tended to become neglected and forgotten, except when some unusually violent outbreak of crime occurred and had to be dealt with. So it was in this unpromising area that Ted Harris, the Community Development Officer, was asked to try to bring about a minor economic and social revolution. The first task was, of course, to try to check the terrible problem of erosion and then to restore the pasture to its former lushness. The task was obviously beyond the powers of individuals but perhaps could be tackled by neighbouring groups.

A Community Development Assistant whose home was in the salubrious highlands agreed to come down and live in the fever-stricken, vice-ridden hell, for so it must have seemed to him. It is greatly to his credit and to the inspiration he received from the Community Development Officer, a tough, indefatigable Englishman who had previously taught agriculture at a South African University, that he was prepared to make this sacrifice.

But his efforts were rewarded. Groups were formed after the preliminary discussions with the elders and a plan of campaign worked out. First of all they started by stopping the gullies with great acacia trees which grew in the area. They were thrust whole into the clefts so that their spreading branches locked into the sides and prevented their being carried away by the floods. This idea proved to be most successful and the soil piled up behind them in a series of steps until the land was restored to its original level.

Next wash-stops had to be established along the contours. Rows of aloes which were also common thereabouts were planted thickly. Then the various fields were enclosed by hedges so that the cattle, sheep and goats could not wander all over the countryside, but were confined to tracks which were properly drained. These measures resulted in a restoration of the grass cover.

Then the groups turned to the question of housing and a start was made to build cattle sheds away from the dwelling houses. It was customary to keep the cattle in the back part of the house so that they could be protected from thieves which were a menace in this part of the country at night.

Next they began to establish sugar plantations of their own and to sell the produce to the factory through a co-operative. Previously they had left the cultivation of sugar to the agricultural Luo across their borders. As in other parts of the District they overcame their prejudices against manual work through the influence of group effort and in so doing were able to provide themselves with a substantial supplementary income instead of merely relying on the yield of their cattle.

The construction of cattle crushes followed to assist the Veterinary Officers to spray and inoculate their cattle against disease.

Step by step therefore the people worked together to restore the fertility of their land and their hope for the future. By so doing they began to recover their self-respect and drunkenness and vice declined. Feuds and quarrels also grew less as a result of the people being thrown together and having to get along with each other.

The final stage was reached when parties of leaders were brought down to the Valley to see the achievements of the inhabitants. These visits not only acted as a further spur to the people themselves but as an object lesson to their kinsmen from the highlands.

They quickly appreciated the fact that if these forgotten people could bring about such an economic and social revolution in such an unrewarding part of the world, how much more easily this could be done in the fertile, healthy country at the top of the escarpment.

In fact on their return the leaders quickly established groups and they had the effect of not only improving pasture but of fencing the land. An interesting discovery was that the groups were composed almost entirely of men. In other areas it had been found that either the members were for the most part women, as in Machakos and Kitui, or half men and half women as in the Nyanza districts. Among the Kalenjin it was the men who chiefly undertook the development work.

This feature was remarkable since at the time that community development was introduced the men were found to be too proud to do ordinary manual work. They were traditionally herdsmen and warriors and they considered this to be their proper role. It was shameful to soil their hands or exert themselves in the fields. The agricultural work had therefore to be undertaken either by the women or by labourers they hired from neighbouring tribes. As a result considerable sums of money left the district annually in the form of wages.

It was probably the influence of the Community Development Officer himself which first of all began to break down this prejudice. He found great difficulty in getting the people to do the work of digging wells and to give them a lead he joined them himself and shared the work of digging. The sight of a white man actually doing hard physical work was a remarkable and almost unique one and the word quickly spread. The men were soon ready to help him with the work.

But mainly it was the practice of group work itself which finally broke down the reluctance of the men to do manual labour. Once all the neighbours had joined together to undertake a task there was no one to despise them for doing so. They were all involved and it had thereby become the accepted thing to do.

Again although the Nandi are not particularly money conscious and their wants in the past had been few there was a growing realisation of the value of money. With it schools could be built and equipped and in so doing the children could be enabled to catch up the leeway they had lost through the previous scorn of education by their parents. Tractors could be bought to speed up the cultivation of the land; sewing machines could be acquired to satisfy the growing dress consciousness of the women.

By working in groups they suddenly realized that they could dispense entirely with the labourers they had been in the habit of hiring. Almost in one season this revolution occurred and the people's income from their crops increased enormously. The burden of the women was also relieved and larger areas could be brought under the plough.

In the highlands also the same phenomenon which had been noticed in the lowland pilot area became apparent. Inter-family feuds and drunkenness lessened. The people apparently appreciated that more was to be gained from working together than by squabbling among themselves. The young men were also kept so busy that they did not take to the bottle to relieve their boredom. A new purpose came into their lives which resulted in a better ordering of society.

As in other areas therefore, almost imperceptibly, and certainly with no preconceived purpose, the introduction of community development through group-work achieved both economic and social reforms. As also in other areas the idea of group-work was not alien to the people. In an undeveloped and limited sense it had existed since time immemorial. It was its revival and modification which provided the means to produce the new dynamism which did so much to bring progress and added prosperity to the district.

The efforts of Baringo District before the appointment of a Community Development Officer or Assistants have already been described. As soon as Richard Jolly was appointed under an American Aid scheme greater progress was made. He was a young man recently down from University with a very good degree. He had felt drawn to make some practical contribution to Africa before settling down in his chosen career. He certainly made his mark.

Being primarily cattle people like the Nandi the first appeal was made to their interest in the health of their stock. One of the chief diseases was liver fluke which was carried by leeches in the stagnant pools where the herdsmen were accustomed to water their animals. It was suggested that if the people helped to protect the springs and to build cattle troughs they could no doubt check the disease.

The Agricultural Officer originally started the scheme to help them to do this work but it was greatly expanded by the Community Development Officer. It was a straightforward grant-in-aid project. The people cut the tracks to enable a truck to get as near to the spring as possible They cleared the undergrowth around the spring, collected stone and sand and dug the trenches to the edge of the spring. The government provided the cement and a mason to build the retaining wall, the outlet pipe and the trough.

There was a great demand for such springs and the only obstacle was the limited number of masons and supplies of cement. No doubt in future years the people could protect springs themselves without the material assistance of government but they would still need technical guidance on the siting and construction of the retaining wall.

Another community development scheme was organized by an Agricultural Officer in the district. It took the form of an irrigation project covering a considerable area. This had been undertaken entirely by the people under his guidance. He had received some cement from the Community Development Department to construct the head works but all the canals had been dug by the villagers themselves. Unfortunately, through lack of technical advice from an irrigation engineer the head-works had been wrongly sited, it was therefore necessary to rebuild them. However, the people with their characteristic perseverance were ready to do so and the scheme was completed successfully.

This is another example of a community development scheme being undertaken by a technical officer. It is also another object lesson in the importance of technical guidance.

Another excellent example of community development by these enterprising people occurred in the arid plain at the foot of the ridge. An agricultural development scheme involving enclosures had been in operation for some time in the area. Progress had not been as fast as had been hoped and the peoples' response had not always been good.

A group of farmers from this area went on a course to Jeanes School. On their return, without any assistance from the government, they started forming groups and rebuilding each others' houses and working on each others' land. This was completely spontaneous and shows again how stimulating residential courses can be to encourage leaders to organise community development. The Agricultural Officer in charge of the scheme was also struck by the changed attitude of the inhabitants as a result of first the course and then the group work.

But the Community Development Officer got group-work going in the highland ridge too. It caught on quickly as it had done in Nandi. The groups needed little encouragement or advice once it had got under way. They helped each other to cultivate and manure and build houses. They established large numbers of vegetable plots too in an effort to improve their diet.

Another young Community Development Officer, Alan Wright in Elgeyo-Marakuet district held a camp of school boys in their holidays. They built a school as their holiday task with the co-operation of the village people. In fact they showed the older people the way to meet their needs.

Taita

The Taita District is a small area of steep hills surrounded by desert about a hundred miles from the Indian Ocean. In the pockets of the hills there is rich soil and the crests are clothed in thick forests. Above the forests tower massive outcrops of rock smoothed by the torrential downpours typical of this island of population.

This is an unusual country inhabited by unusual people. Being on the route which the early explorers took on their dangerous journeys into the interior of Kenya, they were the first to be converted to Christianity after the freed slaves at Mombasa. As a result they have benefitted from education for a longer period than others in the colony and to a greater extent in terms of numbers.

There were many interesting features about the community development campaign in the district. In the first place the Community Development Officer was a woman, thus demonstrating that there are no barriers of sex in the successful introduction of community development. Secondly, the people had adopted a communal system of working for money. This idea had been introduced by the early missionaries who had devised it to enable the members of the different Christian communities to collect funds for the building and maintenance of their branches and schools. Thirdly, in the introduction of communal work by the Community Development Officer the people on their own initiative evolved a system of common cultivation. They would set aside a piece of land on which the community would jointly plant some new crop or method of cultivation, as they knew to their cost that there is always the danger of failure. By pooling their land as well as their resources, the losses would be shared as well as the profits. This meant that the people were much more prepared to experiment in an enterprising way than they would have been otherwise. One of the crops they had tried out was a new type of onion, for this district had a large export trade in vegetables to Mombasa for the provisioning of ships. Another was a trial of tobacco.

But one of the most important achievements was the terracing of the hill sides. As has been mentioned, these were often precipitous and while the magnificent views over the stark hills and desert below were one of the most notable features of the ares, the difficulties of cultivation on such steep slopes without causing erosion was one of the nightmares of the Agricultural Officer.

The work of terracing the hill side was made even more difficult because the vast majority of the male population was out of the district for most of the year working in the docks or in industry in Mombasa. The problem was therefore similar to that confronting the Central Nyanza District described earlier. The women had already more than enough to do to look after their large families, for here as elsewhere the birth rate was high and thanks to western medicine the survival rate increased annually. Such young men as remained in the District were usually regarded as idlers, but nevertheless once the group work got started it was possible to involve them which was no doubt beneficial to both the land and their physique and general state of health.

The hill sides quickly began to take on a new look and although it would be many years before they resembled those of Italy, how many centuries had it actually taken the Italians to transform their mountains. But great strides were made in the protection of the soil and the extension of the area under coffee was accelerated considerably. The planting of coffee trees in the right way is an elaborate process. Large holes have to be dug, manure has to be laid in the holes and finally the seedlings have to be planted neatly in rows with the proper spacing. Group-work, as in the case of the line planting of maize described in the chapter dealing with Elgon Nyanza facilitated this operation enormously and enabled far more rapid progress to be made.

Again as elsewhere, the traditional co-operative idea was there, though long forgotten and neglected. It was revived and elaborated to become the motive force of the various activities. Again the same tendency to progress from one sector of development to another took place. The groups turned to house building during the season when agricultural work was not pressing. Good square houses with corrugated iron roofs began to take the place of the round grass-thatched huts which were the usual type, in ever increasing numbers.

This matter of the phasing in of activity, which was common in all community development areas, might be considered further here. It was undertaken by the groups themselves, who decided what work they intended to undertake and when. They knew only too well, and often better than the technical officers, that certain tasks could be undertaken at one time of year and others at another. For instance it was impractical to try to dig terraces when the soil was dry and hard. Similarly road work was unnecessarily arduous at such seasons. However the same obstacles were not encountered in the building of houses in the dry season. In fact this was when they must be completed, before the start of the rains. Planting had obviously to be tackled at the first onset of the rains and could not be delayed, weeding had to be done as often as possible before harvest, and so forth.

So the groups tended to work out a seasonal timetable for themselves allotting to each month the appropriate activity. The group leaders were in far the best position to know how to work out such timetables and it benefited the technical officers to consult them and to adapt their assistance and guidance accordingly. This was a feature of community development schemes where not only had the group leaders become aware of their proper functions and their initiative been encouraged, but the officers of government had become fully orientated to their particular supporting role.

This changed relationship was a revolutionary one but was to a great extent the secret of success. It is greatly to the credit of the technical officers and particularly of the Agricultural Officer in this area, as in the others, that he appreciated this fact and adjusted his programme accordingly. He could, for instance, arrange courses and technical instruction in the slack season. He would throw all his resources into the field when terracing or planting were the order of the day.

It is worth mentioning in connection with the Taita District, that it is probable that the advanced level of education of the people, together with the contribution made by the women's clubs that created a keener awareness among them of the need to change and adopt new methods of agriculture, new types of housing, new health precautions. The early and later missionaries no doubt contributed much in this way and the example of the responsiveness of the people in the pilot area in Central Nyanza already referred to provides an exact parallel.

There is no doubt that though community development was introduced somewhat later in the District than the others already mentioned, the people gave every sign of catching up and surpassing them. While education is certainly not an essential requirement for successful community development it certainly assists the process considerably.

The Kikuyu

We now return to central Kenya, to the home of the Kikuyu who inhabit the hilly fertile country around the foothills of Mount Kenya and the Aberdare Range. It stretches south westward from the mountains to the outskirts of Nairobi a hundred miles away. It is an area of ridge upon ridge dividing the streams which flow down to the larger rivers which pass through the Machakos and Kitui Districts in the plains below.

The earth is rich and red to match the ripe coffee berries which spread in increasing profusion throughout the area. The ridges are patched with plantations of black wattle from the bark of which tanning extract is made. In the higher areas where the air is colder and only one crop of maize can be grown a year, tree plantations cover more than half the country and present a feathery contrast to the rich emerald pasture which lies between them. In the lower zone, however, erosion has been a perpetual menace and giant efforts have been made by the people under the guidance of technical officers to check its growth and restore fertility.

At the time referred to in this account the people were still in the throes of Mau Mau. They were living in huge villages on the tops of the ridges which had been set up to achieve closer administrative control and to deny the terrorist gangs access to food supplies from the people who had previously lived in scattered homesteads.

The Government then took advantage of the concentration of the people in villages to organise a land consolidation scheme. This was not conducted on community development lines, and in a number of areas ran into difficulties over unjust re-allocations by the local committees set up for the purpose. These abuses were eventually corrected and the time arrived when the security situation had so improved that it was thought safe for the land-holders to return and live on their newly consolidated farms. In fact until they were actually living on their holdings it would be difficult for them to farm or develop them properly.

But it was then found that the land owners were reluctant to move back to their holdings. A number of reasons were given for this. Some said that they were apprehensive that they might suffer reprisals from the gangs which were still operating, though much fewer in numbers, in the nearby forests. Others said that they preferred the life in the villages where schools and other public services such as water supplies were available close at hand. But the principal reason was found to be that the majority could not afford to build their new houses up to the minimum standards which were laid down by the health authorities.

It was then decided to see if a solution could be found along community development lines. Accordingly a party from Nyeri District travelled to Kitui to see the re-housing campaign which had proved so successful there. They were most impressed with what they saw and on their return immediately formed groups to build houses, cow sheds and other auxiliary buildings on their consolidated holdings.

The campaign proved a complete success and houses of an even higher standard than those built in Kitui began to spring up all over the District. They were for the most part built of off-cuts nailed to a timber framework and therefore rather resembled Canadian log cabins. Their roofs were of corrugated iron and their windows usually shuttered, though some were glazed. The carpenters and masons gave their service free to the other members of the group. The groups usually carried the materials down from the nearest forest station. So the only cost for which the household was liable was usually that of the corrugated iron, nails and sometimes petrol for a lorry to carry timber if the forest station was too distant. This proved to be within the means of all the farmers. In some cases the groups would help their poorer relatives to build their homes and pay for the iron and nails.

Soon afterwards a similar scheme was launched in the neighbouring Embu District after teams of leaders had seen for themselves the methods adopted in Nyeri, and later still another campaign was launched in Meru. So the whole thing worked on the basis of chain reaction. Pilot areas in each district were expanded and multiplied until the whole area was covered.

Houses were completed, the groups then turned their attention to fencing the fields in each holding so that a proper rotation of crops could be introduced. Paddocks were provided for the cattle and the whole countryside took on an entirely different character. While previously it resembled a vast patchwork of plantations and irregular strips of cultivation, now it consisted of thousands of small farms with the homestead on the roadside and the fields arranged neatly below it.

Next there was the problem of the landless and of those whose holdings were too small to justify their living on them. They were to continue in the villages, but they could be given larger plots and enabled to build bigger houses. Groups were formed of this section of the population and a campaign to build the new houses undertaken. In due course therefore the villages too completely changed their characters. Instead of martial lines of beehive huts, housing estates of modern cottages appeared, each surrounded by its vegetable garden and flower beds and connected by paths to the school, community centre, playing fields and shops. Most of the transformation which occurred in these latter days of the emergency occurred as the result of the adoption of community development methods.

A word should be said about the Community Development Officers who as elsewhere were the mainspring of the campaigns. One, Don Diment, was a former journalist who turned up in Kenya at the beginning of the Emergency while on a world tour. He was persuaded to join the Community Development Ministry and found the work so interesting that he abandoned his idea of completing his world tour and remained to achieve outstanding success.

Another, Denis Cox, had been a political agent in England but felt drawn to serve in Kenya under a special scheme which was set up to recruit people who were prepared to help in the rehabilitation programme. He showed great imagination and initiative in Embu under most trying conditions. As can be imagined the promotion of community development under conditions almost amounting to civil war was not exactly simple. He not only got the community development re-housing programme firmly established but also got a community development training centre established.

A third was a former District Officer who transferred to the Ministry of Community Development. He built up a most effective training centre at Meru, which will be referred to more fully in the chapter on training, with slender resources, as well as starting a community development housing project.

The fourth was an African, one of those invaluable Kikuyu loyalists who after doing rehabilitation work did outstanding service in building up a widespread chain of youth centres in the Kiambu District. The Community Development Officer in Fort Hall District was a former Indian Army Officer who also did excellent work in the organisation of Youth Centres. Rural community development work was however held up owing to the fact that the land consolidation allocations had to be almost completely revised.

The promotion of Youth Centres will be dealt with in a separate chapter as it is a story of achievement in its own right. Perhaps it is not community development in its true sense but it was nevertheless based on the principles of self-help and was a major part of the activities of a number of Community Development Officers.

Scope and Value of Community Development

A question which will, and in fact should, be asked at this stage is how effective was the work of the groups. What were the economic results of their efforts? What did they actually achieve? How widespread were their activities?

The tables at the end of the book will provide partial answers to these queries but will not give the whole picture. One of them gives a list of a variety of projects undertaken in 1959 in a district which may be regarded as fairly typical. It had not fully developed group-work by any means but it had made a good start. The rate of growth in the number of groups during the year was considerable. Detailed figures were not available from the District where community development had been established longer, but the following facts will give an indication of the impact it had made.

In Machakos, for instance, which is a District of nearly 360,000 people, at one time the entire able-bodied population was engaged on an average of two days a week, firstly on homestead improvement, and later on soil conservation work. About three quarters of the population of Kitui, which numbered over

200,000, was similarly involved when the campaign was at its height. During 1958, 1220 houses were re-built in brick, 507 cattle sheds were constructed, and nearly 114,000 acres of land were ridged against soil erosion in this District.

Although group-work was only introduced in Central Nyanza in 1958, by the end of 1959 more than 740 groups numbering nearly 15,000 people or 7,000 families had got into action, mainly engaged in land consolidation and farm planning activities. In Elgon Nyanza, as is shown in the table more than 500 groups were in operation, although there too the idea had only been introduced the previous year. It was the same story in North Nyanza where more than 300 groups went into action in a single year.

Nandi District showed the most remarkable rate of growth. Although the pilot scheme described was only launched at the beginning of 1958, by the end of 1959 the entire able-bodied population was involved. In its way, perhaps, the performance of Nyeri District, which had so recently been in turmoil through Mau Mau, was equally impressive. In one year 240 groups were formed which were mainly occupied in house building and the improvement of farm holdings.

A few more facts may be of interest. Groups worked on average for two days a week but in certain areas, and notably Nandi at the beginning they were actually engaged for five. The average number in a group was between 15 and 20 representing about a dozen families each, although in Machakos, where the main activity was soil conservation, they averaged 75. As has been pointed out, the size varied with the magnitude of the task.

What now of the actual physical achievements of the group, and would a comparable programme have been completed if group-work had not been adopted? It is more difficult to give an accurate statistical reply. What can at any rate be stated with confidence is that most of it would not have been undertaken at all if it had not been for the introduction of 20 in Machakos and Kitui in the first instance. It has been explained that the scheme would never have got off the ground but for the adoption of group-work. In Kitui the Agricultural Officer reported that the mileage dug by groups was three times that previously achieved on an individual basis. The economic advantages of soil conservation cannot be assessed in numerical terms. The actual benefits were, however, there for all to see in terms of grass cover, healthier crops, and longer lasting springs.

Again, the actual economic benefits of the land consolidation campaign in the Central Nyanza District could only be assessed by a study of the export figures from the District, which are unfortunately not available. The long-term benefits of the project were probably of greater importance than the immediate economic return. For instance, the land-owners achieved a firm title to a compact area of land. This encouraged them to make capital improvements, not only in terms of buildings, but in the establishment of orchards and plantations. In due course they would be able to obtain loans on the security of their land once the process of issuing title-deeds had been completed.

Similarly the economic benefit of the considerable programme of house building and homestead improvement would be difficult to calculate, but the social and health benefits were obvious. Thousands who would otherwise be living in hovels found themselves the occupants of attractive cottages in which they could and did take pride.

This brings us to a consideration of the intangible results of community development. The examples have shown how many and various they were. There was, for instance, the growth, or perhaps one should say the restoration, of a sense of social conscience as evidenced in the readiness of the groups to help their less fortunate or handicapped members in the cultivation of land or the building of houses. There was the inculcation of the idea of what is sometimes tritely termed the dignity of labour, but was really the realisation of the advantages of doing one's own farm work instead of employing labourers, which occurred among the Nandi. There was the reduction of drunkenness and the substitution of a sense of purpose which was noticed in a number of areas.

We should at the same time consider whether group-work achieved more than alternative methods of working. The examples have made it clear that much more could be achieved by a group working together than by individuals working separately. Apart from the extent of soil conservation activities already referred to, Agricultural Officers frequently remarked on the great increase in the amount of weeding of crops achieved, the increased use of manure and the improvement of pasture. It is not necessary to obtain figures to establish the fact that such an intensification of farming activities must have led to increased yields.

The reasons for this greater effort have been indicated already. There was the sense of competition engendered between the groups and within the groups, which resulted in increased exertion and therefore greater achievement. There was the introduction of new methods such as line-planting of maize, which could only be achieved through team work in communities too poor to employ trained labourers. There was the construction of houses which alone could be undertaken by building teams.

There was another intangible advantage. In the years before community development had been introduced it had been the accepted practice for chiefs to call out the inhabitants of an area to undertake essential public works for a certain number of days a year. They would be required to build roads and even to undertake soil conservation measures. So we had revived an older tradition. At times this communal work was even referred to by the traditional term given to community activities.

Chapter Nine

Conclusion

The foregoing account of community development includes examples and experiences from different areas. They show that in many respects they have common problems despite wide differences of culture. It has been suggested that in many ways the solutions are also similar. In working in these widely separated districts one is struck more by the similarities than the contrasts which are to be found. To begin with they had all evolved through the centuries a way of helping each other to overcome their difficulties. This system included not only assistance in domestic matters but in providing the requirements of the whole community. In all the spirit of mutual help has tended to die out with the emergence of government services to meet the needs of the rural populations and with the growth of a cash economy. In recent years the practical value of these traditions of cooperation have been or are being appreciated as a way of accelerating rural development.

In certain instances an awareness of the importance of building on the traditional organizations of the people rather than of introducing sophisticated systems which have only been evolved after centuries of trial and error in more advanced countries has become apparent.

Two schools of thought, of course, exist in relation to the value of indigenous cultures as opposed to modern expertise. Much of it is based on theoretical arguments, or even reluctance to accept that anything which is termed primitive can have value in the modern world.

We are, in the twentieth century, confronted with real and urgent problems of development of the poorer areas of the world. It is suggested that we have not the time to base our plans on theory or experiment. Rural development, and even less community development, are not academic or intellectual exercises. We should be studying the success or failure of actual projects in different parts of the world, evaluating and analysing them and drawing valid conclusions. Rural development through the adaptation of traditional economic and social organisations is worthy of further widespread study. Furthermore, there is little doubt that progress will be found to be much more rapid and the results longer lasting than through the methods which are usually employed in developing countries.

It is hoped that the few examples given will indicate the extent to which energy and vitality can be stimulated and how communities with little further stimulus can advance from one objective to the next through their own efforts.

But one overriding condition governs success in the field of community development. Without the keen interest of the government, and even more that of the field officers in guiding and supporting the village people, success cannot be expected. In almost every example given it will have been noticed that there was one public-spirited person behind the project. Where the government was behind the scheme, its officers were men or women with a vocation. Such people are always rare in any country and if all community development depended upon them progress would be slow. Fortunately, by using traditional organisations they can operate like the starter of the engine. Provided that assistance, in the form of petrol and oil, is maintained, they only need to make their chief effort to get things started or start the engine again if it stops for any reason. They have a hard job but anyone who has had experience of work in community development in the field knows how satisfying it is. Frustrating as it may be to persuade the powers-that-be to support the idea and provide assistance, the village people are seldom difficult to convince.

It is not suggested that development along traditional lines will always be successful. In some countries there are certain aspects of traditional society which have to be altered radically before the people will give their willing support to development projects. The stranglehold of landlordism, indebtedness, religious conservatism, autocratic government, political corruption or official apathy have all, in various countries, either hindered the work of community development or destroyed it. In such countries reforms are often needed before community development can be fully successful. Nevertheless, even where many of these obstacles exist, community development in one field or another is usually possible. In none of the areas described in this book were the conditions ideal for community development yet considerable progress was possible. How much greater progress could be achieved if the road blocks were removed.

The success of community development depends to a great extent on the encouragement of democratic institutions at the village level, whatever the pattern at the national level may be. The traditional framework of village life is almost invariably democratic even though feuds and factions may exist within the community itself. The basing of community development on it is, therefore, a comparatively simple matter. But success must depend upon the positive goodwill and enlightenment of the government and its officials who can, and sometimes do, obstruct the introduction of community development. Approval at the national level is essential and it must be sincere. The establishment of a ministry is not always desirable, and is sometimes ineffective. Some organization is necessary, however to persuade the various agencies of government to work together along community development lines. Account must also be taken of the various jealousies which tend to be created among the various ministries working for village betterment if another body is created to usurp their functions.

Experience also shows that government officials, and particularly those at the top, who are inevitably out of touch with village life and conditions, can only be convinced by actual experience of community development. A whole complex of emotions is sometimes aroused at the very mention of the words. They fear that their positions of authority will be undermined, that a dangerous self assertiveness will be aroused among the villagers. Such attitudes have been encountered in all the districts described. Nevertheless, there are always others with the vision and humility to see the value inherent in community development.

All government officials are naturally concerned with making the greatest progress in their particular fields with the minimum of funds. To put it at its lowest, once they have been convinced that this can be achieved by working with the people's organisations and winning their support, they give up their prejudices.

Administrative and technical officers are seldom impressed by a theoretical approach, and this is not unnatural. They prefer practical solutions to practical problems. All too often, community development has been cloaked in jargon and a form of mysticism, which cuts little ice with those confronted with the realities of development.

It is hoped that the description of actual projects described in this chapter will be of assistance to field officers, and provide them with practical examples which will convince them of the value of community development. It cannot solve all the problems of development but if increased food supplies, roads and public services are required it can make a major contribution. Of greater importance, however, it can help to get rid of choking weeds of apathy, fatalism, and despair, which are the principal obstacles to progress at all levels in the developing countries.

For those who doubt the economic advantages of community development a table is given in the appendices of actual achievements during one year's work in a Kenya District, where, in fact, community development had hardly taken root. Statistical information is always difficult to provide and it would be unwise to judge the success or failure of community development schemes solely on this basis. The increasing support for community development by the government of Kenya when it became aware of its value was, however, an indication of the confidence it placed in its ability to contribute to the national economy. It was, on the other hand, the sense of common purpose which was developed in the various campaigns which was of greater value than the actual physical achievements.

It might be claimed that during the last ten years of the colonial period two victories were won. The first was that over the violence of Mau Mau, through winning the hearts and minds of those concerned, and the second, the physical reconstruction of the country through the agency of community development. Are there some lessons in this for those currently engaged in helping Africans rebuild their lives and communities which have been blighted by violence and neglect?

APPENDICES

APPENDIX I

Achievements of Groups in Elgon Nyanza District during 1959*

6,623	coffee pits dug.
149,383	coffee trees weeded and mulched.
11,405	acres of pasture improved.
3,667	acres of bush cleared.
345	miles of farm boundaries demarcated.
10,093	acres ploughed.
1,777	yards of bench terracing constructed.
93	miles of farm roads built.
15,252	acres of land weeded.
32,231	bundles of thatching grass collected.
2,438	homesteads built.
956	latrines dug.
884	cattle sheds built.
2,629	kitchens built.
6,151	acres harvested.
56	minor springs protected.
31	dams constructed.

In December, 24,441 people were working in 504 groups.

* *Ministry of Community Development Annual Report 1959 Colony and Protectorate of Kenya*

APPENDIX II

Funds Provided For Community Development & Social Welfare*
(In Round Figures)

Government capital grants for social welfare	15,000
Government grants-in-aid towards salaries	48,000
Department of Community Development	147,000
Government grants to community development projects	15,000
Capital expenditure of local authorities	130,000
Recurrent expenditure of local authorities	176,000
Grants from UNICEF (cash and kind)	17,800
Grants from Dulverton Trust	10,000

* *Ministry of Community Development Annual Report 1959*
Colony and Protectorate of Kenya

APPENDIX III

Youth Clubs*
(In Round Figures)

Number of clubs	133
Number of members	15,000
Funds provided by local communities	10,000
Funds provided by local authorities	18,000
Funds provided by Dulverton Trust	10,000
Funds provided by Government	4,600
Total funds provided	42,600

* Ministry of Community Development Annual Report 1959 Colony and Protectorate of Kenya

Retrospect

The purpose of this book has been to cover the colonial period in Kenya and to describe the difficulties encountered and how they were overcome. As such there has been little reference to the post-colonial period. The main emphasis has been on the effects of the population explosion in the '40's and '50's and the consequent landlessness among the Kikuyu. However, it would appear that the battle is not yet won. Some of the conclusions made by Arthur Hazlewood in the 1970s in *The Economy of Kenya, the Kenyatta Era* are worth reproducing in full:

> Kenya is still a very poor country, and there are great inequalities. Despite commitments to the reduction of inequality and the improvement of the welfare of the 'working poor', which is said to be the theme of the Development Plan for the period after 1978, many would argue that policies have been directed to help those who have already helped themselves. A few have certainly 'helped themselves'; in an unrestrained manner. With a less perjorative meaning of that term in mind, it was suggested in the discussion on inequality that to some extent the limitation of resources makes a focus on those who have already made progress inevitable. Agricultural extension and other assistance has been directed towards 'progressive farmers' in the high potential areas. In other words, the benefits have gone to those it has been easiest to benefit, and those, including pastoralists, less able to help themselves and more difficult to help, because of the quality of their location or for other reasons, have been left behind. But they cannot permanently be left behind if Kenya is to continue to progress. Nor can women.

It would seem, therefore, that unless this bias is removed the land now occupied by the one-time landless may deteriorate to the state which so nearly led to the collapse of the tribal agricultural economy prior to Mau Mau. This might well lead to Kenya degenerating to the state of anarchy found in a number of South American states as well as some of its African neighbours today.

I hope I have succeeded in covering the objectives listed in the Introduction and so fulfilled what I set out to do - to confirm the good faith of Britain in her colonising efforts in spite of hiccups of a major nature on the way.

There had always been a yearning hope among certain leading officials and unofficials that it would be possible to return to the status quo ante once 'discipline' among the dissidents had been restored. When it became recognised that this would be impossible even if the British government was prepared to continue to finance the enormous cost of the operation, which after Hola it declined to do, then all concerned settled down to organise a crash course in self-government. It is unlikely that this would have been successful on its own but following the introduction of the essential social economic and political reforms already achieved, all went smoothly.

There are, of course, those who would dispute such claims but what we have to appreciate is that we colonialists, whether officials, unofficials, churchmen or men of business, were confronted with a host of problems to which we alone must find the answers. They were problems which involved assisting the indigenous inhabitants of Kenya to adjust themselves to a world-wide society and economy of which they had absolutely no experience. At the same time, we had to adjust ourselves and learn the nature of a people entirely new to us, to enable us to serve their needs. Settlers in their turn had to discover, at great cost, the secrets of cultivation in unforgiving tropical conditions. Churchmen had to appreciate the religious understanding of people who were, in fact, far from being unenlightened. Business men had to learn how to trade with people who up to quite recently had no need or desire for money.

Inevitably, we all made mistakes and at times took the wrong turning. While doing so we were confronted with natural phenomena and catastrophes for which no one had any proven solution at the time. The measures we took in good faith for the betterment of our adopted home sometimes turned out to conceal a poison, like Cleopatra's asp, hidden in a basket of figs.

We spent our time searching for remedies and antidotes and often failed in the process, but no one could doubt our sincerity. All that we can hope is that, in the end, our efforts were expended in a worthy cause. It will be for the world to judge and time to tell.

Perhaps, however, we may be permitted to hope that coming generations will take the trouble to learn from our experiences and apply the lessons learned, whatever they may happen to be. This is the main purpose of compiling this record of the colonial period in Kenya as I see it, since all history tends to be subjective.

One hopes that at least one general principle may have been established however - that no country can expect to enjoy a peaceful existence if one part of its population is treated unjustly. The standard of living of a community cannot be judged by the prosperity of a single section of it. A small and embittered minority can always, as in the case of Mau Mau, create chaos. The solution of social problems is of greater importance than of economic ones. People can and do all over the world live simple and contented lives in conditions which some wrongly term poverty. The governments of some of Kenya's neighbouring countries have realised this fact. Others have been reduced to a state of anarchy, not always of their own making. It would be tragic if Kenya succumbs to genocide brought about by a disregard of the basic needs of the poorer and less fortunate members of the community. The country people have shown by their response to the call of community development that they can overcome almost insuperable physical and technical problems. Armed with such an experience they should be able to meet most other challenges in the future.

In conclusion, what is the answer to the questions posed at the beginning of this book? I hope I have adequately disposed of the allegation that we colonized Kenya for the purpose of exploitation. A more accurate definition of our activities would, I suggest, be the development of its resources, such at they were. I think there is no doubt that in this we were successful.

But it will be queried whether we were so successful in human terms. The answer to this must be subjective and depend upon the interpretation we give to the words used. The population was certainly healthier and wealthier, but there were, of course, exceptions such as those Kikuyu who found themselves without land as a result of the unexpected growth of population. The British administration could hardly be blamed for this, however, as it came about in consequence of measures taken with the best of motives. It must be accepted, on the other hand, that we failed to convince the inhabitants of the need to limit the size of their families. From this stemmed most of the problems of the latter years. Should we have foreseen these problems? Perhaps we should, but many of us thought that with the spread of education parents would begin to appreciate that large families would become too costly to rear. This unfortunately did not take place.

But was it really necessary for those affected to rebel in order to persuade the Government to provide for the landless? The other tribes who were similarly affected did not go to such lengths. Were their actions simply opportunist and in imitation of those who rebelled in Malaya? The inhabitants of no other dependency followed suit.

However, violence having erupted, did we do everything we could to deal with grievances at the same time as overcoming the violence in as humane a way as possible? War is always a dirty business and civil war, which is what Mau Mau actually became, is probably the dirtiest of them all, but I suggest that non-combatants in particular, such as the passive wing, who were either detained or else concentrated in fortified villages, were treated as fairly as it was possible to do. The fact that exceptional campaigns of agricultural development and even such social activities as schools and youth clubs were undertaken in the Emergency areas at the same time as military operations were being conducted a few miles away, indicates that social and economic development continued and was even accentuated during this time.

A most remarkable sign that the people were themselves becoming opposed to the insurgents was the fact that it was ex-terrorists who finally hunted down and captured Dedan Kimathi, the principal leader, and brought the campaign to a close. Nothing so devastating as the Vietnam conflict ever occurred in Kenya.

Though the opening up of the White Highlands to settlement by Africans seemed to some to be long overdue, nevertheless, when it came, many European farmers stayed on to train Africans to run the farms they had sold to them. Others continued to farm as before as Jomo Kenyatta urged them to do. A number of officials also remained to train their indigenous successors to deal with the complexities of a modern state after Independence. The Swynnerton Plan in the Emergency areas and Community Development throughout the rest of the colony enabled the tendency towards increasing infertility to be reversed and wealth-building crops such as tea and coffee to be introduced.

All in all, therefore, there is much to be proud of in the way that Britain wound up her tutelage, and I hope that readers will, on balance, agree that we did what we reasonably could to fulfil our trust.

Select Bibliography

Elsbeth Huxley, *Red Strangers,* (London, 1939).

Arthur Hazlewood, *The Economy of Kenya: the Kenyatta Era* (Oxford, 1979).

Nigel Pavitt, *Kenya: the first explorers* (London, 1989).

Frank Furedi, *The Mau Mau War in Perspective* (London, 1989).

Robert B. Edgerton, *Mau Mau: an African Crucible* (London, 1990).

Josiah Mwangi Kariuki, *Mau Mau Detainee* (London, 1964).

F. J. D. Lugard, *Dual Mandate in British Tropical Africa* (London, 1965, 5th edn.).

P. T. Bauer, *Equality, The Third World and Economic Delusion* (London, 1981).

T. G. Askwith, *The Story of Kenya's Progress* (East African Literature Bureau, Nairobi, 1958 edn).

Report of the Kenya Land Commission, (Cmd.4556, 1934).

P. E. Williams, *Youth Camps: A Proposal* (Colony and Protectorate of Kenya, 1945).

Norman Humphrey et al, *The Kikuyu Lands* (Colony and Protectorate of Kenya, 1945).

East Africa Royal Commission 1953-55 Report (Cmd. 9475, 1955).

Richard Frost, *Enigmatic Proconsul: Sir Philip Mitchell and the Twilight of Empire* (London, 1992).

Elspeth Huxley, *A New Earth* (London, 1960).

Charles Chenevix Trench, *The Men who ruled Kenya: The Kenya*

Administration, 1892-1963 (London, 1993).

Preston O Chitere, 'The Women's Self Help Movement in Kenya: a historical perspective 1940-80', *Transafrican Journal of History*, 17 (1988) 50-68.

Mary Tiffen, Michael Mortimore & Francis Gichuki, *More People, Less Erosion* (Overseas Development Institute, London, 1994)

T. G. Askwith, *'Young Kikuyu'*, Corona (1951).

INDEX

A

Aberdare Range *202*
adult discussions
    rural issues *141*
Adult Education *83, 96, 125-126, 129, 139, 141, 154, 161, 163, 170-172*
adult literacy *160*
African Administrative Officer *174*
African Advisory Council *50*
African Affairs *22-23, 53, 99, 118*
African Affairs Officer *47–223*
African dancing *181, 183*
African family
    pressure on *42*
African Field Officer *180*
African songs *179*
African unrest
    trade restrictions *83*
African Vagrancy
    memo *60-65*
agrarian administration
    colonial view of *85-97*
Agricultural Assistant *182-183*
Agricultural Extension Officer *186*
Agricultural field officers *128*
Agricultural Officer *184-5, 191, 198-199, 210-202*
alcohol *197*
Alliance High School *53*
American Aid
    for community development *198*
anti-soil erosion campaigns *77*
Arabs *29, 33, 38*
Archbishop *113*
Archdeacon Owen *50*
Asians *50, 73, 75, 82, 90*
    Nairobi *39*
    shopkeepers *40*
Athi River *104, 108, 115*

B
Bantu *27, 28, 31*
Baring, Sir Evelyn *99*
Baringo *111, 119, 138-139, 169-170, 198*
Bauer, T P *33, 39*
Beecher Plan *72*
Bethuel Gecaga *49*
Booth-Clibborn, Stanley *52*
boredom
    African *197*
boy's schooling
    African *71-3*
Brains Trust *142*
Breckenridge, Jim
    Marigat *111*
bride-price, H *73*
British administration
    early *38-9*
Burma *45, 116*

C
Cairo *33*
Castle, Barbara
    visit to Kenya *54*
Central Nyanza *129, 132, 135, 138, 164, 183-190, 201-202, 206-207*
cess
    African areas *70*
Chadwick, E R *160*
Child Care *145, 164*
choral and drama festivals
    women *145*
Christian community *187*
Christian education
    Mau Mau *105*
Church, Memorial *122*
Churches *52-53, 105, 113, 122, 151*
CID *113*
cinematography *89*
citizenship *105-106, 126, 131, 142, 157*
CMS *52-53*
Colchester, Tom *52*

Colonial Development Fund *52*
Colonial Office *112, 121*
    Summer Conference *160*
colonial innovations
    effects of *36*
colonial view of how women saw themselves *29, 42*
colonisers
    early *38*
Commissioner for Community Development *65, 154, 170, 224*
communal rice planting scheme *168*
communal work *191*
community
    tradition of *29-30*
communist influence *29, 75, 78-79, 103, 161*
Community Development *65, 80, 82, 97, 99, 100, 123, 125, 127,*
        129-131, 133, 134, 135, 137, 139-142,
        146-149, 151-152, 154, 157, 159, 174, 178, 180,
        191, 195, 198-200, 204-205, 209-212,
        221, 224
    support of Norman Humphrey *79*
    official policy *88-89*
    early experiments *163-172*
    teams *186-189*
Community Development Assistants
    men *129-30*
Community Development Assistants
    women *130-131, 146*
Community Development Officers *131-132, 134*
Community Development theory *133-137*
community education *140-142*
compulsion
    official view of *87-88*
Cooke, S V *50, 143, 183*
Cox, Denis
    Community Development Officer *205*
craft training
    Mau Mau *104*
crime wage
    World War II *45*

D
debates *141*

demobilised soldiers
    WWII *57, 60, 65*
demonstration farms
    community development *138*
Detention Camp *107*
Detention Camps *63, 101, 106*
Diment, Don
    Community Development Officer *204*
Dini Ya Msambwa *191*
discrimination *46, 49, 54, 73, 76, 99*
displaced Kikuyu *100*
District Commissioner *80, 87, 89, 106, 134, 142, 148, 160, 174, 178, 186*
district shows
    community development *140*
dressmaking *143-144*
Dulverton Trust *152*
Dundas, Charles *87*

E
East Africa *12, 23, 33, 45, 89, 96, 127*
East African Literature Bureau *170*
East Coast *39*
education *37, 46, 53-54, 58, 62, 69, 76, 83, 85-86, 93, 95-97, 100, 102-105, 107-108, 119, 125-126, 129, 137, 139-141, 147-148, 150, 154, 157, 161, 163, 166, 170-172, 184, 195, 197, 200, 202, 220*
    African grievances *71-73*
Electors Union
    address to *99-109*
Egerton, Professor *116*
Egypt *28*
Elgeyo-Marakuet *200*
Elgon Nyanza *129, 190-194, 201, 206*
embroidery *145*
Embu *68, 111, 116, 119, 126, 204-205*
    Community Development Training Centre *133*
Enugu
    Nigeria *160*
erosion *178*
Erskine, Derek *49*
Erskine, General *112*

European beer drinking ban
> Mau Mau *77*

Ethiopia *27, 28, 42*

ex-servicemen
> training of *66*
> training centre *143*

F

family
need for adequate wage *67*
famine *36, 40, 42-43, 57, 173*
Farmers *35, 40, 45, 57, 64, 69, 90, 93, 111, 126-128, 138, 164, 166, 172-173, 175, 185, 189, 191, 193-194, 199, 204, 221*
Farmer's Days *164, 175*
farming demonstrations *128*
Fazan, H S *99*
Fearn, R D *121*
female education
> official view *96*

fertility restoration
> soil *159*

field assistants
> official view *93-94*

field officers
> official view *90-92*

film *139, 171*
football *151, 155*
Fort Hall *80, 106, 149, 171, 205*
force
> use of against prisoners *118-119*

Francis, Carey *52-53*
freedom fighters *116*
Fundamental Education *161*

G

Gardner, Major *151*
Garratt *34*
Ghana *161*
Githunguri *76*
glove-puppets
> community development work *140*

Goa *33*
Gold Coast *78*
Government trade schools *72*
Griffin, Geoff
    Starehe Youth Centre *117, 151*
group leaders
    training course *132*

H
Harris, Ted
    Community Development Officer *195*
Harry Thuku riots *51*
Hayes, Charles *164*
Hazlewood, Arthur *28, 218*
Health *39, 85-86, 125-126, 129, 138, 140-141, 143, 145, 153, 165, 167, 188, 198, 201-203, 207*
    Health Centres *160-161*
Health Assistants *188*
health education *161*
Hola *112, 119-120, 219*
homecraft training centres *141*
Home Guard *115*
Housing *52-53, 83, 85, 108, 135, 142, 156, 179, 196, 202-205*
    African dissatisfaction *70-71*
Humphrey, Norman *59, 67-68, 79*
Hyde-Clarke, Meredyth *58*

I
Independent Schools *72, 76, 103*
India *33, 39, 161*
Information Service *165-166*
inter-racial co-operation *48*
interrogation
    Kikuyu *63*
irrigation schemes
    labour on *119*
Jeanes School *81, 105-107, 125-127, 130-132, 138-144, 154, 164, 166, 170-171, 174, 175, 199*
Jock Scott
    operation *51*
Jolly, Richard *198*

Josiah, S O *50*
juvenile rehabilitation *117*

K
KAU *77*
Kaloleni Hall *47-48*
Karatina *66*
Kenny, Mary *81*
Kenyatta, Jomo *47-49, 75, 78, 84, 221*
Kenya Land Commission *31*
Kiambu chiefs
    campaign against *75*
Kibachia, Cheege *75*
Kikuyu *30, 57, 59-60, 62-63, 65-74, 76, 84, 96, 100, 102-104,*
    113-115, 117, 119-120, 126, 128, 133, 149, 154-156,
    207, 211, 190, 191
    lawlessness in Nairobi *61*
    unrest *78-82*
    loyalists *205*
Kikuyu Central Association *76*
Kikuyu oaths *113-114*
Kikuyuland *50, 58-59*
Kimameta *34*
Kimathi, Dedan *221*
Kings African Rifles *151, 179*
Kirkaldy, Bill *50*
Kisii *2, 94*
Kisuu *33, 50, 53-54*
Kitui *129, 134-135, 173, 178-183, 187, 191, 194, 197,*
    202-204, 206-207
Krapf, Dr
    Swiss missionary *37*
Kubai, Fred *76*

L
La, Hugh Fontaine *48*
Labour Commissioner
    Meredyth Hyde-Clarke *58*
Labour Party *54*
Laikipiak *35*
Lake Victoria *27, 33, 164*
Land Commission *31, 59, 99*

landless *43, 46, 52, 57-59, 61-64, 68, 112, 119-120, 204, 218, 220*
land consolidation *185-186*
    scheme *203*
land exhaustion
    theory of *41*
land pressure *173*
land redistribution *185*
Langata Prison *106*
leadership promotion *125*
Leakey *99*
left-wing politicians
    Britain *78*
literacy
    Mau Mau camps *115, 163*
Livingstone, David *33*
Lugard, Lord *31, 33*
Luo *27-28, 31, 50, 53, 183-190, 196*

M

Maasai *27, 28-31, 34-36, 59, 174, 196, 209*
Machakos *107-108, 129, 149-150, 152-153, 164, 172-173, 178-179, 186, 188, 197, 202, 205-206*
    community development pilot scheme *132-135*
    youth scheme *147*
Mackinnon *111-112*
Makueni settlement scheme
    Wakamba *60*
Maendeleo ya Wanawake *143-145*
Malaha *167*
Malawi *27, 135*
Malayan rehabilitation *102*
Malayan terrorism *78*
Malinda, John *174*
Manda *104, 108*
Manyani *111-112*
Manyassi Valley *164-167*
Marigat *111, 116, 119*
Marxist *101*
Maseno High School *53*
Maseno
    Jeanes School *142*

mass-media
> community development *137-138*

Mathu *82*
Mau Mau *45-46, 51-52, 58, 60, 74, 76-78, 83-84, 99-101, 103, 107-108, 111-120, 122, 145-150, 152, 171, 202-203, 206, 212, 218, 220-221*
Mbagathi Airport *108*
Mbotela, Tom *52*
Mboya, Tom *125*
Meatki, Titus *180*
Meru *68, 126, 204-205*
mikora *46*
missionaries *3, 37-38, 41-42, 50, 90, 200, 202*
Missions *7, 96*
missions *39, 138*
minimum wage *64*
Mitchell, Philip *99*
mobile cinemas *139*
Mohamedanism *103*
Mombasa *33, 37, 52, 60, 111-112, 150, 184, 200-201*
> strike *75*

Moral Rearmament Community *113*
Mount Kenya *27-28, 37, 38, 116, 202*
Municipal Native Affairs *46, 224*
Muranga Memorial Church *121*
music *181*
musicians *191*
mutual help *209*
Mwangi, Josiah Kariuki *115*
Mwea Plains *111*
mwethya *177-180*

N

Nairobi *57, 60, 63, 65, 75-76, 111-112, 115, 117, 126, 148, 150-151, 155, 173-174, 202*
> World War II *46-51,*

Nandi *27, 129, 134, 194-199, 206-207*
newspaper *137, 170*
Ngong *34*
Nigeria *24, 160, 162*
Nile *28, 33*
North African *45*

North Nyanza *69, 133, 167, 174, 206*
Nyanza *28, 33, 41, 53, 68-70, 75, 108, 126, 129, 132-133, 135, 138, 164, 167, 174, 184, 190, 193-195, 197, 201-202, 206-207*
Nyasaland *135*
Nyeri *7, 68, 106, 133, 149, 203-204, 206*

O
oath-reversing *113-114*
Ohanga, Beniah
    Minister for African Affairs *53, 113*
old-age security
    Kikuyu *79*
Olenguruoni
    settlement scheme *59*
Operation Anvil *111-112*
Owen, Bill *52*
Owles, Roger *151*

P
Pearson Commission *38*
Physical Training Officer *154*
pilot scheme
    community development *134*
planting restrictions *73*
police *42, 60, 63, 77, 102, 111, 115, 142, 149, 151, 178-179, 183, 187, 194-195*
Poll Tax *9, 35-36*
population explosion *41, 57, 218*
primary schools *71, 83, 172*
Prisoner-of-War *67*
Probation Officer *81*
progressive farmers' courses *127-128*
propaganda *88-89, 94*
prostitutes *58*
protest
    Government House *173*
Provincial Administration *115*
provincial and district teams
    official policy *89-90*

R
race relations *15, 51*
racial dscrimination *46*
railway *33-35, 47-48, 111, 131, 142, 150*
    origins *38-39*
Rehabilitation Advisory Committee *112*
Rehabilitation Centre *107*
rehabilitation
    programme *111-121*
resettlement
    families *119*
Richards, Charles *170*
Riddoch, John *54*
Rift Valley *27-29, 34, 40-42, 57-58, 76, 169*
rift Valley *34*
rinderpest *35, 39*
Royal Commission on Land and Population *51, 59, 85-97*
rural development *209-212*

S
Screening Teams *111*
Second World War *45, 57, 125*
self-government *160*
self-help *159-172*
sewing and dressmaking *144*
Singh Makham *76*
Sinn Fein *78*
sleeping sickness *164*
spivs
    Nairobi *62*
sport and recreation
    community development *153-157*
social and economic hardship
    Kikuyu *78*
Social Centre *170*
Social Welfare Organisation *125*
Society of Friends *113*
social survey
    need for *80*
Sociological Committee
    Mau Mau *99*
soil *42*

erosion *57, 77, 87, 135, 164-165, 167, 173-174, 176-177, 184, 196-197, 200-201*
conservation *206-208*
Somali *27, 30, 31*
spiritual rehabilitation *105-6*
spivs
Nairobi *62*
Spleenhamland Acts *64*
Sports Officer *154, 171*
Squatter Policy Committee *58*
squatters *36, 40, 46, 57, 59, 68-69, 76, 79, 81, 84, 112, 119*
Starehe Youth Centre *117*
Sturuck, Bill *186*
sub-division of land
problem of *58*
Sudan *28, 42*
Suez Canal *33*
Swahili *53*
Swiss missionary *37*
Swynnerton Plan *116, 120, 185, 221*

T
Taita District *202*
Tanganyika *2, 40, 68, 70, 73, 79, 92*
Tanzania *27-28*
technical teams *188*
techniques
community development *137-140*
Templer, Gerald *99*
terracing *200-1*
Thompson, W
Fort Hall *80*
Thomson, Joseph
explorer *33-35*
traditional co-operation *201*
tribal football leagues *156*
tribal warfare *29, 35, 42*
Turkana *27, 30*

U
Uganda *28, 33, 38, 52, 54, 70, 73, 86-87, 190*

UNESCO *161*
UNICEF *139, 144*
United Kenya Club *48-51*
unrest
    growth of *65-80*
Uplands Bacon Factory *75*

V

Vasey, Alderman *52*
Veterinary *39, 126, 165, 196*
veterinary *91*

W

wages
    African dissatisfaction *62-64, 67-70, 79, 82-83, 197*
Wakamba *37, 60, 154, 173-183, 187, 193*
Wamumu *115, 117, 152*
Waruhiu, Chief
    murder of *58*
weeding *207*
White Highlands *59, 73, 112, 221*
white settlement *35, 39-41, 77*
Williams, Patrick *79*
witches *145*
World Bank *23, 39*
Worker's Federation *75*
works camps
    mental rehabilitation *108, 111*
World War I *40*
women
    extention work - official policy *95-7*
    rehabilitation plan *106-7, 175-176, 178, 218*
women community development assistants *130-131, 146*
women's clubs
    African *138, 141*
women's emancipation
    African *142-146*
women's homecraft training
    Jeanes School *125*
women's transformation *145*
Wright, Alan *200*

Y
youth centres *115, 146-153, 205*
youth
        conflict with elders *74*
youth camps
        proposal *79*
        rehabilitation scheme *150-153*
youth clubs
        Funds *217*

AFRICAN STUDIES CENTRE PUBLICATIONS

Published with James Currey:
K. Hart and J. Lewis (eds) **"Why Angola Matters"**, 1995

J. Lonsdale, (ed) **"South Africa in Question"**, 1988

Monographs in Print
R. Abrahams, (ed), **"Witchcraft in Contemporary Tanzania"**
ISBN 0-902993029-1; £7.00

T.E. Kyei, **"Marriage and Divorce Among the Asante"**
ISBN 0-902993-27-5; £7.00

G.I. Jones, **"From Slaves to Palm Oil. Slave Trade and Palm Oil Trade in the Bight of Biafra"**
ISBN 0-902993-26-7; £6.00

Don Robotham, **"Militants or Proletarians? The Economic Culture of Underground Gold Miners in Southern Ghana, 1906-1976"**
ISBN 0-902993-25-9; £6.00

Christine Fox, **"Asante Brass Casting. Lost-wax casting of goldweights, ritual vessels and sculptures, with handmade equipment"**
ISBN 0-902993-24-0; £7.00

Anne Thurston, **"Smallholder Agriculture in Colonial Kenya: The Official Mind and the Swynnerton Plan"**
ISBN 0-902993-19-4; £5.00

Simon Albrecht and Janet Seeley (eds), **"Teaching Conservation: Proceedings of a Seminar on Teaching Conservation Overseas"**
ISBN 0-902993-18-6; £4.50

Polly Hill, **"Talking with Ewe Seine Fishermen and Shallot Farmers"**
ISBN 0-902993-17-8; £5.00

Janet Seeley, **"Conservation in Sub-Saharan Africa: An Introductory Bibliography for the Social Sciences"**
ISBN 0-902993-12-7; £5.00

A.F. Robertson (ed), **"Uganda's First Republic: Administrators and Politicians, 1961-1971"**
ISBN 0-902993-08-9; £5.00

Occasional Papers in Print

Terence C. Moll, **"No Blade of Grass: Rural Production and State Intervention in Transkei, 1925-1960"**
ISBN 0-902993-22-4; £5.00

G.C. Passmore, **"H.R.G. Howman on Provincialisation in Rhodesia 1968-1969 and Rational and Irrational Elements"**
ISBN 0-902993-16-X; £4.00

G.I. Jones, **"Annual Reports of the Bende Division, South Eastern Nigeria, 1905-1912"**
ISBN 0-902993-14-3; £4.00

RECENTLY PUBLISHED

WHY ANGOLA MATTERS

Edited by
Keith Hart &
Joanna Lewis

AFRICAN STUDIES CENTRE PUBLICATIONS

ORDERS AND ENQUIRES

Please order direct from:
The Secretary
AFRICAN STUDIES CENTRE
University of Cambridge
Free School Lane,
Cambridge, CB2 3RQ,
United Kingdom.

Orders may be sent by:
Phone: (01223) 334396
Fax: (01223) 334396
Telex: 81240 CAMSPL G
E-Mail: african-studies@lists.cam.ac.uk

24-HOUR ORDERING
Ring or Fax at any time